Counseling the
Adolescent

Individual, Family, and
School Interventions

Edited by

Jon Carlson
Lake Geneva Wellness Clinic

Judith Lewis
Governors State University

LOVE PUBLISHING COMPANY
Denver, Colorado 80222

To our adolescents,
Keith, Kirstin, and Matthew

Copyright © 1988 Love Publishing Company
Printed in the U.S.A.
ISBN 0-89108-204-2
Library of Congress Catalog Card Number 88-80105

Contents

Introduction

Jon Carlson and Judith Lewis

The pressing issues surrounding adolescence are among the most challenging faced today by counselors and by our society as a whole. Adolescents are unquestionably at a vulnerable developmental stage as they attempt to navigate the difficult transition from childhood to adulthood. *Any* life transition holds the potential for danger or for growth (Krupp, 1987), but adolescence represents probably the most crucial transition, combining a general life adventure (bidding farewell to childhood and joining the adult world) with a series of specific changes (leaving one school for another, entering the work world, learning to think differently, meeting new expectations, seeking independence from parents—even adapting to a new body).

Most young people manage this transformation successfully, but many do experience major stress and find themselves engaging in behaviors that place their well-being at risk. As Ingersoll and Orr point out in the first article, "Only a recluse could be unaware of the statistics that show an upsurge in adolescent suicide, pregnancy, and venereal disease, as well as continued patterns of drug and alcohol use and abuse, school dropouts, and delinquency."

All of us—whether in our roles as educators, as counselors, as parents, or simply as community members—feel a sense of urgency, a need to do something to help adolescents find healthy ways to deal with the demands they face. Although there are no simple answers to the complex problems of adolescence in modern society, some fresh perspectives can enhance our understanding and give direction to our efforts. The purpose of this book is to give voice to those perspectives, to address the special needs of adolescents at risk, and to provide suggestions for action.

If any action is to be fruitful, it must be based on an understanding of adolescent development and behavior patterns. *Individual Interventions*, the first section of this book, focuses on important concerns such as adolescent risk behaviors, suicide, pregnancy, violence, and loss. It addresses these issues from a developmental frame of reference and provides suggestions for counseling strategies that can interrupt the cycle of self-defeating behavior.

To better understand adolescent development and behavior, we also must examine them within their social context. Asserting that "human development is a product of interaction between the growing human organism and its environment," Bronfenbrenner (1979, p. 16) decries the fact that there is "a marked asymmetry, a hypertrophy of theory and research focusing on the properties of the person and

1

only the most rudimentary conception and characterization of the environment in which the person is found." As Conyne (1985) has pointed out, counselors have tended to ignore Kurt Lewin's formulation that B = f (P × E), or behavior is a function of the interaction between the person and the environment. Instead, counselors have usually acted on the basis of a far more limited formula: B = f (P), or behavior is a function of the person. We believe that any consideration of adolescents and their problems must focus not just on the young people themselves, but also on the settings within which they function. Because the systems that affect children and adolescents most directly and universally are the family and the school, we have placed a major emphasis on interventions in these arenas.

Section Two, *Family Interventions,* describes changes in contemporary family life that may have strong effects on adolescent family members. Section Three, *School Interventions,* is directed at the school climate and suggests activities that can help schools to enhance, rather than deter, adolescents' development.

Whether focusing on the individual, the family, or the school, the authors represented in this book each blend theory and practice. They provide an overview of the issue, followed by workable, implementable suggestions—promising avenues for counselor interventions.

REFERENCES

Bronfenbrenner, U. (1979). *The ecology of human development*. Cambridge, MA: Harvard University Press.

Conyne, R. K. (1985). The counseling ecologist: Helping people and environments. *Counseling & Human Development, 18*(2), 1–12.

Krupp, J. A. (1987). Counseling with an increased awareness of the transition process. *Counseling & Human Development, 19*(7), 1–15.

ONE: INDIVIDUAL INTERVENTIONS

Jon Carlson and Judith Lewis

The five articles that make up this section examine concerns that are important to today's adolescent. Each author combines knowledge of adolescent development with an awareness of the behaviors that tend to place young people in jeopardy.

In the first article, Gary Ingersoll and Donald Orr focus on young people whose maladaptive behaviors place them at risk. They point out that adolescents normally engage in some activities that adults would term risky. Whether a particular set of behaviors is, in actuality, *risk taking* depends on the needs, causes, and dangers involved. Adolescents who can be considered at risk tend to be involved in more than one problem behavior. Here, the authors examine a cluster of behaviors including substance abuse, sexual activity, and delinquency. According to Ingersoll and Orr, intervention strategies can be successful only if they are based on an understanding of adolescent development and a recognition of the linked nature of risk behaviors.

The second article, by Richard Hayes and Nancy Cryer, takes a developmental approach in analyzing a specific issue: teen pregnancy. The urgency of this problem is a function of its serious consequences: Youthful mothers and their children pay a heavy penalty in poverty, medical complications, and lack of opportunity for education. As the authors point out, "Teenage pregnancy may be seen as both a solution to one set of interrelated problems and the cause of similar, interrelated problems." Hayes and Cryer suggest a number of primary prevention strategies based on reconceptualizations of social attitudes and policies. They also recommend implementation of specific programs involving education, family planning, health care, employment, counseling, and referral.

Dave Capuzzi, too, addresses a problem of great urgency: adolescent suicide. His article provides an overview of possible causes of adolescent suicide, identifying common misconceptions and describing the developmental, family, and environmental factors that may relate to the recent increase in suicide rates for this age group. Capuzzi suggests a number of strategies for recognizing and preventing potential suicides; he also provides guidelines for managing crises that could not be prevented.

Violent behavior among adolescents—whether inflicted on self or others—has increased dramatically in recent years. In the fourth article, Raymond Winbush

3

points out that, between 1960 and 1980, juvenile crime rose twice as fast as adult crime. Winbush suggests that, although many theories have attempted to account for violent behavior among adolescents, developmental theory offers the most useful explanations. With developmental theory as a basic framework, this article suggests counseling strategies for dealing with self-inflicted violence (including both suicide and drug use), and other-inflicted violence.

The final article in this section, "Coping with Loss: A Developmental Approach to Helping Children and Youth," deals with a more universal issue. All children and young people must deal with change and loss. As Richard Hayes, the author, states, "Life is a series of goodbyes." In his discussion of adolescence, Hayes points out that the adolescent's transition to adult status may be perceived as "the death of his or her identity as a child." Children and youth can be helped to master and learn from loss experiences if counselors encourage the expression of feelings, provide honest information, communicate understanding, and share a balanced, adult perspective. Successful intervention also depends on the adult's understanding of the child's developmental pace.

The need to understand the nature of adolescent development is made clear through all of the articles in this section. Ingersoll and Orr, in their discussion of adolescents at risk, and Hayes, in addressing issues of loss, underscore the importance of Elkind's (1974) conceptualization of adolescent egocentrism. Those authors, along with Winbush, also discuss the key role and the variability of cognitive, social, and moral development. Adolescents are expected to attain the capacity for formal operational thought. Yet, as Ingersoll and Orr point out:

> Many adolescents—perhaps a majority—do not progress beyond concrete operational thought. In the same fashion, there are no guarantees that older adolescents operate at advanced, or even middle, levels of cognitive social development. Those same adolescents who vary so widely in physical status likewise vary in intellectual and social skills.

Clearly, individual interventions with adolescents require that counselors understand how clients attach meaning to their experiences. Awareness of the developmental level of the adolescent client must be an important component in each counselor-client interaction.

Another theme that unites these chapters is the authors' shared recognition of the interactions among varied problematic behaviors. Ingersoll and Orr cite the research of Jessor and Jessor (1974), Donovan and Jessor (1985), and others to support the idea that drug abuse, delinquency, and early sexual activity are linked, especially by the individual's rejection of commonly held social values. In his analysis of adolescent violence, Winbush addresses such seemingly diverse behaviors as suicide, drug abuse, and criminal behavior. Hayes and Cryer provide a profile of the adolescent who becomes pregnant and keeps her child:

> She is likely to express less acceptance of social norms, be biologically ready for pregnancy and childbirth, possess an inability to use information and an inability to project events into the future, have an unstable family environment, have no clearly defined religious orienta-

tion, have poor school performance and low educational aspirations, and have low self-esteem.

The similarity between this profile and that of the adolescent drug abuser cannot be overlooked by the counselor who hopes to understand and intervene. As Ingersoll and Orr point out,

> The linked nature of many risk behaviors suggests that categorical interventions limited to only one component of a series of problem behaviors and ignoring the others will be unsuccessful. For example, insisting that sexual abstinence is the only way to prevent teenage pregnancy ignores the interactions between drug use, antisocial acts, and early sexual activity. A given behavior may serve multiple personal needs.

Finally, these authors share a vision of counseling that encompasses *prevention* as well as intervention. Each article provides a set of practical suggestions for services to address a particular issue. The guidelines presented have a number of common characteristics, including:

— a recognition that complex problems require multifaceted strategies for their resolution. No single method will always be appropriate.
— an awareness that interventions should fit the developmental level and special needs of the individual at risk, and careful assessment as the basis for the approach to be used.
— a focus on the roles of family, peer group, and other systems in the development and resolution of problems.
— an appreciation of the need to use honest, straightforward, two-way communication in dealing with adolescents.
— a combination of broad, preventive measures and specific, targeted interventions to address each issue.

Adolescence is, for many, a difficult transitional stage. Because of the complexity of the issues involved, counseling clients who are at this stage in their development is demanding. The articles in this section do not oversimplify this challenge, but they do provide some practical, positive strategies.

REFERENCES

Donovan, J. E., & Jessor, R. (1985). Structure of problem behavior in adolescence and young adulthood. *Journal of Consulting & Clinical Psychology, 53,* 890–904.

Elkind, D. (1974). *Children and adolescents: Interpretive essays on Jean Piaget* (2nd ed.). New York: Oxford University Press.

Jessor, S. J., & Jessor, R. (1974). *Problem behavior and psychosocial development: A longitudinal study of youth.* New York: Academic Press.

1

Adolescents At Risk

Gary M. Ingersoll and Donald P. Orr

When G. Stanley Hall (1904) first set the parameters for the psychological study of adolescence and adolescents, he left as part of his intellectual legacy the phrase "storm and stress" as a descriptor of this developmental period. In Hall's vision, adolescence was, by its bio-psycho-social nature, doomed to be tumultuous. Later writers, especially those from a psychoanalytic tradition, not only concurred with Hall's assessment but added that *failure* to show signs of disturbance during adolescence was a symptom of maladjustment. More recent writers, however, have taken that assumption to task. Rather than being the subjects of uncontrolled biologic impulses, stress, and tumult, the vast majority of adolescents fare quite well; only a minority fit the more classic description (Adelson, 1979; Bandura, 1964; Offer & Offer, 1975; Offer, Ostrov, & Howard, 1984).

Still, for those who deal with adolescents in a therapeutic context, there remains a subgroup that *does* experience storm and stress, whose transition to adulthood is marked by turmoil and trial. Further, only a recluse could be unaware of the statistics that show an upsurge in adolescent suicide, pregnancy, and venereal disease, as well as continued patterns of drug and alcohol use and abuse, school dropouts, and delinquency. For some young people, adolescence is an extended period of struggle; for others the transition is marked by alternating periods of struggle and quiescence. During periods of stress and tumult, this latter group's ability to draw on effective adaptive coping behaviors is taxed. The resulting maladaptive behavior risks compromising physical, psychological, or social health. These young people are *at risk*. The present review is directed toward this group.

Although our focus is on at-risk adolescents, we do not intend to review in detail specific at-risk behaviors such as drug and alcohol use, suicide, or promiscuity. Neither will we address issues related to serious psychopathy. Instead, we offer a perspective on adolescents who are likely to engage in at-risk behaviors. To do so, we will touch on selected psychological and social factors that contribute to at-risk behavior.

7

RISK TAKING

In part, the willingness of adolescents to engage in risk-taking behaviors is normative. Use of the term "adolescent" to describe someone's behavior is a perjorative, implying impulsivity and low levels of social maturity. As Baumrind (1987) notes, however, because risk-taking behaviors are common to youth culture does not excuse those behaviors, nor does such knowledge reduce the danger that those behaviors present.

Differences among adolescents in their willingness to engage in risk-taking behaviors seems related to a general personality factor (McNeely, 1986). Those who are more likely to regularly take risks score higher on scales of venturesomeness and sensation seeking. McNeely found that the willingness to be risk taking diminishes across the adolescent years; risk taking appears related to general behavioral maturity. She also found that among those who had actually engaged in risk-taking behaviors that were rated as serious, their reported willingness to engage in future risk-taking behaviors was reduced. Apparently the experience of serious risk was, for some, motive to cease.

An important concept in understanding risk taking among adolescents is drawn from the work of David Elkind (1967) on adolescent egocentrism. In his characterization, Elkind noted that the emergence of advanced thinking skills at adolescence results in adolescents being able to conceive of other people's thoughts. The shortfall of this ability, however, is that, because of their egocentrism, they presume that others have the same thoughts as themselves. They generate an *invisible audience* that is obsessively concerned with the individual's well-being and status. An adolescent may engage in risky behavior because the audience will appreciate his or her bravery.

Adolescents also are likely to engage in the generation of *personal fables*. They presume that they and their personal problems are unique; no one else could possibly understand. Because of their uniqueness, they also make the inference that they are immune to harm, that they are invulnerable and immortal. They see themselves as unique and beyond harm.

The concept of the adolescent as a risk taker, while at times an appropriate descriptor, may be inaccurate to the extent that it tends to oversimplify a complex set of behaviors into a single, unidimensional activity. This is clearly not always appropriate. Risk taking has many meanings. Although there are some unifying themes, one must keep in mind that a single risky behavior or a set of such behaviors may meet several different needs and have various causes. As developmentally normative behavior, risk taking may meet biologic, psychosocial or societal/parental needs, and as such the activity itself may be rewarding and reinforcing for the adolescent (Irwin & Millstein, 1986).

For example, many people view alcohol consumption and sexual activity as socially appropriate adult behaviors. Those same behaviors are illegal among minors solely by reason of chronological age; thus, the same youths may not see them as risk taking. The behaviors become dangerous (place the adolescent at risk) only when the adolescent lacks the experience and knowledge to protect himself or herself from harm. To determine whether a specific behavior or activity represents risk taking, it must be viewed in the context of possible motivations and the potential dangers that may result.

AT-RISK PROFILE

Within the research literature there is ample evidence that those who are identified as falling into one at-risk category (sexually active, school dropout, substance abuse, etc.) are likely to fall into one or more other at-risk categories (see, for example, Donovan & Jessor, 1985). Further, the likelihood of occurrence of at-risk behaviors varies with age and gender. For example, transition into and out of middle or junior high school seems a particularly sensitive time (see, for example, Lipsitz, 1977; Peterson & Crockett, 1985; Irwin & Millstein, 1986; Simmons & Blyth, 1987).

In their longitudinal study of problem behaviors, Jessor and Jessor (1977) found that, among high school and college youths, a variety of problem behaviors clustered together. That is, frequency of engaging in alternative at-risk or problem behaviors was intercorrelated. Later Donovan and Jessor (1985), using multivariate statistical analyses, found a single common trait that they described as "unconventionality," which accounted for much of the common variance among the variables. Unconventionality, in this sense, should not be confused with nonconformist creativity. Rather, it appears to reflect a lack of willingness to conform to conventional social values. This common trait, thus, is of importance, because these problem behaviors risk jeopardizing physical and psychological status.

In data collected from junior high school students (Orr & Brack, in preparation), youngsters were asked to indicate whether they had engaged in specific behaviors or experienced selected feelings. Items addressed issues of substance abuse, sexual activity, health-related behaviors, legal issues, relationships with others, and management of emotions. Factor analysis of their responses yielded two primary factor structures that were stable in content over males and females and between younger and older adolescents. The first factor related to general willingness to engage in problem behaviors; and the second factor related to tendency to report psychological symptoms (see Table 1).

The first factor results from a clustering of three broad categories of problem behaviors—substance abuse, sexual behavior, and delinquent behavior. The structure of this (problem) behavioral factor does not change between males and females, although the magnitude of specific factor loadings may vary. For example, loadings of sexual behavior as representative of problem behaviors were smaller for males than for females, perhaps reflecting less social stigma for males. In contrast, consideration of dropping out of school yielded a higher factor rating among males.

TABLE 1
Behavioral and Affective At-Risk Factors
Among Junior High School Students

Problem Behaviors	**Psychological Symptoms**
Substance Abuse	Loneliness
Use alcohol	Sadness
Use pot	Easily upset
Use other drugs	Nervousness
Sexual Activity	Tension
Sexual intercourse	Consider hurting self
Pregnancy	Sleep difficulties
Delinquent Behaviors	Interpersonal difficulties
Running away	
School suspension	
Considering dropping out	
Arrests	

Based on Orr & Brack (unpublished data)

The second factor is a clustering of emotional variables that are not infrequently, but not uniformly, tied to depression. The psychological factor, if not clearly one of depression, is certainly a configuration of potentially problematic states.

BIOLOGY

It would be naive to automatically dismiss the long-held belief that there are biological antecedents to adolescent risk-taking behaviors. Recent evidence from several laboratories strongly indicates that serum androgenic hormones are important factors in male adolescent aggressive behavior and sexual motivation (Olweus, Mattsson, Scholling, & Low, 1980; Sussman, Inhoff-Germain, Nottelman, et al., in press; Udry, Billy, Morris, et al., 1985). The evidence is less convincing for adolescent females (Udry, Talbert, & Morris, 1986).

Some also consider the timing of pubertal maturation, with respect to peers, to be an important determinant in risk taking (Irwin & Millstein, 1986). Early puberty is disadvantageous for girls; those who begin puberty earlier than same-age peers are more likely to become sexually active and use drugs (Magnusson, Stattin, & Allen, 1985). Late physical development is a risk factor for boys, with increased likelihood of delinquent behaviors, school problems, and other anti-social activities (Irwin & Millstein, 1986; Simmons, 1987). It is not yet possible to separate direct biological effects from indirect ones that result from adolescents' and others' responses to developmental asynchrony.

PARENTS

There are those, especially those from a psychoanalytic framework, who speculate that the willingness of adolescents to engage in at-risk or problem behaviors is related to their struggles for emotional and psychological independence from their parents. Risk taking thus is seen as an assertion of one's individuality and a rejection of parental values (and symbolically the parents).

Establishing adult independence from parents is a socially sanctioned attribute of psychological maturity (Greenberger, 1984). Parents, therefore, expect that as adolescents mature, they will assume increased responsibility for their own behavior. But is it necessary that the process of establishing independence be accompanied by challenge and rejection of parental values? This concept does seem to have some validity because, even among families whose adolescents appear well adjusted, some degree of challenge to parental authority seems normal (Steinberg, 1987a; Steinberg & Silverberg, 1986). Elkind (1984) adds the additional caution that contemporary western society imposes pressures to accelerate this transition, and that young people are being thrust into roles for which they are unprepared.

Adolescents who regularly engage in at-risk behaviors are more likely to come from families with inept parenting styles (Patterson, 1986). Reviews of the impact of parenting style on adjustment of offspring repeatedly demonstrate links between inadequate parenting and psychosocial maladjustment. Conversely, positive parenting styles are associated with positive psychosocial adjustment (see Steinberg, 1987b; Thomas, Gecas, Weigart, & Rooney, 1974).

Olson (Olson, Sprenkle, & Russell, 1979; Barnes & Olson, 1985) has found the dimensions of family adaptability and cohesion to be particularly salient in the analysis of family variables and offspring adjustment. *Cohesion* refers to the degree to which a family "sticks together," and it also reflects the degree to which family members are expected to think alike. What is attractive about this model of family functioning is that it suggests that either extreme of family cohesiveness is unhealthy. At one extreme, a family may be so cohesive that the individual members are enmeshed; they lose individuality. At the other extreme, family members may be disengaged and offer each other little or no social-emotional support. In the same fashion, families may vary in *adaptability* from overly rigid, nonadaptive to overly reactive, chaotic reactions to stress. As family patterns are reflected in one or the other extremity of one or both dimensions, risk of maladaptivity in the offspring increases.

On the other hand, some risk-taking behaviors may be expected as part of the adolescent's attempts at asserting autonomy from parents. Recent research evidence (Steinberg & Silverberg, 1986) suggests that the transition from childhood dependence to adult independence may present unique developmental roadblocks. Rather than moving from one state to the other, adolescents may move from a state of psychological and emotional dependence on parents to a comparable dependence on peers prior to adult independence. If, as Elkind (1984) suggests, there is a societal press for earlier psychological separation from parents, the risks of peer influence on risk-taking behavior are enhanced.

PEERS

Peer influences on adolescent at-risk behaviors may be seen as taking two somewhat divergent forms. In the first form, peer influence in direct; peer acceptance and approval are contingent upon conformity to behavioral standards. Repeatedly, research evidence indicates linkages between the individual adolescent's willingness to engage in at-risk behaviors and the likelihood that peers engage in the same behaviors. This relationship has been demonstrated in substance abuse (see Bachman, O'Malley, & Johnston, 1980; Jessor & Jessor, 1974), sexuality (see Jessor & Jessor, 1974; Sach, Keller, & Hinkle, 1984), school dropouts (see Rumberger, 1987), and delinquent behavior (see Gold & Petronio, 1980; Kazdin, 1987). The more likely at-risk behavior is sanctioned and expected by the peer culture, the more likely the individual adolescent is to engage in that behavior.

The second way in which peer approval plays a role in the tendency to engage in at-risk behavior is in its absence. Children and adolescents who are isolated from peers, and for whom peer approval is lacking, are more likely to engage in behaviors that are antisocial (Hartup, 1983). Failure to establish workable social ties with peers is a major predictor of social and emotional maladjustment during adolescence and adulthood.

STRESSFUL EVENTS

Normal adolescence requires the completion of a variety of socially and psychologically defined developmental tasks. During the progression from childhood to adulthood, a young person may be subject to outside events that interfere with the smooth transition. Some stressful events, such as changing schools as one moves from elementary to middle and high school, are common to most young people. Other events, such as a family separation and divorce, may be shared by many. Other events, of only a few, such as development of a physical handicap or a chronic illness, may be the province of only a few. Any such event, however, taxes the individual's capability of dealing with other normal stresses.

Research studies indicate that major and minor life transitions, both positive *and* negative events, can result in feelings of stress for the individual. Coddington (1972) estimated that the typical adolescent experiences three or more transitional life events each year. Each transitional event requires the adolescent to muster psychological resources to make social and emotional adjustments. There are, however, no universally accepted scales of the degree of impact of transitional life events on adolescents' developmental progress. Wide individual differences exist in reactions to similar life events; not all adolescents respond similarly. The transition from elementary to middle school, for example, may be negative for one child but positive for another. The impact of transitional life events depends on the value given them by the individual (Johnson, 1986; Healy & Stewart, 1984).

Significant life events may, however, have a generalized disruptive effect on an individual's ability to cope. The adolescent who experiences several major life events may be overwhelmed and unable to cope. Likewise, the adolescent who experiences repeated failure in ability to cope over time may develop negative feelings of self as a competent individual and elect to engage in behaviors that are either self-destructive or reflect frustration.

Certainly not all stress is bad. It can serve as an important motivator, and our success at dealing with stressful tasks provides for positive feelings of self-worth. On the other hand, too much stress and failure to deal adequately with stress may result in physical and psychological distress. Further, Lazarus (1966) has offered convincing evidence that the range and number of daily "hassles" in the adolescent's life may be as influential in fostering positive or negative health behaviors as standard life events.

DEPRESSION

Most adolescents experience periods in which they are depressed and uncertain; events seem out of control and they are unable to cope. For most, those feelings are short-lived and, after a period feeling "down," the individual regains feelings of competence. For some, however, the feelings are longer lasting and may lead to serious disruption in one's life. Debate over the character of adolescent depression continues in the clinical literature (Lefkowitz & Burton, 1978; Cantwell, 1982; Chartier & Ranieri, 1984), because it may be masked by behaviors not typical among depressed adults. But depression undoubtedly does occur among adolescents and is a major contributor to poor academic performance, truancy, delinquency and acting out, substance abuse, suicide, and alienation from peers and family (Teuting, Kaslow, & Hirschfeld, 1981).

ANTISOCIAL BEHAVIOR AND DELINQUENCY

Although the focus of this review is not on the subgroup of young people whose behavioral profile is seriously antisocial or sociopathic, we have to recognize that these individuals exist and that minimal intervention is not apt to afford much success. At-risk youngsters in this category may fit the delinquent syndrome described by Achenbach (1985), or as conduct disorders by Kazdin (1987). The profile includes repeated lying or cheating, running away, stealing (at and away from home), excessive obscene language, and associating with others who are regularly in trouble. The key elements that draw together the profile of young people in this group are chronicity of problem behaviors, intensity of the behaviors, and the variety of settings within which the problem behaviors are observed and recorded.

Observers of these youngsters perceive that their problem behaviors reflect a personality profile that is likely to persist into the adult years (Kazdin, 1987). Though some youngsters who display chronic delinquent behavior during adolescence cease such behavior once they enter adult social roles and internalize normative social standards, many do not. Those whose problem behaviors are recorded early, often, and as seriously deviant are more likely to show continued social maladjustment as adults (Kazdin, 1987; Loeber, 1982; Robins, 1974).

In a 22-year follow-up of children who had been rated by peers as aggressive or prosocial, Eron (1987) reports a high degree of stability in behavior. That is, those who were targeted by peers as aggressive in childhood were apt to engage in aggressive acts as adults. Conversely, those rated as prosocial as children were likely to be prosocial as adults.

SOCIAL COMPETENCE

An individual's ability to behave in ways that are socially adept, skilled, and effective is fundamental to good psychological health. Social competence results in positive feedback and acceptance. Conversely, social incompetence is a major early predictor of adolescent maladjustment and adult psychopathology. Those who are socially adept are more likely to receive positive feedback from peers and adults. Those who are socially inept are more likely to be shunned and avoided.

Dodge (Dodge & Murphy, 1983; McFall & Dodge, 1982) suggests that social competence is dependent on the individual's ability to adequately decode and interpret social settings. Persons who are socially competent are able to accurately identify critical cues in a social setting, or are at least able to take their own cues from someone else who has greater sensitivity. Once the social setting is interpreted, the individual must select from among a variety of alternative behaviors; the individual must decide which behavior is appropriate for which situation. Alternatively, in the absence of a clear interpretation of the setting, the socially competent individual may elect to model the behavior of the person seen as socially competent. Once the behavior choice is made, it must be translated smoothly into action. At that time, the individual receives feedback from others in the social setting to indicate appropriateness of the response. Socially adept individuals likewise are more sensitive to the feedback (Dodge, Pettit, McClaskey, & Brown, 1986).

Less socially competent individuals fail to perceive critical cues, or they misperceive the social intentions or the social dynamics of a setting. As a result, their ability to choose among behaviors is disrupted by fundamental errors in social encoding. Second, those who are socially incompetent may lack an adequate repertoire of socially acceptable behaviors. Irrespective of whether they interpret or misinterpret the setting, they lack the social skills with which to respond. Third, their initiation of the behavior may be strained, and they seem unaware of social feedback regarding the adequacy of their behavior.

In the case of at-risk adolescents, there is a strong likelihood that they lack adequate social competence to draw on a reservoir of adequate and appropriate behaviors, or that the stresses of current life events are sufficiently disruptive that they interfere with the individual's ability to decode and respond. In the latter case, knowing what to do and being able to do it are not the same. Anxiety, inexperience, and emotions may interfere.

Social competence, like social cognition, is a developmentally related trait (Selman, 1980). As one matures cognitively, the ability to analyze and decode complex social settings also matures. In dealing with adolescents, we cannot expect a 13-year-old to respond in the same fashion as an 18-year-old. As intellect matures, individuals progress not only in their ability to deal with more information, but they also progress in the quality with which they manage information. In the same fashion, individuals shift in their abilities to interpret social settings.

At early levels of social cognitive maturity, individuals interpret social settings from a hedonic, egocentric, and self-serving view. Their ability to generalize social cues from one setting to another, or to see causal links of their behavior to outcomes beyond the immediate present, is distinctly limited. As individuals move into middle levels of cognitive-social development, their behaviors are more likely to be directed toward what they see as socially desirable or as demanded by those in authority. Interpretation of social settings is categorical and simplistic. They may be able to generalize behavior across settings, but their ability to recognize subtle differentiations that require similar alterations in their own behavior are limited. At advanced levels of social cognition, individuals recognize the complex interdependence of their own and others' behaviors. The abilities to generalize and differentiate have progressed along with their ability to recognize time-related causal relationships of their behavior to outcomes.

A common misconception of adolescent thinking is that advanced levels of thinking—what Piaget (e.g., 1970) refers to as formal operational thought—are automatically part of the adolescent transition. Many adolescents, perhaps a majority, do not progress beyond concrete operational thought. In the same fashion, there are no guarantees that older adolescents, operate at advanced or even middle levels of cognitive-social development. Those same adolescents who vary so widely in physical status likewise vary in intellectual and social skills.

Beyond developmental differences in abilities to interpret social settings, adolescents may vary in personal ability to interpret social cues as a function of their levels of stress. Under stressful transitions in their life course, the ability to respond with social adeptness may be restricted.

DESIGNING A SOCIAL INTERVENTION

Just as there is no single cause or single well defined pattern of at-risk adolescent behavior, neither is there a single intervention strategy appropriate to all who display at-risk behaviors. Nevertheless, our understanding of adolescent development can guide us in designing rational interventions.

1. One must identify, to the extent possible, the underlying basis for the at-risk behavior and determine whether it represents a normative process, a psychopathology, or misguided attempts to meet psychosocial needs. Given the assessment, the appropriate intervention might be education with help in resisting peer pressure, psychological evaluation and therapy, or providing a substitute behavior.
2. The linked nature of many risk behaviors suggests that categorical interventions limited to only one component of a series of problem behaviors and ignoring the others will be unsuccessful. For example, insisting that sexual abstinance is the only way to prevent teenage pregnancy ignores the interactions between drug use, antisocial acts, and early sexual activity. A given behavior may serve multiple personal needs.
3. Interventions must be focused and targeted to specific behaviors and audiences. The format of intervention will vary according to whether the goal is primary prevention or secondary or tertiary interventions. For example, effective programs designed to prevent alcohol-related deaths could include: psychoeducational school instruction; screening to identify individual students with alcohol problems; providing free, nonjudgmental adult transportation for intoxicated youths to discourage driving under the influence; student-initiated programs such as Students Against Drunk Driving; alternatives to expulsion programs for students caught consuming alcohol on school grounds; or legislation to lower the legal driving age so that risk of simultaneous introduction to two dangerous activities (drinking and driving) are reduced.
4. Whatever the format, intervention must be matched to the adolescent's developmental needs. Mismatching the intervention environment and developmental traits will result in treatment failure and further diminish the already low feelings of personal adequacy in the at-risk adolescent.

Hunt (1971; Hunt & Sullivan, 1974) provides compelling evidence that the optimal environment for those at low levels of cognitive social development should be firmly structured, with clear behavioral guidelines. The emotional context of intervention should be warm, with rules firmly enforced. Complexity of behavioral guidelines should be minimized. Too much uncertainty or response ambiguity will result in closure and rejection. In the case of at-risk adolescents, those operating at lower levels of cognitive-social development may be aware enough of their behavioral dysfunction to also have lowered feelings of self-competence. Hence, an important element in an intervention strategy is to provide successful experiences with ample positive reinforcement.

For adolescents at moderate levels of cognitive-social development, the optimal treatment environment is less structured than for those at lower levels, but still constrained. Because adolescents at middle levels of cognitive social development are oriented toward authority for guidance, they have a tendency to want adults to "Tell me what to do." Our temptation in dealing with these youngsters is to acquiesce to their desire. But these youngsters have the rudiments of appropriate behavioral repertoires, so what they need is assistance in improving their cue attending and response selection skills. Although they may prefer highly certain tasks, unlike their less socially mature peers they can manage with some element of situational ambiguity. Treatment modalities should take the form of "guided discovery."

Adolescents at advanced levels of cognitive-social maturity are basically autonomous thinkers who possess complex cognitive skills. Typically, they are not only tolerant of ambiguity, but they prefer settings that are multifaceted. At-risk adolescents in this category are more likely undergoing acute situational crises and have the capability to deal with analysis of complex interpersonal relationships. Treatment modalities may include complex problem analysis.

Matching the intervention modality to the level of cognitive-social maturity admittedly is complicated by the lack of clear definitional boundaries between levels of development and the lack of generally agreed-upon instrumentation for its measurement. In our own work with chronically ill and at-risk middle school children and adolescents, however, we have found the Paragraph Completion Method (Hunt, Butler, Noy, & Rosner, 1971) to be useful. The PCM is semi-projective instrument composed of six open-ended questions assessing the adolescent's concepts and attitudes regarding conflict, rules, and authority. The resulting score reflects a global measure of cognitive-social maturity.

Beyond providing interventions in response to specific behavioral crises, for effective change to occur, intervention should flow from planning. At present, we typically mount intervention programs in response to some presenting crisis such as multiple suicides or drug overdoses. These programmatic interventions, while well intentioned, are usually short-lived. And, meanwhile, other, less salient at-risk behaviors are ignored. In other situations, categories of at-risk behaviors are dealt with separately. A pregnancy prevention program may be initiated, and several disparate dropout prevention programs may be offered in the same school district. Although these alternative programs do exist, they often fail to share resources and end up competing with each other. Programmatic intervention for at-risk behaviors should result from coordinated efforts.

CLOSING COMMENTS

At the outset, we noted that the generalized image of adolescence as a period of storm and stress was misleading. Yet, as practitioners dealing with adolescents, we are aware that this period of development is not conversely a period of peace and tranquility. For most young people who have a behavioral crisis that places them at-risk for physical, social, or psychological harm, our interventions are short-term crisis intervention strategies. For some, however, more intensive, long-term interventions are advisable. In cases of school-based counselors, for example, adequate resources may not exist for such intensive responses. Counselors in these settings should establish a referral network built on expected needs.

The preceding discussion begs the question, "Which treatment techniques best fit the needs of which at-risk adolescents?" The unfortunate reality is that theory and research have not yet progressed adequately to offer a clear answer. But, it does appear reasonable to speculate that therapeutic techniques aimed at developing coping mechanisms to deal with stress and to learn cue attending and social skills are in order.

REFERENCES

Achenbach, T. M. (1985) Assessment and taxonomy of child and adolescent psychopathology. *Developmental Clinical Psychology & Psychiatry* (No. 3). Beverly Hills: Sage.

Adelson, J. (1979). The myth of the generation gap. *Psychology Today, 12*(9), 33–34, 37.

Bachman, J. G., O'Malley, P. M., & Johnston, L. D. (1980). *Correlates of drug use: 1. Selected measures of background, recent experiences, and lifestyle* (Monitoring the Future Occasional Paper 8). Ann Arbor, MI: Institute for Social Research.

Bandura, A. (1964). The stormy decade, fact or fiction. *Psychology in the Schools, 1,* 224–231.

Barnes, H. L., & Olson, D. H. (1985). Parent-adolescent communication and the circumplex model. *Child Development, 56,* 438–447.

Baumrind, D. (1987). A developmental perspective on adolescent risk-taking in contemporary America. In C. E. Irwin (Ed.), *Adolescent health and social behavior: New directions in child development* (No. 37) (pp. 93–126). San Francisco: Jossey-Bass.

Cantwell, D. P. (1982). Childhood depression: A review of current research. In B. Leahy & A. Kazdin (Eds.), *Advances in Clinical Child Psychology.* New York: Plenum.

Chartier, G. M., & Ranieri, D. J. (1984). Adolescent depression: Concepts, treatment, preventions. In J. Karoly & P. Steffan (Eds.), *Adolescent behavior disorders: Foundations and contemporary concerns* (pp. 168–196). Lexington, MA: Lexington Books.

Coddington, R. D. (1972). The significance of life events as etiologic factors in the diseases of children: 2. A survey of a normal population. *Journal of Psychosomatic Research, 16,* 205–213.

Dodge, K. A., & Murphy, P. R. (1983). The assessment of social competence in adolescents. In P. Karoly & J. J. Steffan (Eds.), *Adolescent behavior disorders: Foundations and contemporary concerns* (pp. 97–132). Lexington, MA: Lexington Books.

Dodge, K. A., Pettit, G. S., McClaskey, C. L., & Brown, M. M. (1986). Social competence in children. *Monographs of the Society for Research in Child Development, 51* (2, Serial No. 213).

Donovan, J. E., & Jessor, R. (1985). Structure of problem behavior in adolescence and young adulthood. *Journal of Consulting & Clinical Psychology, 53,* 890–904.

Elkind, D. (1967) Egocentrism at adolescence. *Child Development, 38,* 1025–1034.

Elkind, D. (1984). *All grown up and no place to go: Teenagers in crisis.* Reading, MA: Addison-Wesley.

Eron, L. D. (1987). The development of aggressive behavior from the perspective of a developing behaviorism. *American Psychologist, 42,* 435–442.

Gold, M., & Petronio, R. J. (1980). Delinquent behavior in adolescence. In J. Adelson (Ed.), *Handbook of adolescent psychology.* New York: Wiley.

Greenberger, E. (1984). Defining psychosocial maturity in adolescence. In P. Karoly & J. J. Steffan (Eds.), *Adolescent behavior disorders: Foundations and contemporary concerns* (pp. 61–96). Lexington, MA: Lexington Books.

Hall, G. S. (1904) *Adolescence: Its psychology and its relations to physiology, anthropology, sociology, sex, crime, religion and education.* New York: Appleton.

Hartup, W. W. (1983). The peer system. In E. M. Heatherington (Ed.), *Carmichael's manual of child psychology: Vol. 4. Socialization, personality, and social development* (pp. 275–386). New York: John Wiley.

Healy, J. M., & Stewart, A. J. (1984). Adaptation to life changes in adolescence. In P. Karoly & J. J. Steffan (Eds.), *Adolescent behavior disorders: Foundations and contemporary concerns* (pp. 39–60). Lexington, MA: Lexington Books.

Hunt, D. E. (1971). *Matching models of teacher education: The coordination of teaching methods with student characteristics*. Toronto: Ontario Institute for Studies in Education.

Hunt, D. E., & Sullivan, E. V. (1974). *Between psychology and education*. Hinsdale, IL: Dryden.

Hunt, D. E., Butler, L. F., Noy, J. F., & Rosner, M. C. (1978). *Assessing conceptual level by the paragraph completion method*. Toronto: Ontario Institute for Studies in Education.

Irwin, C. E., & Millstein, S. G. (1986). Biopsychosocial correlates of risk-taking behaviors during adolescence. *Journal of Adolescent Health Care, 7,* 825–965.

Jessor, S. J., & Jessor, R. (1977). *Problem behavior and psychosocial development: A longitudinal study of youth*. New York: Academic Press.

Johnson, J. H. (1986). Life events as stressors in childhood and adolescence. *Developmental Clinical Psychology & Psychiatry* (No. 8). Beverly Hills, CA: Sage.

Kazdin, A. E. (1987). Conduct disorders in childhood and adolescence. *Developmental Clinical Psychology & Psychiatry* (No. 9). Beverly Hills, CA: Sage.

Lazarus, R. S. (1966). *Psychological stress and the coping process*. New York: McGraw-Hill.

Lefkowitz, M. M., & Burton, N. (1978). Childhood depression: A critique of the concept. *Psychological Bulletin, 83,* 716–726.

Lipsitz, J. (1977). *Growing up forgotten*. Lexington, MA: Lexington Books.

Loeber, R. (1982). The stability of antisocial and delinquent behavior. *Child Development, 53,* 1431–1446.

Magnusson, D., Stattin, H., & Allen, V. (1985). Biological maturation and social development: A longitudinal study of some adjustment processes from mid-adolescence to adulthood. *Journal of Youth & Adolescence, 14,* 167–184.

McFall, R. M., & Dodge, K. A. (1982). Self-management and interpersonal skills learning. In P. Karoly & K. H. Kanfer (Eds.), *Self-management and behavior change* (pp. 353–392). Elmford, NY: Pergamon.

McNeely, S. L. (1986, April). *Components of risk-taking behavior in adolescence*. Paper presented at the annual meeting of the American Educational Research Association, Washington, DC.

Offer, D., & Offer, J. (1975). *From teenage to young manhood*. New York: Basic Books.

Offer, D., Ostrov, E., & Howard, K. I. (1984). The self-image of normal adolescents. In D. Offer, E. Ostrov, & K. I. Howard (Eds.), *Patterns of adolescent self-image: New directions in mental health services* (No. 22) (pp. 5–16). San Francisco: Jossey-Bass.

Olson, D. H., Sprenkle, D. H., & Russell, C. S. (1979). Circumplex model of marital and family systems: 1. Cohesion and adaptability dimensions, family types, and clinical applications. *Family Process, 11,* 365–455.

Olweus, D., Mattsson, A., Scholling, D., & Low, H. (1980). Testosterone, aggression, physical and personality dimensions in normal adolescent males. *Psychosomatic Medicine, 42,* 253–269.

Orr, D. P., & Brack, K. (In preparation). *Structure of problem behaviors in young adolescents*.

Patterson, G. R. (1986). Performance models for antisocial boys. *American Psychologist, 41,* 432–444.

Peterson, A. C., & Crockett, L. (1985). Pubertal timing and grade effects on adjustment. *Journal of Youth & Adolescence, 14,* 191–205.

Piaget, J. (1970). Piaget's theory. In P. H. Mussen (Ed.), *Carmichael's manual of child psychology*. New York: Wiley.

Robins, L. N. (1974). *Deviant children grow up* (2nd ed.). Huntington, NY: Krieger.

Rumberger, R. W. (1987). High school dropouts: A review of issues and evidence. *Review of Educational Research, 57,* 101–121.

Sach, A. R., Keller, J. F., & Hinkle, D. E. (1984). Premarital sexual intercourse: A test of the effects of peer groups, religiosity, and sexual guilt. *Journal of Sex Research, 20,* 168–185.

Selman, R. (1980). *The growth of interpersonal understanding: Developmental and clinical analyses*. New York: Academic Press.

Simmons, R. G. (1987). Social transition and adolescent development. In Irwin, C. E. (Ed.), *Adolescent health and social behavior: New directions in child development* (No. 37) (pp. 93–126). San Francisco: Jossey-Bass.

Simmons, R. G., & Blyth, D. A. (1987). *Moving into adolescence: The impact of pubertal change and school context*. New York: Aldine/Hawthorne.

Steinberg, L. (1987a). Bound to bicker. *Psychology Today, 21*(9), 36–39.

Steinberg, L. (1987b). Single parents, stepparents, and the susceptibility of adolescents to antisocial pressure. *Child Development, 58,* 269–275.

Steinberg, L., & Silverberg, S. B. (1986). The vicissitudes of autonomy. *Child Development, 57,* 841–851.

Sussman, E., Inoff-Germain, G., Nottelman, E., et al. (in press). Hormones, emotional dispositions, and aggressive attributes in young adolescents. *Child Development.*

Teuting, P., Kaslow, S. H., & Hirschfeld, R. M. A. (1981). *Special report on depression.* Bethesda, MD: National Institute on Mental Health.

Thomas, D. L., Gecas, V., Weigart, A., & Rooney, E. (1974). *Family socialization and the adolescent.* Lexington, MA: Lexington Books.

Udry, J., Billy, J., Morris, N., et al. (1985). Serum androgenic hormones motivate sexual behavior in boys. *Fertility & Sterility, 43,* 90–94.

Udry, J., Talbert, L., & Morris, N. (1986). Biosocial foundations for adolescent female sexuality. *Demography, 23,* 217–227.

Gary Ingersoll is associated with the Department of Counseling and Educational Psychology, Indiana University. Donald Orr is with the Department of Pediatrics, Indiana University School of Medicine.

2

When Adolescents Give Birth to Children: A Developmental Approach to the Issue Of Teen Pregnancy

Richard L. Hayes and Nancy Cryer

The magistrates are God-fearing gentlemen, but merciful overmuch—that is a truth. . . . At the very least, they should have put the brand of a hot iron on Hester Prynne's forehead. Madam Hester would have winced at that, I warrant me. But she—the naughty baggage— little will she care what they put upon the bodice of her gown! . . . This woman has brought shame upon us all, and ought to die. (Hawthorne, 1850/1983, p. 162)

In the more than 125 years since Hawthorne wrote those words, the prospects for and the popular perception of young, unwed mothers has shown little real improvement. True enough, young, unmarried women who become pregnant today will not have to stand trial before a magistrate, nor will they be prevented legally from seeking meaningful employment. Nonetheless, the reality for a young woman who may "go astray" in this day and age is that her prospects for living a full, productive life in this society are as relatively limited as if she had been condemned to wear an "A" embroidered upon her breast.

Despite a more open and accepting public policy on the part of Americans toward sexual behavior and teenage pregnancy, the sad reality is that premature parenthood places great limitations on the possibilities for a sizeable portion of each new generation to participate fully in realizing the American Dream. How teenage pregnancy is both a cause and an effect of the limited opportunities available to today's adolescents is the subject of this article. How an understanding of human development can help to explain this "maturational crisis" (Martin, 1973) and can form the basis for new approaches to coping with teenage pregnancy will be explored.

THE EXTENT OF TEENAGE PREGNANCY

Of the more than 29 million teenagers in this country, approximately 12 million have had sexual intercourse. Of this group, more than 1.1 million can be estimated to become pregnant this year (Alan Guttmacher Institute, 1981) and bear nearly one half million infants (Children's Defense Fund, 1982). Another 434,000 will terminate their pregnancies with an abortion (Alan Guttmacher Institute, 1984). Teenagers bear nearly 20% of all babies born in the United States, more than half of which are to unwed mothers, accounting for 44% of all births to unmarried women (Children's Defense Fund, 1982; Lachance, 1985).

Although the number of teenagers who became sexually active during the 1970s rose by nearly two thirds, the teenage birthrate has declined over the past two decades (Alan Guttmacher Institute, 1981). In the 1950s, 90 of 1,000 women under age 20 gave birth, as contrasted with 52 of 1,000 in 1978 (Polit, 1982). This situation has resulted, in part, because of teenagers' increased use of contraceptives to avoid pregnancy and of abortion to avoid giving birth. Nonetheless, three fourths of teenage pregnancies are unintended, with 78% of births to teenagers being first births (Alan Guttmacher Institute, 1984). Although the birthrate for mothers aged 15–19 is declining, the rate for those 14 and younger is actually increasing. Understanding that the sooner a teenager gives birth after initial sexual intercourse, the more likely she is to have subsequent births while still in her teens, one should not be surprised to learn that 19% of births to teenagers are second births and 4% are the third birth or more (Lachance, 1985).

Estimates show that 1.3 million children under age 5 are living with an adolescent parent and that public aid to teenage parents and their children will consume over $16.65 billion (Studies Target Teen Pregnancy, 1986, p. 1). Given that 96% of teenage mothers—90% of white and nearly all of black mothers—are choosing to keep their babies to rear (Lachance, 1985), the need to provide services for these young mothers and their children should be of immediate concern to counselors and other human service professionals.

CONSEQUENCES OF TEENAGE PREGNANCY

That SCARLET LETTER, so fantastically embroidered and illuminated upon [Hester's] bosom . . . had the effect of a spell, taking her out of the ordinary relations with humanity, and enclosing her in a sphere by herself. . . . Could it be true? She clutched the child so fiercely to her breast, that it sent forth a cry; she turned her eyes downward at the scarlet letter, and even touched it with her finger, to assure herself that the infant and the shame were real. Yes!—these were her realities—all else had vanished! (Hawthorne, 1850/1983, pp. 164–168)

The transition to adulthood has few markers for today's adolescents. Instead they are encouraged to participate in adult rituals. Consequently, premarital sexual activity has become part of the process for socialization into adult life. Yet, this learning is intended to be anticipatory rather than experiential. The young person today is bombarded with images of the successful, sexual adult (but is offered few and often ambiguous external sanctions for behaving inappropriately (Kantner, 1983). As a result, when teenagers are unsuccessful in their sexual negotiations to achieve adult status, the social response has been their exclusion from the society they have tried so hard to join. After a thorough review of the literature, Phipps-Yonas (1980) concluded that despite popular views to the contrary, no data suggest that any groups within American society view teenage childbearing positively. The promise of social inclusion vanishes in the reality that comes with being a pregnant teenager.

Socioeconomic Realities

Beyond the immediate effects to be realized with the birth of any child, teenage pregnancy involves many interrelated problems. These include substandard. housing, poor nutrition and health, unemployment, social isolation, incomplete education, inadequate vocational training, psychological and developmental difficulties, excessive fertility and large single-parent families, and socioeconomic dependency (Anastasiow, 1983; Cobe, 1976; Johnson, 1974; Klerman, 1975; Miller & Miller, 1983; Phipps-Yonas, 1980; Washington & Glimps, 1983).

The likelihood of living in poverty, for example, is seven times greater for a teenager who becomes pregnant and gives birth at a young age (Illinois Caucus on Teenage Pregnancy, 1983; Johnson, 1974; Miller & Miller, 1983; Phipps-Yonas, 1980). In fact, the mean family income of white women who gave birth at or before age 16 is about half that earned by families in which the mother delayed birth until her middle to late 20s (Alan Guttmacher Institute, 1981).

Women who bear their first child before age 20 are at greater risk for poverty and dependency on welfare. Nearly one half of all government expenditures through Aid to Families with Dependent Children (AFDC) are to households with women who were teenagers when their first child was born (U.S. Department of Health and Human Services, 1979). Results of a study by Presser (1979) indicate that 72% of mothers aged 15–17 required assistance, compared to 41% of mothers aged 17–19, 17% of mothers aged 20–23, and 9% of mothers aged 24–29.

Low-income pregnant adolescents have limited opportunities to emerge from their present economic status. A review of the literature reveals that the probability of a family living in poverty is related positively to the number of children in the family. This relationship between fertility and poverty appears especially cogent in terms of young teenage girls (Phipps-Yonas, 1980). As noted, the adolescent who first conceived and gave birth at a young age has more children than she desires or can afford. "Early pregnancy may contribute to the initiation and/or perpetuation of poverty conditions" (Johnson, 1974, p. 402).

In addition, the teenager's incomplete education adversely affects her ability to provide for herself and for her child. Because of limited resources, skills, education, and experience, pregnant adolescents have little to offer or provide for their future children. These children are cast in the same mold as their impoverished parents, and the poverty cycle is repeated again and again.

Educational Realities

Research has revealed that a substantial portion of adolescents who do not return to high school soon after the birth of their children do not complete their high school education (Miller & Miller, 1983). In a comprehensive review of the literature, Phipps-Yonas (1980) found that pregnancy was the most common reason for girls to fail to complete high school, with some 50%-67% of female drop-outs being pregnant.

Notably, these studies revealed that girls who become pregnant in adolescence were below average in their school performance and achievement test scores *even before* they conceived. This poor academic picture was often coupled with a history of difficulties and disinterest in school, as well as with low educational and vocational aspirations (p. 407). Importantly, the level of education appears to be related directly to factors associated with the maintenance or improvement of socioeconomic level, such as employment status, personal and social competencies, and income level.

Medical Realities

Complications arising from pregnancy have long been held to be exceptionally high for women under the age of 18. "The rates of anemia, toxemia, urinary tract infections, uterine dysfunction, cephalopelvic disproportion, abruptio placenta, prematurity, and other labor and delivery complications were reported to decrease as a function of age" (Phipps-Yonas, 1980, p. 405). Nonetheless, data to support this view have only recently begun to emerge and are confounded by the fact that illegitimacy and lower social-class status are associated with inadequate health care.

Although evidence supports the view that teenagers over age 14 are ready medically to become mothers, poor nutritional habits and inadequate prenatal care are more likely (Phipps-Yonas, 1980). Teenagers are less likely to seek prenatal care than are their older counterparts and, when they do, it is later in their pregnancy. In fact, nearly 50% of all teenage mothers seek no prenatal care in their first trimester. Beyond the medical complications mentioned, the death rate from these complications is 13% higher than the national average for mothers aged 15–19 and rises to 60% for mothers 15 or younger (Levering, 1983).

Marital Realities

Of course, these young women did not get pregnant by themselves. Nonetheless, only one in five premarital pregnancies is resolved through marriage (Kantner, 1983). Of teenagers who do marry, 54% of adolescent wives are not living with their husbands within 15 years of marriage, compared to 14% of women who married at later ages (Alan Guttmacher Institute, 1981). As a consequence, 70% of children born to mothers aged 17 or younger, compared to 25% of children born to mothers in their 20s, will spend part of their lives in single-parent homes (Alan Guttmacher Institute, 1981).

The role of male partners of these young women has been little explored in the literature. What is known tends to be contradictory. In a study reported in the recently released Congressional report on teen pregnancy (U.S. Congress, 1986), a nationwide survey of 400 teenage fathers reported that 82% of the respondents claimed to have daily contact with their child, even though they lived apart, and 74% claimed to be contributing to the child's support. Other studies were cited, however, suggesting that fewer than one in four teenage fathers is in contact with his child even once per week and that only one in six single women between the ages of 18 and 24 even receives child support (p. 17). In households where the father is present, he is likely to have dropped out of school and to hold an unskilled job, further limiting his ability to support a family (Furstenberg, 1976).

The Children

Despite the medical studies indicating that there should be no developmental differences between the offspring of teenage mothers and those of older mothers, most researchers agree that infants born to teenagers are a high-risk population. Phipps-Yonas (1980) found that these children have a higher risk of neonatal health problems. The journal of the Alan Guttmacher Institute (1981) contains a report that mothers aged 15 and younger are still two times more likely to have low birth weight babies than are those aged 20–24. Even those aged 19 have rates 27% higher than those who wait to give birth until they are in their early 20s.

Because low birth weight is a major cause of infant mortality, along with other serious childhood illnesses, birth injuries, and neurological defects, children born to teenagers are considerably at-risk. Some of the outcomes of adolescent pregnancies are: an increase in the number of failure-to-thrive infants, emotional disturbance among pre-schoolers, lower academic performance, and more frequent grade retention for children born to adolescents (Bennet & Bardon, 1977).

A disproportionate number of children of these young mothers, who frequently live in poverty, will become future members of the group of students referred to as exceptional or handicapped (Anastasiow, 1983). In addition, offspring of adolescent mothers tend to repeat the pattern, becoming adolescent parents themselves.

Studies reveal that adolescents in general, and adolescent mothers in particular, are ignorant of the usual course of infant development. Further, adolescent mothers' attitudes have been shown to resemble the attitudes of emotionally disturbed and abusive mothers. These mothers' need for independence appears to be in conflict with their own children's needs for independence, interfering with the normal process of attachment (Miller & Miller, 1983).

Young women who are subjected to isolation, poverty, and racism and who are ignorant of child-care techniques tend to have children who are normal at birth but who become handicapped by school age. Several factors are implicated in the normal infant's transformation into a handicapped child: disruption in the attachment process, inadequate stimulation and responsiveness on the part of the primary caregiver (usually the mother) in the first two years of life, and various forms of neglect and abuse. As a result, the adolescent mother is at-risk for producing an at-risk infant and may provide an environment that fails to fulfill what may be genetically possible for her child (Bennet & Bardon, 1977).

Finally, as previously noted, the earlier a teenage mother has her first child, the more children she is likely to have and the closer spaced they will be (Trussell & Menken, 1978). More disturbing, perhaps, are studies reported by Phipps-Yonas (1980) that found 60% of one sample of girls who delivered before age 17 were pregnant before age 19 and 8% of another sample were pregnant again within 6 months after they delivered (p. 415).

ALTERNATIVE EXPLANATIONS

To this point in the discussion, the prospects for teenage mothers and their children appear painfully bleak. Further, the implication is that these young mothers have pathological reasons for becoming pregnant and for continuing to do so. This focus on the negative outcomes of teenage pregnancy has obscured the reality that more than one half of all teenagers are *not* sexually active and, among those who are, more than 90% do *not* become pregnant. Of the teenagers who do become pregnant, three fourths will have done so *un*intentionally. Further, nearly 95% of all teenagers will reach their 20s *without* having given birth. Of the teenagers who do bear children, one fourth of those aged 15–17, and more than one half of those aged 17–19, do *not* receive public aid. Finally, of pregnant teenagers who do marry, nearly one half are *still married* more than 15 years later.

To understand teenage pregnancy in all its complexity, one must understand the resources—economic, social, physiological, and psychological—available to teenage mothers and fathers. The issue becomes whether and in what ways pregnant teenagers are different or whether they are different because they are pregnant.

Part of the problem in finding answers to these questions lies in the nature of the studies that have been done to find the answers. Because the teenagers who are the object of most studies are already experiencing some stress, it is difficult to tell whether they are feeling or acting differently than they did in the past (Phipps-

Yonas, 1980). Further, the major theoretical frameworks that have been advanced to explain teenage pregnancy have offered psychological explanations primarily for whites and sociological explanations for blacks and other minorities (Aug & Bright, 1970; Johnson, 1974). What evidence there is refutes the notion that teenagers are pregnant because they are different or because they wanted to become pregnant (Parker, 1971; Vincent, 1961).

As an alternative, teenage pregnancy may be seen as both a solution to one set of interrelated problems and the cause of similar, interrelated problems. Consequently, sociological explanations may be most appropriate at the group level in accounting for the high incidence of teenage pregnancy among the poor and poorly educated, who are disproportionately represented by blacks. Psychological explanations may be most appropriate on the individual level in accounting for the motivation to become sexually active and for the variation in responses to becoming pregnant as a result. How these sets of factors are interrelated seems to be different from one case to the next.

Clearly, the teenager who is already poor and who becomes pregnant perpetuates a cycle of poverty from which she and her offspring are unlikely to find any escape. Set against the backdrop of the normal course of adolescent growth and development, however, the set of responses that are unique for each individual can help to explain why this crisis is a disaster for some and an opportunity for others. Viewed within this context, teenage pregnancy poses a developmental crisis, which can serve as a stimulant for some teenagers and as an impediment to further development for others.

ADOLESCENT DEVELOPMENT

A developmental analysis of teenage pregnancy may be conducted from a variety of perspectives. As I have discussed elsewhere (Hayes, 1986), three fundamental views—maturational, behavioral, and structural—dominate contemporary approaches to human development. These views differ primarily in the emphasis each gives to the balance between environmental and organismic conditions in determining the individual's developmental course. Although none of the many variables associated with each of these perspectives may be said to *explain* teenage pregnancy, an understanding of the potential relationship between variables can help to explain why some teenagers become pregnant and, more important, suggest how prevention programs might be developed.

A Maturational View

For maturationists, development is characterized by the unfolding of prepatterned stages that are genetically limited, if not determined. The nature of the teenager's experience in adolescence is determined by the conflict between the demands of the instincts and the limitations imposed by the teenager's environment.

Although biology is not entirely destiny, biological changes signal the beginning of adolescence.

A necessary but not sufficient condition for teenage pregnancy is fertility. It is commonly believed to be attained at first menarche for girls, which occurs on the average in the United States at age 12.6 years (Bullough, 1981), but fertility actually is not reached until 1–3 years later. For boys, the entrance into "manhood" is not as dramatic. Beginning on average at age 12.5 years, the testes and pubic hair begin to grow, followed by a lengthening of the penis, with ejaculation occurring approximately a year later (Fischer, 1984).

Other changes brought on by hormonal stimulation effect changes in physical growth and the development of primary and secondary sex characteristics in both boys and girls. The biological demands of puberty are set against social demands to control one's sexual appetites. Driven by genital urges, the adolescent attempts to cope with these sexual feelings by alternately denying their existence through retreats to more infantile behaviors and claiming their resolution by adopting new, more adult behaviors that create the appearance of an end to the conflict.

Sexual activity can serve both these functions by providing caring support for one's efforts while simultaneously signaling that one has reached a certain plateau in the search for adulthood. Both males and females may look to one another for confirmation of their changed bodies. Similarly, a sexual partner may be seen as a way to fulfill one's dreams or to test one's own values against those of one's parents.

Such experimentation has been described by Erikson (1968) as a period of "psychosocial moratorium" during which the adolescent is encouraged to try out various roles without commitment. By experimenting with different people through new and different relationships, the adolescent gradually establishes a more mature identity. Failure to do so results in a condition of "role confusion" wherein the adolescent may engage in delinquent or antisocial behavior when his or her fragile identity is threatened.

From a purely psychoanalytic perspective, the emergence of the adolescent from childhood involves relinquishing the parents as "love objects" and reviving earlier and unresolved Oedipal struggles (Blos, 1962). Successful negotiation of this challenge involves a repudiation of one's sexual interest in the parent of the opposite sex and its redirection to members of one's peer group. A consolidation of sexual identity and personality takes place such that feelings of isolation and grief that accompany the loss of childhood attachments are replaced by new attachments.

As with each period of life, the adolescent is faced with the problem of accomplishing a set of "developmental tasks" (Havighurst, 1972) whose completion is eased by successfully completing other tasks in earlier periods. The tasks of adolescence include: achieving new and more mature relations with agemates of both sexes; achieving a masculine or feminine social role; accepting one's physique and using the body effectively; achieving independence of parents and other adults; preparing for marriage and family life; preparing for an economic career; acquiring a set of values and an ethical system as a guide to behavior; and desiring and achieving socially responsible behavior (pp. 43–82). Although sexual activity can serve as a testing ground for the eventual accomplishment of nearly all of these tasks, pregnancy and marriage are best entered into upon their completion.

To complicate the situation further, Duvall (1957) has pointed out that newly married couples need to accomplish certain developmental tasks of the family prior to introducing children into the family. Pregnancy or marriage introduces psychosocial issues related to establishing a healthy balance between the more adult concerns of "intimacy and isolation" and of "generativity and stagnation." Coupled with the ongoing struggle to establish an identity and to accomplish family tasks for which earlier periods were to be preparatory, the pregnant teenager (and her mate) is overloaded and developmentally out-of-phase in accomplishing these tasks.

Rather than taking on these tasks in order, the teenage parent must undertake to negotiate dating and educational, vocational, and familial tasks simultaneously. The "normal" pattern has been disrupted for the teenage parent, who must now work overtime to "catch up" with his or her own developmental course. As difficult as this developmental correction appears to be, a variety of strategies makes use of personal and familial resources, "including rearrangement of schedules, educational aspirations, and avoidance of further ill-timed pregnancies" (Russell, 1980, p. 51).

Furstenburg (1976) noted that teenage mothers who had had a longstanding and exclusive relationship with the child's father and quickly married them upon realizing the imminent birth or those who postponed marriage indefinitely and returned to school were better able to cope with their situations than were teenage mothers in other circumstances. When they succeeded in avoiding further pregnancies and were able to make suitable child-care arrangements, they often were able to achieve some measure of economic independence.

A Behavioral View

From a behavioral perspective, development involves the internalization of copies of reality that form elementary impressions on the mind. These impressions are associated to build up images of the real world through exposure to external conditions that reinforce the repetition of specific behavior. How a given teenager behaves is both a reflection of his or her reinforcement history and determined by what he or she wants. Knowing what models a teenager has or has had and what he or she values can serve as useful guides to what has been reinforcing in the past and to how he or she is likely to behave in the future.

Accompanying the maturational changes of adolescence are certain socially determined changes that place new demands upon the teenager's efforts to negotiate adolescence. As noted, the popular culture of the 1970s and its so-called sexual revolution ushered in new freedoms that set new and often unattainable standards of adult behaviors. "The upsurge of the feminist movement and a push toward equality in sexual behavior, a rapid rise in the divorce rate, a growing acceptance of 'alternative life-styles,' and a generally free and open sexual climate" (Chilman, 1979, p. 492) are trends that continued into the 1980s. When teenagers are exposed to few, if any, public examples of the negative consequences that follow such behavior, the ingredients are there for dramatic change in the behaviors related to attaining such values.

Added to these values is the notion that bearing children holds the visible promise of having achieved adult status. Indeed, studies suggest that the "self-enrichment and development" that are presumed to come with parenthood might be particularly salient reasons among teenagers for having children (Fawcett, 1978; Hoffman, 1978). For poor and undereducated teenagers, parenthood may be particularly attractive. Indeed, pregnancy may not always signal an interruption in one's education or career. In fact, education seems to be correlated negatively with perceived gratification for both men and women (Thibault & Kelley, 1967).

Presumably, as education increases, so do one's aspirations and income, widening the range of one's choices. As Buchholz and Gol (1986) pointed out, however, career aspirations are not the norm in lower socioeconomic groups. Teenage mothers from working class and depressed communities are not dramatically worse off than their peers and may view childbearing as an acceptable alternative to school and the middle-class expectations associated with it (p. 354). And in a study by Furstenberg (1976), teenagers who were successful in adapting to motherhood were supported by families that held their babies in "universal esteem." These results support the view that there has been a shift in values related to rearing children that is reflected in the low adoption rate. As a corollary, Guyatt (1978) reported that pregnant teenagers' decisions to have an abortion were influenced by their desire to complete school and to fulfill their vocational aspirations.

The primary source of sexual (mis)information among teenagers is their peers. Moreover, the adolescent female's partner plays a primary role in her decisions about sexual activity and contraceptive use (Thompson & Spanier, 1978). After reviewing a particularly disturbing set of studies on contraceptive use by teenagers, Phipps-Yonas (1980) concluded that, unlike so many of their female partners, teenage males who were sexually active simply did not care what happened as a consequence of their activity. Two thirds of one group of teenage males believed that saying "I love you" was acceptable as a means to persuade a girl to have sex; yet over two thirds also were anti-abortion, believing that the girl should be left to pay the consequences. Finally, black males, who are overrepresented as a group among teenage parents, were found to perceive children as personal and social assets despite these adolescents' tendency not to marry the mothers of their children. Nonetheless, a study of adolescents' support networks found that husbands and boyfriends can serve as a significant source of support and influence (De Anda & Becarra, 1984).

A Structural View

For the structuralists, development consists of the reorganization and redefinition of basic mental structures through exercise and confrontation by opposing ideas. Inherent in human nature are certain structuring tendencies, which attempt to make sense of people's experiences within themselves and the world in which they live. In effect, people are meaning-makers, and the course of the changes in the process by which they make meaning is developmental. From this perspective, adolescence represents a psychological epoch in which the realization of certain cognitive processes is first possible (Okun & Sasfy, 1977).

For Inhelder and Piaget (1958), the principal causal agent in the appearance of the adolescent personality is the development of formal operational thought—the ability not only to perceive the world as it is but also to perceive the world as it could be. This new cognitive capacity permits adolescents to construct a world out of their own existence. As adolescence proceeds, teenagers become increasingly more competent in the use of abstract thought and build their personalities in attempts at assuming adult roles.

Unfortunately, full formal operational thought is not achieved until late adolescence, and then by only 50% of the American population (Dulit, 1972). Nonetheless, this view of adolescent cognition helps to explain the wishful thinking and romantic fantasies of teenagers in this period. Rather than thinking of the inability to plan ahead or to take the perspective of others as indicative of some pathology, a structural view of adolescent thought suggests that the contraceptive practices of adolescents, especially younger ones, are a function of their inadequate cognitive development. Faced with adult opportunities and possessing adult bodies, early adolescents are cognitively ill-equipped nonetheless to make complete sense of their sexual experience.

The seeming insensitivity of teenage males (Phipps-Yonas, 1980) to the consequences for their partners of their sexual activity may be explained, in part, by their limited cognitive abilities to appreciate the possible outcomes fully. A similar explanation may account for why 23% of the teenagers in a recent study, who had their first coitus without contraception, explained they had not expected to have intercourse (Zelnik & Kantner, 1979). Elkind (1974) has called the complex of beliefs in the adolescent's uniqueness of thought or presumed immortality "*a personal fable,* a story which he tells himself and which is not true" (p. 93). Certainly the beliefs many teenagers hold regarding pregnancy, that "it can't happen to me" or that "we only did it once" (Zelnik & Kantner, 1979), provide poignant examples of their limited cognitive capacities.

One final issue related to teenage pregnancy that merits discussion from a structural perspective is cognitive moral development. Kohlberg (1969) has argued that adolescence is a critical period for the transition from a system of moral reasoning based on fear of punishment and an orientation to reciprocity and exchange to a system of moral judgments based on a need for approval and conformity to cultural stereotypes and an orientation to maintaining the social order.

Over the course of adolescence, therefore, one can expect to find teenagers with several different moral orientations. Significantly, as the age of first sexual involvement is lowered, the proportion of teenagers who desire to maintain the expectations of family and the social group should also be getting lower. In its place, a "morality of the marketplace," in which personal advantage determines real value, is likely to prevail. From a structural perspective, there are likely to be several distinctly different moral orientations within any group of teenagers to justify involvement in sexual activity, a subsequent pregnancy, and resolution of it.

In a particularly appropriate application of the structural-developmental approach to the nature of teenage sexual behavior, D'Augelli and D'Augelli (1979) argued that because sexual behavior occurs between two people, it has meanings for both parties. "Furthermore, the consequences of sexual interaction for the relationship between the partners differ depending upon the meanings they attach to the interaction" (p. 308). "Relationship reasoning," those authors' term for the underlying interpersonal decision-making process, logically evolves through a series of phases that move from egocentric, self-centered forms to committed and mutually gratifying forms.

Their thesis is that at each step in the process, personal decision making about sexual involvement within the relationship is influenced by the individual's level of moral reasoning and sexual philosophy as well as by externally set behavioral standards for sexual conduct and by internalized standards of guilt. In examining teenagers' motives for engaging in sexual activity, therefore, one must recognize that their reasoning about relationships is likely to be qualitatively different from that of adults and of children and that early adolescents are likely to reason about relationships in qualitatively different ways than are later adolescents.

TOWARD AN INTEGRATION OF VIEWS

A simple example may prove useful in showing how these different approaches may be brought to bear upon a single issue. Each of these perspectives may be seen to focus on a different primary concern. The maturational, behavioral, and structural views tend to address emotions, behaviors, and cognitions, respectively. For example, guilt over sexual activity is an emotional variable, prior sexual experience is a behavioral variable, and moral reasoning is a cognitive variable (D'Augelli & D'Augelli, 1979, p. 308).

In examining any one issue, such as bodily changes in puberty, each of these approaches may be brought to bear on an explanation of the associated events. Suffice it to say that rapid and ongoing changes to the adolescent's body (a biological event; Higham, 1980) prompt a revision of body image (an emotional event; Money & Ehrhardt, 1972) that is accompanied by a new self-consciousness (a cognitive event; Elkind, 1974). How adolescents react to the changes in their own bodies depends in large part upon what they have learned to expect (a behavioral event; Peterson & Taylor, 1980).

PROFILE OF A PREGNANT TEENAGER

Although it is difficult to separate the motivation to engage in sexual activity from the motivation (or lack of it) to become pregnant from the motivation to bear children (or not), some things may be said about the teenager who does become pregnant and who then keeps her child. She is likely to express less acceptance of social norms, be biologically ready for pregnancy and childbirth, possess an inability to use information and an inability to project events into the future, have an unstable family environment, have no clearly defined religious orientation, have poor school performance and low educational aspirations, and have low self-esteem (Kantner, 1983; Levering, 1983; Washington & Glimps, 1983).

Importantly, no single teenager is likely to fit this profile. Nor do those who do fit the profile necessarily become sexually active, or pregnant, or give birth. What does seem to be true, however, is that "if we consider all of the points at which a choice is made along the path that leads to teenage motherhood, it is possible to build the case that it is the least appropriate candidate for that role who moves forward at each conjunction" (Phipps-Yonas, 1980, p. 422). Or, put in a more positive light,

> Increases in sexual activity, unintended pregnancy, and a string of negative consequences notwithstanding, most young women are able to negotiate adolescence adroitly enough to avoid the more serious of these pitfalls. In the general view of how life should proceed, they see childbirth, ideally as coming after age 20 and after marriage; and again in the idealized conception of things, they have tended to postpone both of these events farther into their futures, a plan that is in keeping with their growing educational aspirations. (Kantner, 1983, p. 193)

IMPLICATIONS FOR POLICY

A number of policies to reduce the incidence of teenage pregnancy are indicated by the research (see especially Chilman, 1979; Johnson, 1974; Phipps-Yonas, 1980). The following guidelines are intended as primary prevention strategies for both adolescents and for their families of origin:

- Increased emphasis on primary prevention through postponement of sexual activity for teenagers who are not pregnant or not yet sexually active.
- Reconceptualization of the problem as a normal developmental crisis for which causes and solutions are to be found in an understanding of the social ecology of adolescence.
- Provision of contraception for sexually active teenagers, preferably with parental encouragement and support.

- Increased public discussion and examination of social attitudes and practices that may exacerbate the problem, including governmental, media, personal, and familial policies and behavior.
- Reduction of poverty through adequate income maintenance, vocational training and placement, and creation of needed jobs.
- Welfare reform making public assistance equally available to one- and two-parent families and couples with or without children, and subsidizing inadequate wages.
- Provision of child care for parents who work outside the home.
- Increased affirmative action for equalizing pay and housing opportunities for minorities and women.
- Increased access to high quality health care financed by comprehensive health care insurance.
- Development of broad-based educational programs that place sex education within the larger context of life-skills development.
- Increased participation of parents in the schools; improved staffing for student services such as counseling, school psychology, and health services, especially elementary school guidance.
- Federal intervention to withhold funds from schools that exclude pregnant females, and incentives to involve parents and grandparents in caring for their pregnant teenagers and their families.
- Increased community mental health services addressed to issues such as poor family communications, single parenting, conflicts between parents and adolescent children, and early identification of abuse and abusive patterns.
- Policy and programs focusing on the family as well as on the individual level.

SPECIFIC PROGRAMS

Any program aimed at reducing the incidence of teenage pregnancy must be responsive to a host of variables, including socioeconomic level, race, gender, familial status of both the family of origin and of procreation, level of cognitive and moral development, values and personal aspirations, extent of social skills, level of self-esteem, relations with peers, identity development status, health/nutritional habits, level of biological maturation, knowledge of sexual reproduction/childcare/development, and degree of accomplishment of individual and familial developmental tasks. Clearly no program can (or has!) been able to meet such a lengthy list of demands—in part because so few programs consider the range of variables with which they must deal. Instead they take characteristically reductionistic approaches to the problem of teenage pregnancy, citing single causes, which lead to single, straightforward solutions.

Any group considering an attack on the problem of teenage pregnancy would be well advised to ask *which* teenagers and to *what* ends? Having determined whom one wants to help and to do what, one may begin the complex task of manipulating one or a few of the most important variables that might be expected to effect some change with *these particular* teenagers. Successful programs tend to be those that weave the topic of teenage sexuality into the broader context of teenage life. From such an approach, pregnancy becomes just one of a rich array of needs for which services may be provided. Any program should consider including at least some of the following elements: education, family planning and health care, employment, counseling, and staff development/training.

Education

Sex education classes should begin prior to the teen years and should focus on communication and decision making rather than on pregnancy prevention. These programs should take into account the developmental needs and abilities of the students in the class and should use developmentally appropriate curricula. In working with adolescents, these techniques might include role playing, biographical scripts, family diagrams, developmental charts, and classroom debates (Catrone & Sadler, 1984). The program emphasis should be on the development of life skills, including life planning, vocational and career development, and vocational training and placement.

Every effort should be made to minimize interruption of the academic progress of pregnant teenagers. Special courses should be offered dealing with child care and development, preparation for labor and delivery, the parenting process, remedial academic programs, and communication and assertiveness training. Courses should be offered for parents and children to learn more effective ways to communicate with one another. All programs should make concerted efforts to involve males. Finally, sex education should be included in the agenda of all social organizations that serve children—public and private schools, human service agencies, religious organizations, parent groups, and recreational groups such as the YMCA, 4-H, and Boy and Girl Scouts.

Family Planning and Health Care

Although in-school clinics may be the most controversial issue discussed here, 70% of Americans believe that contraception should be taught in the schools, and the provision of contraceptive services to teenagers is approved by most teenagers and adults (Alan Guttmacher Institute, 1981). Family planning services geared to the special needs of adolescent males and females should be located in or near schools and be open before and after school. Medical care should be provided at little or no cost to pregnant teenagers, both pre- and post-natally.

Employment

Job search information, on-the-job training, work experience, and government subsidies for teenagers should be made available. Programs should publicly promote the idea of a society with full employment and one in which all people, including adolescents, perform meaningful, productive, and interesting tasks.

Counseling

Confidentiality looms as the most important issue in establishing effective working relationships with teenagers who seek help from counselors for sex-related concerns. Counselors who become involved with parents, school administrators and teachers, and other helping professionals in the development of programs are more likely to be in a position to maintain their clients' trust, knowing that they also have the trust and support of other concerned adults. Counselors should include personal, vocational, and rehabilitation counseling in addition to classroom guidance and small-group work among their services. A referral network should be established, a center for information resources developed, and a peer counseling program instituted. Family counseling with the teenage parents and their parents, focusing on identifying and building family strengths, should continue after birth.

Staff Development

Staff development/training for all personnel involved in educational and service delivery programs should be instituted. The focus should be to sensitize professionals to the developmental dimensions of adolescence generally, and of pregnant teenagers specifically, and to increase their knowledge in providing accurate information on sexuality and referrals.

RESOURCES

Adolescent Family Life Program funds care projects to help pregnant teenagers and their children and families, as well as prevention projects to reach teenagers before they become sexually active. In addition, research and evaluation grants and contract funds are authorized to investigate the consequences of adolescent sexual behavior, contraceptive use and early childbearing. For further information about the program, contact: Office of Adolescent Pregnancy, Room 736E Hubert H. Humphrey Building, 200 Independence Avenue, S. W., Washington, DC 20201.

American Association for Counseling and Development's Family Communication Project is a 3-year effort to train parents to discuss sexuality with their children. To obtain information on training, contact: AACD Family Communication Project, 5999 Stevenson Avenue, Alexandria, VA 22314.

Children's Defense Fund, a private lobbying group, has launched a 5-year campaign to prevent teenage pregnancies through increased public awareness and state and federal lobbying efforts aimed at passage of legislation to facilitate teen pregnancy prevention. For information on CDF efforts, contact: Children's Defense Fund, 1520 New Hampshire Avenue, N. W., Washington, DC 20036.

Planned Parenthood Federation of America has available a variety of counseling and educational materials on family planning and reproductive health care at a minimal cost. For information on obtaining these and other resources, contact: Planned Parenthood Federation of America, Marketing Department, 810 Seventh Avenue, New York, NY 10019.

Teen Pregnancy: What is being done? is a state-by-state report of the House Select Committee on Children, Youth, and Families. It includes demographics, health, education, economic indicators, adoption and foster care, programs and resources, and statewide initiatives and recent policy changes related to teenage pregnancy for each state. This report may be obtained from the U.S. Government Printing Office, Washington, DC.

REFERENCES

Alan Guttmacher Institute. (1981). *Teenage pregnancy: The problem that hasn't gone away.* New York: Author.

Alan Guttmacher Institute. (1984, March). *What government can do about teenage pregnancy.* New York: Author.

Anastasiow, N. J. (1983). Adolescent pregnancy and special education. *Exceptional Child, 2,* 396–401.

Aug, R., & Bright, T. (1970). A study of wed and unwed motherhood in adolescents and young adults. *Journal of the American Academy of Child Psychiatry, 9,* 577–594.

Bennet, V. C., & Bardon, J. I. (1977). The effects of a school program on teenage mothers and their children. *American Journal of Orthopsychiatry, 3,* 671–678.

Blos, P. (1962). *On adolescence.* New York: Free Press.

Buchholz, E. S., & Gol, B. (1986). More than playing house: A developmental perspective on the strengths in teenage motherhood. *American Journal of Orthopsychiatry, 56,* 347–359.

Bullough, V. L. (1981). Age at menarche: A misunderstanding. *Science, 213,* 365–366.

Catrone, C., & Sadler, L. (1984). A developmental model for teen-age parent education. *JOSH, 54,* 63-67.

Children's Defense Fund. (1982). *America's children and their families: Key facts.* Washington, DC: Author.

Chilman, C. S. (1979). Teenage pregnancy: A research review. *Social Work, 24,* 492–498.

Cobe, P. (1976). Parenting as a teenager. *Forecast for Home Economics, 2,* 54–55, 70–71.

D'Augelli, J. F., & D'Augelli, A. R. (1979). Sexual involvement and relationship development: A cognitive developmental approach. In R. L. Burgess & T. L. Huston (Eds.), *Social exchange in developing relationships* (pp. 307–349). New York: Academic Press.

De Anda, D., & Becarra, R. M. (1984). Support networks for adolescent mothers. *Social Casework, 65,* 172–181.

Dulit, E. (1972). Adolescent thinking a la Piaget. *Journal of Youth & Adolescence, 1,* 281–301.

Duvall, E. (1957). *Family development.* Philadelphia: Lippincott.

Elkind, D. (1974). *Children and adolescents: Interpretive essays on Jean Piaget* (2nd ed.) New York: Oxford University Press.

Erikson, E. H. (1968). *Identity: Youth and crisis.* New York: W. W. Norton.

Fawcett, J. T. (1978). The value and cost of the first child. In W. Miller & L. Newman (Eds.), *The first child and family formation.* Chapel Hill, NC: Carolina Population Center.

Fischer, K. (1984). *Human development.* New York: W. H. Freeman & Co.

Furstenberg, F. F. (1976). *Unplanned parenthood: The social consequences of teenage childbearing.* New York: Free Press.

Guyatt, D. (1978). *Adolescent pregnancy: A study of pregnant teenagers in a suburban community in Ontario.* Unpublished doctoral dissertation, University of Toronto.

Havighurst, R. (1972). *Developmental tasks and education*. New York: McKay.

Hawthorne, N. (1983). *The scarlet letter*. In M. Bell (Ed.), *Nathaniel Hawthorne* (pp. 115–345). New York: Library of America. (Original work published 1850)

Hayes, R. (1986). Human growth and development. In M. Lewis, R. Hayes, & J. Lewis (Eds.), *An introduction to the counseling profession*. Itasca, IL: F. E. Peacock.

Higham, E. (1980). Variations in adolescent psychohormonal development. In J. Adelson (Ed.), *Handbook of adolescent psychology* (pp. 472–494). New York: Wiley.

Hoffman, L. W. (1978). Effects of the first child on the woman's role. In W. Miller & L. Newman (Eds.), *The first child and family formation*. Chapel Hill, NC: Carolina Population Center.

Illinois Caucus on Teenage Pregnancy. (1983). *Teenage pregnancy*. Chicago: Author.

Inhelder, B., & Piaget, J. (1958). *The growth of logical thinking from childhood to adolescence*. New York: Basic Books.

Johnson, C. L. (1974). Adolescent pregnancy: Intervention into the poverty cycle. *Adolescence, 9*, 391–403.

Kantner, J. F. (1983). Sex and pregnancy among American adolescents. *Educational Horizons, 61*, 189–194.

Klerman, L. V. (1975). Adolescent pregnancy: The need for new policies and new programs. *Journal of School Health, 45*, 263–267.

Kohlberg, L. (1969). Stage and sequence: The cognitive developmental approach to socialization. In D. Goslin (Ed.), *Handbook of socialization theory and research* (pp. 347–480). New York: Basic Books.

Lachance, L. (1985). *Teen pregnancy: An ERIC/CAPS fact sheet*. Ann Arbor, MI: ERIC Clearinghouse on Counseling & Personnel Services. (ERIC Document Reproduction Service No. ED 266–340)

Levering, C. S. (1983). Teenage pregnancy and parenthood. *Childhood Education, 59*, 182–185.

Martin, C. (1973). Psychological problems of abortion for the unwed teenage girl. *Genetic Psychology Monographs, 88*, 23–110.

Miller, E. K., & Miller, K. A. (1983). *Personnel & Guidance Journal, 9*, 15–20.

Money, J., & Ehrhardt, A. (1972). *Man and woman, boy, and girl: The differentiation and dimorphism of gender identity from conception to maturity*. Baltimore: Johns Hopkins University Press.

Okun, M., & Sasfy, J. (1977). Adolescence, the self-concept, and formal operations. *Adolescence, 12*, 373–380.

Parker, J. D. (1971). Girls pregnant out-of-wedlock. *Journal of Operational Psychiatry, 1*, 15–19.

Peterson, A. C. & Taylor, B. (1980). The biological approach to adolescence. In J. Adelson (Ed.), *Handbook of adolescent psychology* (pp. 117–155). New York: Wiley.

Phipps-Yonas, S. (1980). Teenage pregnancy and motherhood: A review of the literature. *American Journal of Orthopsychiatry, 50*, 403–431.

Polit, D. F. (1982). *Need and characteristics of pregnant and parenting teens: The baseline report for project redirection*. New York: Manpower Demonstration Research Corp.

Presser, H. (1979). *The social and demographic consequences of teenage pregnancy for urban women*. College Park, MD: University of Maryland Press.

Russell, C. S. (1980). Unscheduled parenthood: Transition to "parent" for the teenager. *Journal of Social Issues, 36*, 45–63.

Studies target teen pregnancy. (1986, March). *Guidepost, 28*(14), 1, 16.

Thibault, J. W., & Kelley, H. H. (1967). *The social psychology of groups*. New York: Wiley.

Thompson, L., & Spanier, G. (1978). Influence of parents, peers, and partners on the contraceptive use of college men and women. *Journal of Marriage & the Family, 40*, 481–492.

Trussell, J., & Menken, J. (1978). Early childbearing and subsequent fertility. *Family Planning Perspective, 10*, 184–190.

U.S. Congress. (1986). *Teen pregnancy: What is being done? A state-by-state look. A report of the select committee on children, youth, and families (December, 1985)*. Washington, DC: U.S. Government Printing Office.

U.S. Department of Health and Human Services. (1979). *The status of children, youth, and families* (DHHS Publication No. OHDS 80–30274). Washington, DC: Author.

Vincent, C. E. (1961). *Unmarried mothers*. New York: Free Press.

Washington, V., & Glimps, B. (1983). Developmental issues for adolescent parents and their children. *Educational Horizons, 61*, 195–199.

Zelnik, M., & Kantner, J. (1979). Reason for non-use of contraception by sexually active women aged 15–19. *Family Planning Perspectives, 11,* 177–183.

Richard Hayes and Nancy Cryer are associated with the College of Education and Health Sciences, Bradley University.

3

Adolescent Suicide: Prevention and Intervention

Dave Capuzzi

Adolescent suicide has become a critical problem in the United States. Recent yearly estimates (Haffen & Frandsen, 1986) report as many as 400,000 attempts and 7,000 completions among the adolescent population in this country. The extent of the adolescent suicide problem is difficult to identify with an exact number because many suicides are confused as accidents or reported as accidents because of family embarrassment, religious beliefs, community discomfort, or denial of the adolescent suicide problem. During the last five years adolescent suicide has moved from being cited as the third leading cause of death among the 11- to 24-year age group to the second leading cause. Only accidents—quite often automobile accidents—rank higher.

UNDERSTANDING THE PROBLEM

Myths About Adolescent Suicide

One of the first steps in developing an understanding of adolescent suicide is to identify the commonly believed myths regarding teenagers who attempt or complete the act of suicide. Some of the most typically cited misconceptions are discussed briefly in the following paragraphs.

• *Adolescents who talk about suicide never do it.* This is probably one of the most widely held misconceptions. In reality almost all suicidal adolescents have made an attempt (verbally or nonverbally—and usually verbally) to let someone else know that life seems too much to handle. A suicide attempt is a cry for help to

41

identify options other than death that will decrease the pain of living. Verbal threats should always be taken seriously and never assumed to be only for the purpose of attracting attention or manipulating others.

● *Suicide happens without warning.* Most suicidal adolescents leave numerous hints and warnings about their suicidal ideations and intentions. Clues can be verbal or in the form of suicidal gestures such as taking just a few sleeping pills or becoming accident-prone. Quite often the social support network of the suicide-prone adolescent is small. As stress escalates and options other than suicide seem few, suicidal adolescents may withdraw from an already small circle of friends, making it more difficult for others to notice warning signs.

● *Adolescents from affluent families attempt or complete suicide more often than adolescents from poor families.* This, too, is a myth. Suicide is evenly divided among socioeconomic groups.

● *Once an adolescent is suicidal, he or she is suicidal forever.* Most adolescents are suicidal for a limited time. In my experience, the 24- to 72-hour period around the peak of the "crisis" is the most dangerous. If counselors and other mental health practitioners can monitor this crisis period and then get the adolescent into regularly scheduled, long-term counseling/therapy, there is a strong possibility that another suicidal crisis will never occur. The more effort that is made to help an adolescent identify stressors and develop problem-solving skills during this post-suicidal crisis period and the more time that passes, the better is the prognosis.

● *If an adolescent attempts suicide and survives, he or she will never make an additional attempt.* There is a difference between the adolescent who experiences a suicidal crisis but does not attempt it, as in the situation above, and the adolescent who actually tries to bring an end to life. An adolescent who carries through with an attempt has identified a plan, had access to the means, and maintained a high enough energy level to follow through. He or she knows that a second or third attempt would be in the realm of possibility. If counseling/therapy has not taken place or has not been successful during the period following the attempt, additional attempts may be made. Most likely, each follow-up attempt will become more lethal.

● *Adolescents who commit suicide always leave notes.* Only a small percentage of adolescents who complete the act of suicide leave notes. This myth is common and is one of the reasons why many suicides are classified and reported as accidents by friends, family members, physicians, and investigating officers when suicide actually has taken place.

● *Most adolescent suicides happen late at night.* This myth is not true for the simple reason that most suicidal adolescents actually want help. Mid to late morning and mid to late afternoon are the time periods when most attempts are made, since a family member or friend is more likely to be around to intervene than would be the case late at night.

● *The word* suicide *should never be used when talking to adolescents, because using the word gives some adolescents the idea.* This is simply not true. One cannot put the idea of suicide into the mind of an adolescent who is not suicidal. If an adolescent is suicidal and the word "suicide" is voiced, it can invite him or her to verbalize feelings of despair and help establish rapport and trust. If a suicidal adolescent thinks someone knows that he or she is suicidal and realizes the person is afraid to broach the subject, it can bring the adolescent closer to the point of making at attempt by contributing to feelings of despair and helplessness.

● *Every adolescent who attempts suicide is depressed.* Depression is a common component of the profile of a suicidal adolescent, but depression is not *always* a component. Many adolescents simply want to escape their present set of circumstances and do not have the problem-solving skills to cope more effectively, reduce stress, and work toward a more promising future.

● *Suicide is hereditary.* Suicide, like physical and sexual abuse, tends to run in families, which has given rise to this myth. Although suicide is not genetically. inherited, members of families do share the same emotional climate since parents model coping and stress management skills as well as a level of high or low self-esteem. The suicide of one family member tends to increase the risk among other family members that suicide will be viewed as an appropriate way to solve a problem or set of problems.

Causes of Adolescent Suicide

The causes of suicide among teenagers in the United States have been discussed by a number of experts (Haffen & Frandsen, 1986; Davis, 1983; Husain & Vandiver, 1984; Fairchild, 1986). The parameters commonly identified for consideration are (a) the adolescent struggle to develop and integrate a unique identity, (b) familial factors, and (c) environmental factors.

The Adolescent Experience

Early adolescence is second only to infancy in terms of physical growth and emotional development. It is a time during which many of the assumptions of childhood must be left behind as the demands and expectations of others increase with each stage of physical and sexual maturity bringing the adolescent closer to the world of "adults." Even though adolescents may look like young adults quite early, they cannot approach relationships and analyze life circumstances until they have had time to assess a number of areas. Rather than discussing the developmental tasks of adolescence in the traditional sense, the areas of adolescent development that seem to be factors in the development of suicidal tendencies in adolescents will be overviewed.

● *Self-esteem.* In general, adolescents who become suicidal experience feelings of low self-esteem. These feelings have been present since early childhood, and such a young person may have been other-directed, rather than inner-directed, for a number of years prior to adolescence. Parents of adolescents such as these typically comment that their child seemed to lose control and judgment in the presence of peers, and that quite often they dreaded the arrival of their child's friends for an afternoon visit or a weekend stay.

● *Poor communication.* Besides low self-esteem, many suicidal adolescents have developed a pattern of poor communication with parents, other adults and, quite often, friends. These adolescents never have been at ease with the prospect of sharing their feelings about parents, siblings, teachers, and friends. As time passes, it becomes easier and more acceptable simply to keep their feelings inside and experience frustration and discomfort than to attempt to deal with those feelings as they arise. Teachers, parents, and neighbors seldom have many verbal cues that relationships, circumstances, or expectations have been upsetting to these children.

● *Achievement orientation.* In addition to low self-esteem and poor communication skills, suicide-prone adolescents may be quite achievement-oriented. Although it would be a mistake to assume that *all* achievement-oriented adolescents may become suicidal, experience with counseling the suicidal adolescent points to the realization that high achievement is one way to compensate for feelings of low self-worth. Achievement can be focused on any of a number of modalities—high grades, participation in athletic activities, developing a reputation as the "class clown," the best-dressed, most popular. All of these are ways to achieve prominence among peers.

● *Poor problem-solving skills.* Poor problem-solving ability is also characteristic of many adolescents who become suicidal. This trait is usually observable prior to adolescence, epitomized by a lack of resourcefulness in generating options for solving a problem, coping with a difficult relationship, or planning for the future.

● *Narrow commitments.* Lack of resourcefulness is particularly troublesome in conjunction with another trait that often is part of the developmental pattern of the suicidal adolescent—total commitment to a relationship or to a goal for the future. Suicidal adolescents often develop a tunnel-visioned perspective. A relationship may become so important that other friendships are dropped. A goal may begin to dominate every decision, allocation of time, and thoughts about the future. Commitment, total and unwavering, often becomes the theme for patterning daily, weekly, and monthly activities and priorities. When an important relationship ends or a goal becomes unachievable, self-esteem is lowered, feelings are kept secret and left unexpressed, achievement is roadblocked, and problem-solving skills are frozen in past and current maladaptive patterns, resulting in escalation of stress and anxiety.

● *High stress*. Most suicidal adolescents have a history of high stress. As they move from childhood to adolescence and the demands of the peer group and the expectations of adults become even greater, they become even less resourceful in their ability to manage stress. During periods of high stress, they may spend more and more time considering the option of suicide and planning for the time, place, and means.

In addition to the above traits that contribute to an adolescent's inclination to consider, attempt, or complete the act of suicide, two other traits should be noted. In my experience, many (though not all) suicidal adolescents have a relatively small network of social support. Friendships that provide opportunities for self-disclosure may be lacking or few in number since the act of sharing feelings or thoughts is usually quite difficult. Finally, I believe that many suicidal adolescents have been bothered by feelings of guilt and not quite "measuring-up" for most of their lives. Adolescents who have low self-esteem and are other-directed usually are never quite satisfied with anything they do, say, or achieve and are likely to feel guilty about their perceived lack of "achievement."

Family Factors

A number of authors (Bigrar, Gauthier, Bouchard, & Jasse, 1966; Jacobziner, 1965; McAnarney, 1979; Otto, 1972; Truckman & Connon, 1962) have discussed family disorganization as a characteristic of the families of suicidal adolescents. Divorce, death, unemployment, drug abuse, physical and sexual abuse, and mental illness are all factors contributing to disorganization. McAnarney (1979) stated that, "In societies where family ties are close, suicidal rates are low and conversely, where families are not close, suicidal rates are high." A number of family factors have become apparent to me as contributing causes of the adolescent suicide crisis in the United States.

● *Poor communication*. In many families of adolescents who have attempted or completed suicide, family members seem to be lacking in communication. Families report that they have great difficulty communicating clearly and consistently with one another (whether between parents or between parent and child). Even when the family eats breakfast or dinner together, quite often the meal is eaten in silence or with family members' attention directed to a television program. Very often, parents have not modeled a positive, articulate communication style for their children to imitate and develop skills. Parents may have little knowledge of the tribulation their adolescent children experience, and adolescents may have difficulty talking with peers and siblings, while talking with parents may seem unthinkable.

• *Loss.* Loss is something that requires a grieving and adjustment process before daily frustrations and responsibilities can be coped with as before. Losses involving dissolution of the nuclear family because of divorce, death of a family member or close friend, termination of employment, changes in health status, or moves to a new community require the energy to develop changed perspectives and the problem-solving skills to make new beginnings or change life styles. Frequently, suicidal adolescents are from families that have experienced one or more major losses in the preceding one or two years.

• *Dual-career families.* More and more American families are finding that two incomes are necessary to support a family. When both parents work, two adults may be bringing the stresses of employment back into the family system. In addition, time to accomplish household tasks, shop for groceries, schedule medical and dental appointments, and complete necessary errands is reduced. Parents may be too tired to spend as much time with their adolescent children as they would like or unable to give undivided attention to an adolescent at a time when he or she needs to talk.

Unless all family members are good at managing both time and stress, saying "no" to unnecessary work-related or other responsibilities, helping one another and meeting each other's needs at the time the needs arise, the family climate may be one of tension and lack of receptiveness. Adolescents may not think they can turn to family members for comfort and assistance.

• *Single parenting.* The role of the single parent has long been characterized by escalated responsibility, lowered income, high stress, and lack of time. A single parent may be so busy attempting to make a home for his or her children that little time is allotted to the basics of a parent-child relationship. Many troubled adolescents come from single-parent homes.

• *Blended families.* When two adults who have custody of the children from a previous marriage decide to form a new family, the dynamics of the family constellation can become quite complex. Some adolescents have great difficulty adjusting to a "substitute" parent, a new set of guidelines for behavior and discipline, additional siblings, less personal space, or a different home in a new neighborhood or community. Parents should be encouraged to seek family counseling when adolescent children show signs of depression and poor adjustment to the new family group.

• *Mid-life transition.* Parents of adolescent children are usually between the ages of 35 and 50. As parents see their children mature to the point of looking like young adults, they may begin the process of assessing themselves as personalities and as partners. They may evaluate their careers and financial progress and begin thinking about employment changes. Issues between partners may surface or re-surface if they were not dealt with earlier. Just at the time when children need more time and attention than ever, parents may be too focused on their own status and too concerned about "time running out" to notice and respond to the needs of their adolescent children.

- *Abuse.* Families in which physical or sexual abuse is occurring or in which substance abuse is problematic may be at high-risk for adolescent suicide. Parents who are abusive of each other, themselves, or their children are typically low in self-esteem, stressed, poor communicators and problem-solvers, and financially distressed. Children of these parents have not been taught to feel good about themselves and to problem-solve effectively. During adolescence, escaping the pain of this type of family atmosphere or the self-deprecating viewpoint they have probably developed may become the most predominant motivation for suicide.

Environmental Factors

Adolescents of the late 1980s may be concerned and upset about a number of trends in today's society.

- *Pressure to achieve.* The pressure to achieve academically and vocationally in our culture is often felt keenly by today's adolescents. When families and teachers pressure teenagers to achieve, some may choose to commit suicide rather than to fail and disappoint others.

- *Mobility.* Groups with the greatest amount of mobility are those living in central or rapidly changing portions of a city, immigrants, and families working for large companies that transfer them to different cities every few years (Mc-Anarney, 1979). In addition, adolescents are more mobile than ever before because of improved public transportation and access to private vehicles. Families and their adolescent children often experience alienation, isolation, and loneliness when cir-cumstances result in their changing communities or moving constantly from one neighborhood to another.

- *Uncertainty about the future.* Many adolescents feel that school and work will only become more competitive and difficult. Many believe that they must pre-pare for a much lower standard of living than that of their parents because of the escalating costs of housing, utilities, automobiles, and so on in relation to the slower rise in salaries. Some are afraid that no matter how much effort they exert, they already are destined for failure and, perhaps, should not even make a try at life.

- *Graduation from high school.* Although high school students often com-plain about the expectations of teachers, principals, and school boards and talk frequently about the anticipated joys of finishing school, many teenagers are threatened by the approach of high school graduation. For many, graduation symbolizes the transition to young manhood or womanhood and the initiation of a life more independent of other family members. Even though adolescents tell friends, family members, and other adults that they can hardly wait to finish secondary school and that they have everything under control for later, they may be quite apprehensive. The transition to the next stage of development can be a period of extremely high stress.

● *Nuclear threat*. Most of today's young people are totally aware of the reality that no nation or component of the world community can be independent or safe from the actions, and the consequences of those actions, of another country. The recent nuclear accident in Chernobyl and resultant radioactive fallout reinforces the fact that no one will be safe during a nuclear war no matter where nuclear detonation takes place. Some adolescents cite these observations as reasons for "opting out."

● *Drug abuse*. The United States is experiencing an epidemic of drug use and abuse. Opportunities to experiment with marijuana, alcohol, and other drugs are presented to fifth and sixth graders in most school districts. Pressure from peers, a mistaken sense of autonomy and feeling of well-being, and lack of funding to provide school-based prevention, intervention, and after-care programs often result in heavy use and abuse of drugs during the early high school years. Since problem-solving ability, self-esteem, and communication skills—which already may be inadequate—are never enhanced through drug use, suicide-prone adolescents usually become even higher risks as drug experimentation and dependency increase.

APPROACHES TO PREVENTION

The Role of Families and Friends

In addition to understanding the myths connected with adolescent suicide, as well as the impacts of adolescence as a developmental stage and of certain familial and social factors, family members and friends should familiarize themselves with the signs and symptoms of impending suicide. The four following areas should be assessed by anyone concerned about the welfare of an adolescent child or teenage friend: changes in behavior, verbal cues, themes or preoccupations in thinking, and personality traits.

Noticing Changes in Behavior

In general, any behavior that is decided change for a particular adolescent should be noted. Warning signs include: sudden drops in grades for a good student;

difficulty with concentration; loss of interest in friends, hobbies, or goals; changes in patterns of sleeping and eating; experimentation with marijuana, alcohol, and other drugs; lack of cooperation at school or at home; running away; and sexual promiscuity.

Depression is also a symptom of an impending suicidal crisis. When depression, combined with other behavior changes, occurs repeatedly, for periods lasting longer than a week, it is a cause for concern. Family members and friends should realize that when an adolescent who has been struggling with periodic depressive episodes suddenly improves, the possibility of a suicide attempt or completion may be imminent. It is not logical for an adolescent who has seemed troubled for some time to change overnight. Quite often an abrupt change in emotional tenor results after the individual has made the decision about when and how to make a suicide attempt.

Listening for Verbal Cues

Changes in behavior, such as the ones described above, also may be accompanied by a number of verbal warnings. Always listen for statements such as the following:

- I can't go on.
- I'm going to kill myself.
- I wish I were dead.
- I'm not the person I used to be.
- The only way out is to die.
- You won't be seeing me around any more.
- You're going to regret how you've treated me.
- Life is too much to put up with.
- Life has no meaning any more.
- I'm getting out.
- I'm tired.
- If (such and such) happens, I'll kill myself.
- If (such and such) doesn't happen, I'll kill myself.
- I'm going home.
- Here, take this (cassette, jewelry, etc.); I won't be needing it any more.

Although the "language" of adolescents varies from year to year and from one part of the country to another, the above statements convey the meaning that adolescents communicate as their stress and discomfort make suicide seem like an acceptable problem-solving option. Statements similar to the ones listed above invite additional disclosure and description of the person's circumstances and feelings.

Listening for Themes or Preoccupations in Thinking

Themes or preoccupations also seem to dominate the thinking pattern of young persons who are contemplating suicide. Although suicidal adolescents often have difficulty sharing feelings and thoughts, self-disclosure should be encouraged for the following themes:

- Wanting to escape from a situation that seems intolerable (e.g., physical abuse, difficulty at school, drugs, lack of friends).
- Wanting to join a friend or family member who has died.
- Wanting to gain the attention of others.
- Wanting to manipulate others.
- Wanting to be punished.
- Wanting to avoid being punished.
- Wanting to control when death will occur.
- Wanting to end a seemingly unresolvable conflict.
- Wanting to become a martyr for a cause.
- Wanting to punish the survivors.
- Wanting revenge.

Noticing Personality Traits

Traits that often characterize suicidal adolescents were discussed earlier. Low self-esteem, poor communication skills, high achievement orientation, poor problem-solving skills, total commitment to a relationship or a goal, high stress, small social support networks, and feelings of guilt should all be noted, especially if they are observed in conjunction with behavior changes, verbal cues, and preoccupations that could serve as motivations for a suicide attempt.

The Role of School Counselors

Suicide prevention measures can and should be taken at the elementary level and continue through middle and high school years. Traits such as low self-esteem, weak problem-solving ability, high stress, and poor communication skills are noticeable in first and second graders. At this level, counseling programs can be initiated for the purpose of enhancing self-esteem or improving communication skills. These services can be continued or begun at middle and high school levels as well. Because these traits are so often part of the profile of suicidal adolescents, early intervention and prevention would seem essential.

Further, counselors who work with students in grades five through twelve can provide information about the signs and symptoms of an impending suicidal crisis through classroom presentations on the topic. These presentations should be direct (the word "suicide" should be used) and should focus upon encouraging students who are concerned about themselves or their friends to ask for assistance. Students should be made aware that when they are concerned about a friend, someone in the school, as well as the friend's parent or parents, should be alerted. The reason for involvement outside of the family is that parents, when told that their child is in difficulty and may be suicidal, often react in the same way as parents who are told that a child is using or abusing drugs—with denial or anger.

Faculty/staff and administration must participate in inservice education on the topic of preventing adolescent suicide prior to presenting programs to students. Not only must school personnel understand the dynamics of the suicidal adolescent, but they also must be sensitive to the necessity of being able to provide or refer a person to counseling services quickly so that attempted suicides can be averted.

APPROACHING CRISIS MANAGEMENT

When called upon to assist an adolescent who is suspected of being in a suicidal crisis, the counselor can take a number of steps to ascertain the severity of the crisis and the lethality or risk that must be monitored.

1. *Be a good listener.* Understanding and respect must be conveyed for everything that is being shared by the young person. Whatever the circumstances, concerns, and feelings are, they are, for this client, reality. Counselors must begin with reality as perceived by the client even if the counselor would not interpret the circumstances in the same way.

2. *Be nonjudgmental.* If an adolescent is suicidal, he or she may have great difficulty communicating the thoughts and feelings that have led to the current feelings of desperation and hopelessness. Rapport cannot be built through comments such as, "You can't be thinking such thoughts," "It's against the teachings of your religion" or, "It would be such an embarrassment to your family."

3. *Be supportive.* When talking with an adolescent who may be at risk, it is important to be reassuring. This does not mean that the counselor should convey messages such as, "Things aren't really that bad" (for the client, things *are* bad) or "The situation will take care of itself" (circumstances usually do not become better without effort on the part of both client and counselor). Being supportive *does* mean that the counselor communicates understanding, reinforces the client for seeking assistance, and outlines some counseling options for the near future. (If the client is experiencing a high level of stress and suicidal preoccupation, counseling will not be effective until the crisis subsides.)

4. *Ask questions to assess lethality.* The following questions will help determine the degree of risk:

● *What has happened to make life so difficult?* The more circumstances the client describes, the higher is the risk.

- *Are you thinking of suicide?* Use the word *suicide*. Doing so will not put the idea of suicide into the thoughts of an adolescent who is not suicidal. Being direct will let the client know that the counselor has listened, is concerned, and is interested in helping.
- *Do you have a suicide plan?* The more specific the client is about the method, the time, the place, and who will or will not be nearby, the higher is the risk. If the client describes using pills, a gun, a knife, or other specific means, ask if he or she has that item in a pocket or purse, and require that the suicide "weapon" be left with you. (Firearms and highly lethal items, however, should be handled by the police.) Most clients will cooperate since they are most likely at low point, "other-directed," and responsive to taking directions from a trusted adult.
- *How much do you want to live?* The more difficulty the client has in giving reasons for continuing with life, the higher is the risk.
- *How much do you want to die?* The more the client discusses ending life, the higher is the risk.
- *When you think about suicide, how often do these periods of suicidal preoccupation occur, how intense are they, and how long do the periods last?* The more frequent the episodes, the more dysfunctional is the client's behavior during periods of intense preoccupation, and the longer the preoccupation, the more lethal is the situation for the client. Frequent episodes of suicidal preoccupation that are lasting longer and longer mean that the periods of preoccupation with suicidal thoughts are moving closer together and consuming more and more of the client's time.
- *Have you ever attempted suicide in the past?* If the answer is yes, the client is more lethal. In that case, ask: *How long ago was that attempt?* The more recent the attempt, the greater is the current risk.
- *Has a family member, neighbor, or friend ever attempted or completed suicide?* If the answer is yes, the client is more lethal because he or she may have learned or come to believe that suicide is an acceptable form of decision making.
- *On a scale of 1 to 10, with 1 being low and 10 being high, what is the number that depicts the probability that you will attempt suicide?* The higher the number, the higher is the lethality.
- *Is there anyone to stop you?* This question is extremely important for two reasons. First, if the client has a difficult time identifying a friend, family member, or respected adult who would be worth living for, the risk is higher than if as few as one or two people are named. Second, it is important to obtain specific information about the people identified in response to this question. Names, addresses, phone numbers, and the nature of the current or past relationship may be needed to organize a suicide watch.

5. *Remember the meaning of* crisis management. The word *crisis* means that the situation is not normal or usual because the adolescent you are concerned about

is self-destructive. The word *management* means that, for a short time (24 to 72 hours), the client must be directed and monitored. Definite steps must be taken to safeguard the client's well-being, and these steps must be explicated in an assertive, direct manner while conveying concern and empathy. If a young person were in an accident that resulted in life-threatening physical injury and loss of consciousness, paramedics and hospital emergency room physicians and nurses would take decisive action without the permission of the patient to save the patient's life. Managing a suicidal crisis is no different.

6. *Make a decision relative to needed interventions.* If, as a result of the counselor's assessment, the risk factor or lethality is judged to be high, the counselor should develop a management plan to follow until the crisis subsides and long-term counseling can be initiated. If the client is in proximity to a hospital with a psychiatric unit, hospital personnel can undertake additional assessment to determine if hospitalization for a 2- or 3-day period is advisable. Often, if a client has not been eating and sleeping or does not have family or friends to provide a suicide watch, a brief hospital stay will facilitate subsiding of the crisis to the point at which counseling can be initiated.

If hospital services are not available in the community and the counselor believes the risk is high, a suicide watch should be organized by contacting the individuals that the client has identified in response to the question: "Is there anyone to stop you?" After receiving instructions from the counselor, family members and friends should take turns staying with the client until the crisis has subsided and counseling has begun. Under no circumstances should an adolescent in crisis leave the counselor's office until arrangements have been made to monitor the client at all times. Contacting friends and family does break confidentiality, but it does not violate ethical codes of professional groups such as the American Association for Counseling and Development and the American Psychological Association. These steps must be taken to potentially save the client's life.

At times a written contract can be developed with the client, to be used along with a suicide watch (or in place of a suicide watch if the risk is low). The contract should specify activities, time with friends, and the like to which the client will commit, along with phone numbers of individuals to contact if preoccupation with suicide begins again.

A high-risk adolescent never should be left unmonitored, and the counselor should not assume that the client will have the initiative and energy to arrange and arrive for needed counseling when the crisis has subsided enough for counseling to be beneficial. This means that the counselor must be willing to cancel appointments and other scheduled activities to assist if no one else is available to be of support to the client.

7. *Be flexible enough to work with colleagues or crisis center staff.* Responding to a suicidal adolescent and assessing lethality requires patience, energy, and decision making. If another colleague has received training in crisis management,

that colleague could help to make an assessment and decide upon the most appropriate crisis management plan. Or it may be necessary to call upon a local crisis center to provide assistance. This is especially true if a suicidal adolescent is on the telephone and someone needs to go to the caller's location to remove firearms, provide transportation to a hospital, or other intervention. The crisis center staff can help determine whether to involve the police and whether emergency medical assistance may be needed prior to arrival at a hospital emergency room.

After a suicidal crisis has subsided, the services of an agency counselor or private practitioner may be necessary to provide follow-up counseling on a consistent and rather long-term basis. Never assume responsibilities that you do not have the expertise to carry through with or the time to provide.

PROVIDING FOLLOW-UP OR POST-VENTION SERVICES

As many as six to 10 people are affected, on a long-term basis, for each adolescent suicide attempt or completion. Therefore, planning and offering either individual or group ("survivor group") counseling experiences for family members and friends of the suicide victim or attempter is necessary. On a short-term basis, hundreds of people, if not entire communities, may be in need of assistance ranging from information about the dynamics of suicide to individual or group counseling.

In a school setting, providing information about suicide and offering counseling assistance as a follow-up to an actual suicide are appropriate measures. If an adolescent who has attempted suicide is returning to the same classrooms in the same school, however, suicide prevention programs should not be provided for the first time until a few months have passed, so that the returning student will not be focused upon. But individual or group counseling still can be provided for those who seem to need to talk about their feelings related to the suicide attempt of one of their peers.

Members of both school and community groups must realize that the end of a period of suicidal crisis or the return of an adolescent who has made an unsuccessful attempt does not signify the end of responsibility of school and community groups to provide counseling assistance. The only hope for improved mental health of the adolescent is long-term counseling focused upon overcoming low self-esteem and other traits so that life and its options can be viewed differently.

An adolescent who attempts suicide is reaching out for the help that can be provided only in the context of the helping relationship. School and community groups must plan, network, and fund services to cope with the increasing problem of adolescent suicide in the same way that provisions are made for interventions related to physical and sexual abuse and drug abuse. Family members and friends must affirm the self-worth of all adolescents by being sensitive to their developing individuality, as well as the stresses of the complex, changing society of which they are a part. Only then will the promise of a new tomorrow become the reality of today.

REFERENCES

Bigrar, J., Gauthier, Y., Bouchard, C., & Jasse, Y. (1966). On the depressive illness in childhood: Suicidal attempts in adolescent girls. A preliminary study. *Canadian Psychiatric Association Journal, 11* (Supplement), 275–282.

Davis, P. A. (1983). *Suicidal adolescents.* Springfield, IL: Charles C Thomas.

Fairchild, T. N. (1986). Suicide intervention. In T. N. Fairchild (Ed.), *Crisis intervention strategies for school-based helpers* (pp. 321–369). Springfield, IL: Charles C Thomas.

Haffen, B. Q., & Frandsen, K. J. (1986). *Youth suicide: Depression and loneliness.* Provo, UT: Behavioral Health Associates.

Husain, S. A., & Vandiver, T. (1984). *Suicide in children and adolescents.* New York: SP Medical and Scientific Books.

Jacobziner, H. (1965). Attempted suicides in adolescents by poisoning. *Journal of the American Medical Association, 191*(1), 101–105.

McAnarney, E. R. (1979). Adolescent and young adult suicide in the United States—A reflection of societal unrest? *Adolescence, 14*(56), 765–774.

Otto, U. (1972). Suicidal acts by children and adolescents: A follow-up study. *Acta Psychiatrica Scandinavica, 233* (Supplement), 5–123.

Truckman, J., & Connon, H. E. (1962). Attempted suicides in adolescents. *American Journal of Psychiatry, 119*(3), 228–232.

PROFESSIONAL RESOURCES

Bradley, J., & Rotheram, M. J. (no date). *Assessment for risk and imminent danger of suicide among runaways: A training manual for shelter staff.* New York: Columbia University, Division of Child Psychiatry.

Catalog. Kidsrights, 401 South Highland, P.O. Box 851, Mount Dora, FL 32757, pp. 3, 15, 22.

Sunburst Communications, 39 Washington Ave., Pleasantville, NY 10570. *Preventing teen suicide: You can help* (filmstrip) and *Teenage blues: Coping with depression* (filmstrip and video).

Dave Capuzzi is Professor of Counselor Education, Portland State University, and President of the American Association for Counseling and Development.

4

Growing Pains: Explaining Adolescent Violence with Developmental Theory

Raymond A. Winbush

On a hot July afternoon in 1977, "B" was struck and killed by a Long Island Railroad train. Eight days later, his 23-year-old girlfriend died—killed by a train driven by the same engineer. The *New York Times* ("Three Struck and Killed," 1977) reported that moments before the train struck the girl, she was observed extending her hands toward it while making the sign of the cross. Then, as the train whistle blew, she covered her ears with her hands.

The dramatic increase in violence among adolescents has grown to epidemic proportions. Violence by adolescents—self-inflicted as well as that perpetrated on others—has given a new and deadly meaning to the phrase "kid stuff." More than half of all serious crimes in the United States (murder, rape, aggravated assault, robbery, burglary, larceny, motor vehicle theft) are committed by youth aged 10 to 17.

Between 1960 and 1980, juvenile crime rose twice as fast as adult crime. In northern California, children of 17 and under are arrested for 57% of all felonies against people (homicide, assault, rape, etc.), and 66% of property crimes. In Chicago, one third of all murders were committed by persons aged 20 or younger—a 29% jump over 1975 (*Uniform Crime Reports,* 1980).

The increase of adolescent violence is not limited by sex of offender. From 1970 to 1975, the arrest rate of girls under 18 for serious crimes rose 40%, versus 24% for boys. In 1975, 11% of all juveniles arrested for violent crimes were females. Law officers often react with surprise to the increase of violent crime among females—most likely because of sexist stereotypes involving women. Many officials offer the gloomy forecast that, at the current rate, violence among adolescent females will equal that of males by the mid 1990s.

The forms of violence among youth are also becoming more diverse and deadly. The inevitable cost to the public is that these students often commit felonies and violent crimes, especially toward older Americans, during school hours. Young criminals tend to prey on vulnerable victims such as the elderly, sick, or inebriated. The victims are often too weak to resist, or too confused to report the crime to the proper authorities. Moreover, these persons are often the victims of repeated offenses because of their immobility and relatively predictable behaviors. The perpetrators simply return to continue the victimization because the victims pose little threat to the youthful offender's behavior.

THEORIES ON YOUTHFUL CRIMINAL BEHAVIOR

Theories on criminal behavior among youth are as varied as the crimes the youth commit, and appear to be a function of the economic, political, racial, or sexual values held by those who offer them. In this sense, offering a comprehensive theory of juvenile criminal behavior is difficult because of the ubiquitous nature of the phenomenon itself. In any case, the theories appear to fall into two categories—economic and cultural/ecological. The two categories overlap at many points, but they do offer a useful framework for examining these theories.

Economic Theories

Marxist Theory

Karl Marx wrote very little on crime and held the radical view that all privately held property was a form of "theft" (Hirst, 1975). Marx was characteristically unsympathetic toward juvenile criminals, referring to them as "scum." Early Marxist criminologists such as William Barger (1905-1969) offered the traditional Marxist view that juvenile crime was the inevitable result of young persons' realizing that they were being exploited in a capitalistic society (Barger, 1969).

Contemporary Marxists such as Taylor, Walton, and Young (1973, p. 174) have stated that crimes among young people tend to involve property and, therefore, thievery could be eliminated if society would abolish the precondition for theft—private property. The problem with Taylor's thesis, as Glaser (1979) noted, is that the premise is wrong; all societies experience property crimes by youth regardless of political ideology. Therefore, although there may be a slight correlation between the political philosophy of a nation and juvenile crime, youthful violence is far more universal than Marxist theory allows for.

Capitalist Theory

Conservative sociologist Robert Merton has argued that crime in American society, especially among youth, is inevitable because children in American culture are imbued with the importance of ambition, status, and acquisition of "things" associated with prosperity (Merton, 1952). More recent studies, however, have questioned the widely held assumption that lower socioeconomic classes have higher rates of delinquency than higher classes do. In a review of 35 studies on juvenile delinquency, Tittle, Villemez, and Smith (1978), stated that the significant decline in the relationship between class and crime during the past 40 years has rendered that relationship negligible.

Where class does seem to play a significant role among adolescents is in the area of violent versus "white-collar" crime. Poorer classes commit more violent crimes; middle and upper classes commit more white-collar crimes. Property crimes are simply not class-linked. This is an important point because it aids in eliminating stereotypes associated with juvenile crime (e.g., black adolescents are more likely to steal than are their white counterparts).

Elsewhere (Winbush, 1980), I have argued that macrocosmic views of violent behavior in the African-American community provide a much more accurate understanding of the nature of crime in a specific locale. This view takes into account racism, poverty, and unemployment as important variables in the equation for understanding criminal activity. It changes the focus on violent behavior from the perpetrators to understanding society's complicity in encouraging that behavior.

Ecological Cultural Theory

Plotting the correlations between a nation's prosperity and violent behavior, which dates back to the early 19th century, continues to be a popular sociological method of studying violent behavior among youth. More recently, economists have taken a keen interest in understanding the relationship between crime and unemployment. Fleisher's (1966) study marked the beginning of this type of analysis. Upon examining offenses of persons 24 years of age and under, he found significant correlations between rates of unemployment and juvenile delinquency in 101 American cities.

In an intriguing analysis of the relationship between business trends and black juvenile delinquency, Glaser (1979) argued that the civil rights movement of the 1960s created among black youth a set of expectations that have gone largely unfulfilled. He noted, as others have, that the homicide rate for blacks increased steadily from 1965 to 1970 (9.6 to 18.4 per 100,000 in cities over 1 million) but declined slightly thereafter. Given the fact that homicide is the leading cause of death among black males aged 15 to 34 (U.S. Department of Health, Education & Welfare, 1979), Glaser explained this slight drop in the early 1970s as the last period when black youth "had faith" in the perceived gains that would accrue from the civil rights movement. As a consequence, the black community earnestly sought to avoid internally sanctioned violence (Winbush, 1981) that would be disruptive to the community. Unfortunately, as Glaser noted:

The lag in realization of these hopes, especially in the metropolitan ghettoes, is alleged to have been the main factor in precipitating a series of riots in these locales, beginning with the Watts riot in Los Angeles in 1965. These disturbances intensified following the assassination of Martin Luther King and Robert F. Kennedy in 1968, *but were largely terminated in the early 1970s.* (italics mine)

Glaser also noted that youth in Latino barrios in the 1980s may well be comparable to mid-1960s black youth in terms of their expectations of advancement in education, employment, and business opportunities.

COUNSELING VIOLENT YOUTH

Despite the plethora of theories associated with youthful violence, the nagging question remains as to what can be done for youth who inflict violence upon themselves and others. Even more specifically, what can counselors do for these youths? In many instances, the counselor is at a loss when attempting to use existing intervention methods to counsel violent youth. Distinguishing between two types of violence among youth can aid in structuring intervention strategies that would prove useful in counseling these children. One form of violence is *self-inflicted,* including suicide, drug abuse, and alcoholism. *Other-inflicted* violence refers to that perpetrated on other people and also includes vandalism and what the public often calls "senseless violence."

Self-inflicted Violence

Suicide

When examining youthful anger, the increase of suicide among juveniles is one of the most alarming of all statistics. Tragically, this anger is turned toward the self, and it leaves helpers in a quandary as to how they can help its victims. More than 4,000 juvenile suicides were recorded in 1978. The National Office of Vital Statistics documented suicide rates among 10- to 14-year-old children in the United States as increasing from 0.4 per 100,000 in 1955 to 1.2 per 100,000 in 1975. Klagsbrun (1976) reported that more young people die by suicide than from cancer and heart ailments combined. She further suggested that suicide statistics tend to be on the low side because suicides are often hidden or misidentified. Medical examiners often list these deaths as questionable or accidental. Klagsbrun also estimated that juvenile suicide *attempts* range between 200,000 and 400,000 each year.

Increasing suicide rates also have been noted in studies of ethnic groups. Dizmang, Watson, May, and Bopp (1974) studied the Shoshone Indian in Idaho for a 7-year period and found the suicide rate to be 98:100,000. More than half of these victims were under age 25. Similarly, Allen (1974) reported that the highest rates of suicide among black people are in the 20- to 24-year-old age group for both males and females. The alarming increase in adolescent suicide extends cross-culturally, but its most dramatic escalations seem to occur among ethnic groups that have experienced a history of racial discrimination. In a penetrating comment on this point, Smith (1976) stated that:

> A white person does not realize until middle age that he may not reach goals he has set for himself; he then must accept his limitations or resign himself to a life of quiet desperation. Such resulting depression occurs earlier among nonwhites.

Lee (1978) listed three probable, though extremely controversial, causes of the increase of youthful suicides. The first is the *interaction of sex, sibling position, and family constellation.* She quoted Cantor (1972), who postulated that the probability of an adolescent's committing suicide is predetermined by earlier stages of development that include, but are not limited to, the interaction of sex, birth order, and family constellation. Citing flawed Adlerian studies (Balser & Masterson, 1959), Cantor suggested, among other things, that firstborn females with younger brothers have the least satisfactory dyad during development. As a consequence, they are the most submissive, dependent, anxious, and competitive of all children in the family. They are, therefore, more prone to commit suicide during adolescence. Conclusions like these are dubious, at best, and do reflect a sexist view of a serious problem.

Lee's second probable cause is *family disorganization.* She noted that adolescent attempters usually have experienced the death of a close relative; in fact, death of the relative occurred 75% of the time prior to the adolescent reaching adulthood. She concluded that abandonment, either by death or divorce, is a major factor in determining adolescents who are at-risk for suicide.

Finally, Lee listed the *women's movement* as a determining factor in youthful suicide. She cited sociologists Star and Steiner (1976), who argued that women are just now beginning to face circumstances that were once the exclusive domain of men, such as loss of self-esteem resulting from poor job performance. Furthermore, in adolescent girls the increased emphasis on competition engendered by the women's movement can lead to the same frustrations and, hence, suicidal behavior that were once strictly male phenomena. These explanations serve only to reinforce destructive stereotypes of the women's movement and make light of a more complex situation. More complete answers must be provided for counselors who are seeking substantive input toward solutions to the adolescent suicide problem and how to deal with it.

Additional reasons given for youthful suicide include loss of love object, personality characteristics, and depression. Only general information is offered, however, as to why these are important variables.

Counseling Strategies for Suicidal Adolescents

A few practical suggestions for counselors in the school setting are listed as follows:

1. The school counselor should develop a close working relationship with mental health facilities in the vicinity of the school district. This will prevent unnecessary delay if a student attempts suicide during school hours.

2. The counselor should be watchful for any potentially disruptive changes that occur in families of students within the school. Divorce, death of a family member, and severe illness are some of the stressors that can lead to suicidal behavior. Too often, schools ignore family circumstances in general. In the case of a death in the family, for example, the school may merely provide a few days of excused absence. The alert school counselor also might implement a program of primary prevention within the school by letting the students know that the counseling office is available for divorce counseling and working through bereavement.

3. The counselor should be knowledgeable of developmental issues that can provide insight into and lead to solutions to life crises. In a brief but enlightening discussion of this point, Lee (1978) quoted Kohlberg (1976), who stated that cognitive conflict can occur through participating in decision-making solutions by exposure to the moral reasoning of significant others. This realization can be useful for counselors who work largely with adolescent populations. Presentation of moral dilemmas can aid the child in examining his or her strategies for coping with stress. Hopefully, these discussions can lead to higher levels of moral reasoning, which would seek to abandon suicide as a solution to a life crisis.

Petronio (1980) argued that Kohlberg's (see Figure 1) stages of moral development can be used in defining levels of delinquency among adolescents. In an intriguing study on the moral development of juvenile offenders, he found that repeater delinquents had *higher* levels of moral development than those who did not return to court. Repeater delinquents, on the average, had a major orientation in Stage 3 and a minor orientation in Stage 2 of Kohlberg's hierarchy. He argued that delinquents prone to violent behavior may not be as amoral as is generally thought. In regard to juveniles who engage in self-destructive behavior such as attempting suicide, he reasoned that they may rationalize their behavior by blaming "social controls" for the problems they face, and thus feel that their deviance is justified because of the inequities of society.

Drug (and Alcohol) Abuse

The prevalence of illegal drug use among adolescents has been well documented in a number of studies. A false dichotomy exists in the literature, however, in separating discussions of drug abuse and liquor abuse. Each is a form of substance abuse stemming from often similar causes. In their survey of 160,000 adolescents, Norman and Harris (1981), found that adolescents themselves fail to make the distinction that adults do between smoking, drinking, and drug taking.

FIGURE 1   Stages of Kohlberg's Moral Development Theory

Level I: Preconventional or Premoral

Stage 1 —*Punishment and Obedience.* Goodness or badness of an act is judged in terms of its physical consequences. Power and deference to authority are emphasized.

Stage 2 —*Instrumental Relativism.* Moral value resides in the instrumental gratification of one's needs. Value is placed on the concrete exchange of favors.

Level II: Conventional

Stage 3 —*Interpersonal Concordance.* Moral reasoning is guided by gaining approval and meeting expectations of others.

Stage 4 —*Law and Order.* Emphasis is placed on maintaining the social order for its own sake, and showing respect for authority.

Level III: Postconventional or Principled

Stage 5 —*Social Contract.* Moral reasoning revolves around rights of the individual, and rational considerations of social utility and welfare guided by democratic principles.

Stage 6 —*Universal Ethical Principles.* The person feels attracted to principles that embody universality and comprehensiveness.

From Kohlberg (1976)

"They smoke or drink what is available," according to the survey, with an overall goal to get high.

Statistics for substance abuse are alarming, to say the least, and reflect the commonplace use of drugs among adolescents. Table 1 illustrates this point. These data indicate not only that over half of the sample consumed alcohol, but also show polydrug usage among this group. In their survey, the researchers arbitrarily classified "drinkers" as those who, by their own admission, drank more than once per week. The youths themselves defined "pot smokers" as those who smoked marijuana at least "two or three times a month." Using these criteria, Norman and Harris uncovered several patterns in their sample. In their sample, the average beginning age of drinking was 12.5, and although boys drank more than girls, the differences were not that great.

Adolescents' reasons for drinking are remarkably similar to those of their adult counterparts. Enjoying the sensation, wanting to relax and forget, and peer pressure were the most frequently given reasons for drinking in the Norman and

TABLE 1
Drug Consumption by Age
(during the past three months)

	13–15 Year Olds	16–18 Year Olds
Alcohol	53%	78%
Marijuana	32%	55%

From Norman and Harris (1981), p. 88.

Harris study. Many parents of teenage alcoholics are well aware that their child is drinking (see Table 2) but feel helpless to do anything about it. Norman and Harris cited the common case in which a 15-year-old's boy's parents allow him to drink beer at home with the hope that he will not drink it outside of the home. He comments: "I've never gotten drunk, but I would if I had a good reason to. Like if you're having troubles and getting confused and the pressure's just too much, then I guess it's not a bad idea to waste yourself for a day." The issue here is this: Counselors may not have the obvious parental support they may think when dealing with a teenage alcohol abuser. Indeed, many parents, like those of the 15-year-old in the above example, may actually encourage their children's drinking behavior, following the rationale that they can serve as monitors over their child's alcohol intake.

In many cases, counselors may be wise to involve the entire family in counseling for the drinking child. School counselors should be aware that parents of drinking adolescents are often frustrated and have a sense of helplessness with regard to their children's drinking habits. Parents alone may be of little help in rehabilitating their adolescents. Moreover, the parents may themselves drink and, therefore, have difficulty imposing limitations on their children's drinking for fear that the children will deem them hypocritical. Counselors who care about curbing self-destructive behavior among their students should challenge attitudes such as these.

Drug use among adolescents has patterns that resemble their drinking behavior. Table 3 provides an overview of marijuana use by teenagers in the Norman and Harris study. The difference by sex is not that great. These data reinforce the idea of a declining significance in sexual differences when analyzing demographic data over the past decade or so. What is remarkable about these data is that 7 of 10 teenagers smoked marijuana by age 16–18. Even by age 15, nearly half (42%) of all teenagers experimented with marijuana.

The implications for counseling intervention should be clear on this point: By the time most school counselors can structure an intervention program for adolescents who are heavy drug users, these teens may be far more sophisticated in their use of drugs than the intervention programs may be in presenting their ideas. I believe that greater linkages should be established between elementary school counselors and high school counselors in educating children about the use of drugs. This often has been neglected by school counselors, many of whom content themselves to bring in a few guest speakers for talks to the student body on the "evils" of drugs, and to have pamphlets available at the counseling office for students who may be interested in the subject.

Major drug intervention programs for adolescents clearly must be established in schools where the students are at high risk for drug abuse. Primary prevention strategies beginning as early as the fifth grade, with workshops for parents and teachers, could begin the work of sabotaging heavy drug usage during adolescence. Interventions by the American Cancer Society in the mid-1970s contributed to a significant decline in cigarette smoking among teenagers during the latter part of that decade. Unfortunately, information on how to develop effective school drug rehabilitation programs has been lacking. One item of advice is to avoid being "preachy." *Facts* are needed. And drug use relates to *cause*. Counselors, other professionals, and parents must realize that teens are abusing drugs for *reasons*. Communication must be a part of getting at those reasons.

Other-Inflicted Violence

The youthful violence that receives the most attention in the media is the violence that is usually captured by the word "senseless" or "unprovoked." Most adults fear this form of violence because it is often spontaneous, unexpected, and difficult to predict. The case of Lawrence illustrates this. He was 15 when he was charged with murdering two brothers in his neighborhood—Kenneth, 11, and Ronald, 12. Lawrence tied up Kenneth, castrated him, and stabbed him twice in the heart. Then he cut off the boy's head, which he left about 50 feet from the body. He also admitted killing Ronald, whose body was never found, in similar fashion. Like all other offenders in juvenile facilities in Texas, Lawrence was released from prison when he turned 18 ("Youth Crime Plague," 1977). Many additional examples of this type of violence could be cited.

A false assumption surrounding this form of violence is that it is limited largely to poorer classes and relates to the economic conditions these groups face.

TABLE 2
If You Drink, Do Your Parents Know?

	All	13–15 Year Olds	16–18 Year Olds
Yes	46%	38%	55%
No	27%	30%	25%
I don't know	27%	32%	20%

From Norman and Harris (1981), p. 103.

TABLE 3
Who Has Tried Marijuana?

	All	Boys	Girls
13–15 year olds	42%	47%	37%
16–18 year olds	70%	74%	67%

From Norman and Harris (1981), p. 95.

Linden (1978) has provided an intriguing theoretical analysis of the assumption that class variables are important in understanding rates of delinquency among male and female adolescents. He argued that:

> Rather than trying to develop new theories which did not emphasize class position as a cause of crime and delinquency, social scientists decided that middle- and lower-class delinquency were two separate phenomena which required two very different explanations. (p. 410)

He went on to say that violence among middle-class boys, for example, is often seen simply as "raising hell" or "having fun," when in reality violent behavior occurs at essentially the same level in middle classes as in other classes.

Table 4 presents delinquency data on various crimes. The sample was drawn from the 17,500 students entering the 11 public junior and senior high schools of Western Contra Costa County in the San Francisco-Oakland metropolitan area. The final sample consisted of 4,077 males and females in grades 7 through 12. The data in Table 4 represent the 1,588 white boys in the sample. No remarkably sharp differences are revealed between the type of crime committed by the boys and their social class as represented by father's occupation. The study also indicated that violent behavior among middle-class delinquents, while trailing that of poorer classes, is growing at a rate that exceeds that of economically disadvantaged youth. As Linden argued, more comprehensive theories of violence among juveniles must be offered to account for the *why* of violence among youth. Class arguments, he asserted, merely salve the consciences of those who believe that achieving middle-class status equips the individual with the ability to transcend violent behavior. Data from the study simply do not support this contention.

TOWARD A DEVELOPMENTAL EXPLANATION OF YOUTHFUL VIOLENCE

If class issues regarding the causes of juvenile delinquency are replaced by developmental explanations, one discovers many more plausible arguments concerning reasons for youthful violence. Heise (1976) found that 18- and 19-year-old college students were more condemnatory of a list of 30 deviant acts than were students aged 20 and over. Gold and Petronio (1979) found that variables representing an adolescent's involvement in teen roles (for example, number of dates in the previous month) and flexibility concerning the morality of deviant acts (for example, taking a short-cut across someone else's property or lying about your age to get into the movies cheaper are not so bad) account for the most variance in frequency of delinquent behavior. In an early study, Ruma and Mosher (1967) found that higher moral reasoning was associated with *higher* guilt among a group of male delinquents.

Much of the violent behavior among youth can perhaps be better understood by adopting a developmental paradigm in understanding their behavior. Counseling strategies with these youth could then concentrate on increasing the moral reasoning of the young by presenting moral dilemmas similar to those suggested earlier with suicidal adolescents.

Two Case Examples

SOARs

I have commented elsewhere on my use of Seminars on African-American Relationships (SOAR) (Winbush, 1980) as a means of deliberate psychological education with black adolescents. These groups meet once per week and discuss a wide range of issues confronting African-American youth, such as dating behavior, relationships with parents and peers, and the prevention of violence in predominantly black communities.

The SOARs were first introduced while I taught on a campus at which several incidents of violence had occurred among blacks from different cultural backgrounds. Representatives from each group agreed to meet once a week to discuss issues related to the cultural similarities of the various West Indian, African, and

TABLE 4
Specified Delinquent Acts
By Father's Occupation

| Type of Delinquency | Father's Occupation | | | | |
	Unskilled Manual %	Semiskilled Manual %	Skilled Manual %	White Collar %	Professional %
Theft under $2.00	55	53	51	65	52
Theft $2.00 to $50.00	21	21	20	20	13
Theft over $50.00	6	7	7	4	5
Auto Theft	10	9	12	10	10
Property Damage	23	28	25	25	26
Battery	44	40	45	42	35

From Linden (1978). Used by permission of the author.

African-American groups on the campus. After the SOARs had met for 8 weeks, violent episodes among the groups who had met to discuss their differences *and* similarities declined notably.

Umoja House

Similar results were achieved by David and Falaka Fattah of Philadelphia, who became alarmed over gang-related deaths involving black adolescent males in the Philadelphia area (Whittemore, 1980). This prompted them to create an extended family home, modeled on the principle of *umoja* (unity) for members of rival gangs in the northern section of the city. In 1969, 40 boys had been killed in gang-related violence when the Fattahs invited 15 members of the Clymer Street Gang into their home (the four-room house already had eight members—Mr. and Mrs. Fattah and their six sons). Through dialogue, an emphasis on African values, and dedication, gang-related deaths dropped to 32 in 1974, 15 in 1975, 6 in 1976, and only 2 between 1977 and 1983.

All of the boys are encouraged to get involved in community service and to understand the meaning of being a black adolescent in a society that is often hostile to their very existence. Falaka Fattah told me that the principles upon which Umoja House was founded can easily be applied to other African-American communities that have high rates of violence. She added that the principles inculcated at Umoja House have implications for stemming family violence as well.

Application of Developmental Theory

School counselors who are interested in addressing incidents of violence among their students should increase their familiarity with developmental theorists such as William Perry (1970), Lawrence Kohlberg (1975), Robert Kegan (1982), Carol Gilligan (1982), James Fowler (1981), and Jane Loevinger (1976). This knowledge will help them formulate practical ways of addressing the violence they wish to eliminate among their students. Primary prevention strategies involving these theorists as points of departure can serve to increase the evaluative capacity of adolescents engaged in violent behavior.

Jurkovic (1980) has provided a comprehensive review of literature on structural-developmental approaches to juvenile offenders, including discussion of the ways in which Piaget's and Kohlberg's theories can be used to address delinquency problems among adolescents. Ironically, Kohlberg (1958), one of the first to investigate the moral reasoning of delinquents, has devoted little to this topic since writing his doctoral dissertation at the University of Chicago. In that study he compared the moral reasoning of delinquents to that of nondelinquents and found that the former group reasoned primarily at the preconventional level (Stages 1 and 2), in contrast to the controls, who relied heavily on conventional level (Stages 3 and 4) judgments. Fifteen years later Hudgins and Prentice (1973) found no correlation between moral reasoning and delinquency status. They also found that the mothers of the delinquents earned lower moral maturity scores than did the mothers of nondelinquents.

Drawing on Piagetian theory, mixed results on developmental issues involving delinquents are also evidenced. Johnson (cited in Eshel, Keegelmass, & Breznitz, 1968) found that delinquents had moral reasoning scores similar to those of a comparable group of "normal" children. In a subsequent study by Eshel et al. (1968), however, delinquent boys were found to be more oriented toward material consequences than were the nondelinquents. Jurkovic concluded, as did others (e.g., Petronio, 1980), that stereotypes concerning the moral development of violent youth are dysfunctional when intervention strategies are concerned, because mental health workers may typecast these young people as incorrigible.

Counselors can best serve these individuals by erasing their own doubts about the efficacy of counseling juvenile delinquents and by providing settings that can encourage youths to examine the values they hold regarding violence. These settings can be groups, such as the previously mentioned SOAR experience, involving youths with a history of delinquent behavior, meeting once or more per week for an hour in groups of 10 to 15. Counselors could utilize moral dilemmas such as those provided in the Defining Issues Test *(DIT)* (Rest, 1974) to aid the adolescents in refining their moral reasoning. Pairing the teenagers in the group for 5 minutes, before discussing their opinions openly with the other members, can be an effective way of encouraging discussion of feelings by these youth—which often challenges the values held by the counselors themselves.

Counselors who lead groups of this nature must possess a working knowledge of theorists who deal specifically with developmental issues of adolescents. They also must be aware of recent studies challenging some of the traditionally held assumptions on adolescent and moral development. Gilligan (1982), for example, has widened the views of moral development by revealing distinct differences in the ways boys and girls solve ethical dilemmas. Erikson's notions about identity formation in black adolescents fail to provide an adequate picture of the diversity of development cross-culturally (Winbush, 1976).

Developmental theory provides an unprecedented opportunity for counselors to develop new intervention strategies for curbing the plague of youthful violence. Counselors can ill afford to neglect these opportunities, the rewards of which will be seen in alleviating pain in the lives of both the victims and the perpetrators of youthful violence.

SUMMARY

Various theories on juvenile violence appear to account for the increase of this phenomenon, but closer examination of these theories often reveals that they are superficial in their analyses. Developmental theory offers a way of reassessing juvenile violence and allows for a better explanation of delinquent behavior than do traditional sociological analyses.

To help combat the alarming increase in juvenile violence in America, counselors can address the problem using developmental theory as a means of understanding how this behavior may be related to predictable developmental milestones. Intervention can include the use of moral dilemmas, in groups, as a means of giving adolescents insight into their "growing pains" and on their effects on others.

REFERENCES

Allen, N. (1974). *Suicide*. Los Angeles: Department of Health.

Balser, B., & Masterson, J. (1959). Suicide in adolescents. *American Journal of Psychiatry, 116,* 400–404.

Barger, W. A. (1969). *Criminality and economic conditions*. Boston: Little, Brown (and Bloomington, IN: Indiana University Press).

Cantor, P. (1972). The adolescent attempter. *Life Threatening Behavior, 2,* 3–17.

Dizmang, L., Watson, J., May, P., & Bopp, J. (1974). Adolescent suicide at an Indian reservation. *American Journal of Orthopsychiatry, 44,* 43–49.

Eshel, Y., Keegelmass, S., & Breznitz, S. (1968). Moral judgments of lower-class delinquents. *British Journal of Criminology, 8,* 69–74.

Fleisher, B. M. (1966). *The economics of delinquency*. Chicago: Quadrangle.

Fowler, J. (1981). *Stages of faith: The psychology of human development and the quest for meaning*. New York: Harper & Row.

Gilligan, C. (1982). *In a different voice: Psychological theory and women's development*. Cambridge, MA: Harvard University Press.

Glaser, D. (1979). Economic and sociocultural variables affecting rates of youth unemployment, delinquency, and crime. *Youth & Society, 11* (1), 53–82.

Gold, M., & Petronio, R. (1979). In J. Adelson (Ed.), *Handbook of adolescent psychology*. New York: John Wiley.

Heise, D. (1976). Norms and individual patterns in student delinquency. *Social Problems, 16,* 78–92.

Hirst, P. Q. (1975). Marx and Engels on law, crime, and morality. In I. Taylor et al. (Eds.), *Critical criminology*. London: Routledge & Kegan Paul.

Hudgins, W., & Prentice, N. M. (1973). Moral judgment in delinquent and nondelinquent boys and their mothers. *Journal of Abnormal Psychology, 82,* 145–152.

Jurkovic, G. J. (1980). The juvenile delinquent as a moral philosopher: A structural-developmental perspective. *Psychological Bulletin, 88*(3), 709–727.

Kegan, R. (1982). *The evolving self*. Cambridge, MA: Harvard University Press.

Klagsbrun, F. (1976). *Too young to die*. Boston: Houghton Mifflin.

Kohlberg, L. (1958). *The development of moral thinking and choice in the years ten to sixteen*. Doctoral dissertation, University of Chicago.

Kohlberg, L. (1975). Counseling and counselor education: A developmental approach. *Counselor Education & Supervision, 14,* 250–256.

Kohlberg, L. (1976). Moral stages and moralization. In *Moral development and behavior*. New York: Holt, Rinehart & Winston.

Lee, E. E. (1978). Suicide and youth. *Personnel & Guidance Journal, 57*(4), 200–204.

Linden, R. (1978). Myths of middle-class delinquency: A test of the generalizability of social control theory. *Youth & Society, 9*(4), 407–432.

Loevinger, J. (1976). *Ego development*. San Francisco: Jossey-Bass.

Merton, R. (1952). *Social theory and social structure*. Glencoe, IL: Free Press.

Norman, J., & Harris, M. W. (1981). *The private life of the American teenager*. New York: Rawson, Wade Publishers.

Perry, W., Jr. (1970). *Forms of intellectual and ethical development in the college years*. New York: Holt, Rinehart & Winston.

Petronio, R. J. (1980). The moral maturity of repeater delinquents. *Youth & Society, 12*(1), 51–59.
Rest, J. (1974). *Manual for the defining issues test: An objective test of moral judgment development.* Available from author (330 Burton Hall, University of Minnesota, Minneapolis, MN 55455).
Ruma, E. H., & Mosher, D. L. (1967). Relationship between moral judgment and guilt in delinquent boys. *Journal of Abnormal Psychology, 72,* 122–127.
Smith, F. (1976). Adolescent suicide: A problem for teachers? *Phi Delta Kappan, 57,* 539–542.
Star, C., & Steiner, S. (1976, January). Why more women are committing suicide. *McCall's,* p. 47.
Taylor, I., Walton, P., & Young, J. (1973). *The new criminology: For a social theory of deviance.* London: Routledge & Kegan Paul.
Three struck and killed by Long Island train (1977, August 8). *New York Times,* p. 26.
Tittle, C. R., Villemez, W. J., & Smith, D. A. (1978). The myth of social class and criminality. *American Social Review, 43,* 643–656.
Uniform Crime Reports. (1980). Washington, DC: FBI, Dept. of Justice.
U.S. Department of Health, Education & Welfare. (1979). *Health.* Washington, DC: U.S. Government Printing Office.
Whittemore, H. (1980). One family conquers. *Parade,* pp. 4–5.
Winbush, R. A. (1976). *A quantitative exploration into the theoretical formulations of Erik H. Erikson concerning black identity.* Doctoral dissertation, University of Chicago.
Winbush, R. A. (1980). Toward a macrocosmic view of crime in African-American communities. *Public Health Reports, 95*(6), 557.
Winbush, R. A. (1981). *The two faces of violence in the African-American community.* Unpublished manuscript, Vanderbilt University.
Youth crime plague. (1977, July 11). *Time,* pp. 18–28.

SUGGESTED READINGS

Fowler, J. (1981). *Stages of faith: The psychology of human development and the quest for meaning.* New York: Harper & Row.
Gary, L. (1981). *Black men.* Beverly Hills, CA: Sage.
Gilligan, C. (1982). *In a different voice: Psychological theory and women's development.* Cambridge, MA: Harvard University Press.
Kohlberg, L. (1958). *The development of modes of moral thinking and choice in the years 10 to 16.* Unpublished doctoral dissertation, University of Chicago.
Levinson, D. (1978). *The seasons of a man's life.* New York: Ballantine Books.
Loevinger, J. (1976). *Ego development.* San Francisco: Jossey-Bass.
Perry, W., Jr. (1970). *Forms of intellectual and ethical development in the college years.* New York: Holt, Rinehart & Winston.
Rest, J. (1976). New approaches in the assessment of moral judgment. In T. Lickona (Ed.), *Moral development and behavior* (pp. 198–220). New York: Holt, Rinehart & Winston.
Rodgers-Rose, L. (1980). *The black woman.* Beverly Hills, CA: Sage.
Staub, E. (1979). *Positive social behavior and morality (Vols. 1 and 2).* New York: Academic Press.

The author wishes to thank his graduate assistant, Sandra Washington, for her diligence in securing the bibliographic sources for most of this paper, and for her organizational skills.

Raymond Winbush is an Assistant Professor of Psychology and Education at Vanderbilt University.

5

Coping with Loss: A Developmental Approach to Helping Children and Youth

Richard L. Hayes

Eight was a very special age for me. I got a new bicycle. Nearly 4 years had passed—half a lifetime—since my new tricycle had been stolen only 2 days after I had gotten it. Then I watched, green with envy, as my twin rode his trike about. Oh, he was generous in letting me use it from time to time, but it was his, and mine was gone. I pleaded with my parents to get a new one, arguing that it "just wasn't fair." And always the reply would come back from one or the other of them: "It doesn't seem fair, does it? But caring for your trike was your responsibility. You didn't put it away as asked, and it was stolen."

Now I had a bicycle. And every night I put it away. When it was scratched, I painted it. When it was broken, I fixed it. And when I was 15, I sold it. What friends that blue Columbia and I had been! But I was interested in cars now, "too old for just a bicycle." I said "goodbye" and "thanks" to the kid who bought it, and for just a moment I thought about saying the same to that bike as it and my childhood went rolling down the driveway together.

Life is a series of "goodbyes." Yet, like a doorway that marks the passage of our lives, loss presents the opportunity to say "hello" to new learning experiences. The crises that form the context of our goodbyes are the natural consequence of living so as to preserve the present in the face of change. As Kegan (1982) pointed out:

> The Chinese draw "crisis" with two characters: one means "danger," and the other "opportunity." This, literally, is the character of crisis; for crisis *is* in the transformation of meaning,

73

the costs of evolution, and the death we hear may be, as much as anything, the death of the old self that is about to be left behind. (p. 266)

In each step forward in our evolution, we must necessarily leave something behind. Through these losses we gain new opportunities to learn about the selves we are becoming.

I learned a lot in those bicycle years. I learned to ask strangers for directions and how to sit next to them on a bus; I learned to talk with relatives who knew all about me but whom I had never met; I learned how to start a conversation with classmates who were new to school or I to theirs. I also learned that robins die when they fall from their nests; I learned to wait by myself when my mom was late in arriving home from work; I learned to be patient when shopping with my father.

This article is about the losses in life, how we learn about them and how we learn to live with them. Some are predictable, as when relatives leave after a visit, or when grandparents die after a long illness. But many come as a surprise, especially to the minds of children whose years of experience are as limited as the sense they make of such events. Toys that break, stores that are closed, and friends who don't call are as mysterious to the minds of children, when first encountered, as premature death, divorce, and company-ordered moves are to the minds of adults. Each loss challenges us to rethink our world view and to learn from it or be lost ourselves.

This article is also about how we can help others to learn from the losses in their lives. Much has been written lately about death and death education (see Bernstein, 1983), and no attempt will be made here to improve upon that literature. Instead, the focus will be less on death per se than on those *little deaths* that confront each of us in the enterprise of being human. The discussion is organized around three related areas: (a) loss as a part of life, (b) loss as a cumulative experience, (c) mediating in the experience of loss—and how counselors, teachers, and parents can help children to grow within the context of this universal, developmental experience.

LOSS AND LIFE

Death is our new obscenity. In a society attempting to rebuild itself from a decade of rampant individualism, it should come as no surprise that Americans see death around every corner. Jeffrey Schrank (1972) has a theory that "What a particular culture considers obscene reveals its most threatening fear" (p. 126). With sex now "out of the closet" in which our Victorian forebearers put it, death and related losses have become the latest preoccupation.

Consider the current interest in the holocaust, nuclear disarmament, environmental protection, and the almost fanatical pursuit of wellness in this country. Selling fitness is big business in America today because it appeals to a recurring fear that the self may be overwhelmed at any moment by forces beyond one's control.

This is an old theme in Western civilization—"man against nature"—but its form now pervades American culture. As the *Peanuts* character Snoopy once remarked, "It doesn't matter whether you win or lose . . . until you lose." In a country where 10% of its working force is estimated to have some difficulty with alcohol, beer companies proclaim that, "You only go around once in life" and challenge consumers to "grab for all the gusto" they can.

Americans are at war with more than their own bodies—events acted out in the recent, so-called sexual revolution; they are at war with life itself. Beyond the more than $260 billion estimated to be spent on defense each year, Americans spend in excess of $6 billion on coffee, $8 billion on cigarettes, $10 billion on alcohol, and $85 billion on health insurance premiums, 80% of the medical benefits from which are used to postpone death in the last 6 months of life (U.S. Bureau of the Census, 1983).

Advanced technology has made death the province of the hospital, while the natural life cycle of the farm is as remote an experience for most children as a field trip to the museum to see animals that *once lived*. But today's children are not without loss. One third of all children growing up today will spend at least part of the first 18 years of their lives living with only one parent; 1 in 20 will lose a parent by death during the same period; and 1 in 5 families will move this year alone.

Even if by some miracle these big losses could be prevented, or if we could at least protect our children from them, how could we protect them from all of those other losses that so inevitably come their way: the loss of a pet through death, or of one's place in the family through the birth of a sibling; the loss of one's culture as the result of a change in the social order; the loss of older siblings through the natural progression of their leaving home; the loss of function through illness; the loss of self-esteem that can come with failing in school; the loss of direction that comes when expectations are unmet; the loss of security that accompanies the loss of a treasured object; the loss of one's innocence in choosing to grow up.

Change and Pain

The question is not how to help children to avoid the losses they might experience but, rather, how to help them to experience the loss, to get *through* instead of *over* it. Change is constant, and with every change there is the accompanying experience of loss. But the concern here is not so much with loss as it is with pain, which is so often the experience of loss. Pain, Kegan (1982) has told us

> . . . is about the resistance to the motion of life. Our attempt to deny what has happened and is happening causes us pain. . . . In defense against the losses which have already occurred, in defense against the experience of grief and mourning, we inflict on ourselves a pain which is greater than the loss itself. (pp. 265–266)

In essence, it is the self which loses and which is lost. Our identities, the selves we have chosen and to which we are committed, are out of balance. "Rather than acknowledge the loss and our lack of control over it, we often . . . defend against the reality to insist that the loss be manageable. The 'stages' of grief, then, are best understood as the result of trying to maintain our illusions of omnipotence in the face of lack of control" (Davenport, 1981, p. 333). The anticipation of continued or enduring pain leads to suffering and to chronic stress. As can be seen in Figure 1, change, loss, pain, and stress are linked by a sequence of self-regulated events.

The nervous system is designed to tell us what's different. It analyzes change. So it is that we cannot smell ourselves, or after a time, our own cologne or the fish we may be cooking. But when others enter the room, they may immediately take notice of these scents. What we have long since failed to notice in its presence, others now recognize as a change in their own environment. This system has a simple logic: It acts to protect us against the possibility of harm. By monitoring the changes that take place about us, we are ever alert to the dangerous and the fresh opportunities that can exist for us. Yet, by the very recognition of change, we must acknowledge the loss of a way of being that was, to this point at least, self-sustaining.

Choices

If change is constant, loss is inevitable. But pain and suffering—especially the sort that accompany chronic stress—are optional. Although we must be responsive as living organisms to change, we nonetheless have some options in the choices we make. These choices are at the core of what it means to be a human *being*. As Dewey (1960) argued:

> In committing oneself to a particular course, a person gives a lasting set to his own being. Consequently, it is proper to say that in choosing this object, rather than that, one is in reality choosing what kind of a person or self one is going to be. . . . The self reveals its nature in what it chooses. (pp. 148–151)

Just as our choices reveal the kind of self we would like to be, so they reveal the kind of self we have been. In the course of our evolution toward a new self, each

FIGURE 1 The Relationship Between Change, Loss, Pain, and Stress

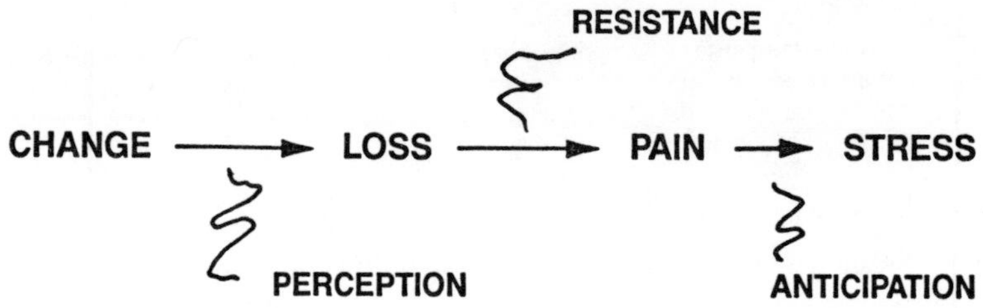

choice presents an opportunity to speculate on a future self and represents the danger in giving up a familiar past.

LOSS AS A CUMULATIVE EXPERIENCE

Life holds predictable psychosocial crises in store for us over the course of our development. These crises do not pose a threat of catastrophe as much as they represent "crucial periods of increased vulnerability and heightened potential" (Erikson, 1968, p. 96). When worked out in a constructive manner, the resolution of these crises can result in a new balance of forces within the individual. Failure to negotiate the crisis limits the individual's capacity for further development.

Human development represents the course of our attempts to make sense of the changes going on around us. If adults are to help children realize their possibilities, they must help children make better choices and help them better organize their experiences.

> What a human organism organizes is meaning. Thus it is not that a person makes meaning, as much as that the activity of being a person is the activity of meaning-making. . . . And the most fundamental thing we do with what happens to us is organize it. We literally make sense. (Kegan, 1982, p. 11)

The challenge for those who would intervene in the lives of children is to help them face life directly. Helping children make better choices involves helping them acknowledge loss rather than fight it, and necessitates increasing their responsiveness to change. If adults are to help children understand the losses they experience, they must understand the child's efforts to make meaning of the events.

Well meaning but protective adults often view children as too delicate or too young to handle information about loss directly. Also, adults often succeed in insulating themselves by their actions from their own concerns about unresolved or anticipated events. This self-protective and misinformed approach to helping children often reflects the cumulative experience, or more properly the lack of experience, of the adult in dealing with similar issues. How we handle the greater disappointments of adulthood is influenced by our understanding of the smaller losses experienced in childhood. To be effective in helping children cope with loss, adults need to understand how children make sense of loss.

Two Misunderstandings About Children

David Elkind (1974) has written about some of the "self-evident assumptions" adults make about children which, upon reflection, turn out to be incorrect. "One of the most serious and pernicious misunderstandings about young children is that they are most like adults in their thinking and least like us in their feelings. In fact, just the reverse is true" (p. 51).

This type of misunderstanding prompts parents to tell a 4-year-old child that "everything will be all right" while simultaneously encouraging the child to "stop that crying." Children who believe that the moon follows them when they walk will make little sense of an unhappy event that can somehow make everything "all right." In contrast, a husband would not think of saying to his grieving wife that somehow things will be better if only she would stop crying. To be able to help children cope with the inevitable separations and losses they experience, adults must understand that children feel as we do in these circumstances, but they make a different sense of the events.

"A second misunderstanding about young children" Elkind (1974) went on, "is that they learn best while they are sitting still and listening" (p. 52). So often adults ask children to think about the consequences of their loss, telling them to "go to your room and think about what has happened." Certainly adults do learn by sitting quietly and reflecting upon their actions or by listening to the shared wisdom of others. But for children the activity of learning is of a different kind than that of most adults. With children the idea of active learning must be taken quite literally, for only in acting and experiencing the concrete effects of their actions do children truly learn.

Thus, the child who has lost a tricycle, had a pet die, or dropped a scoop of ice cream from the top of a cone must be helped to confront the loss directly. Adults who replace the tricycle, bring home a new pet, or offer another ice cream cone in consolation, without an intervening period to allow the child to experience the full impact of the associated loss, deny the child a significant opportunity to learn about change and oneself. In contrast, helping the child to make better sense of the event and to experience the loss in its entirety does nothing less than stimulate development itself.

Grief and Loss

Researchers (Bowlby, 1973; Freese, 1977; Kavanaugh, 1974; Kubler-Ross, 1969; Westberg, 1962) have independently identified emotions commonly associated with loss. Drawing upon this work, Davenport (1981) has proposed a list of assumptions that seem to underlie these feelings:

- *Denial:* This couldn't *possibly* happen to me without my permission!
- *Anger:* How *dare* this happen? It's not fair and I won't allow it!
- *Bargaining:* The only circumstances under which I'll go along with this are . . .
- *Depression:* I'm not worth much if this could happen. I must have some irremedial inadequacy that caused this.
- *Panic:* My psychological survival depends on keeping this loss from occurring.
- *Guilt:* If only I had done differently, I could have prevented this from happening.
- Worry: If I plan things carefully enough, I can at least make sure nothing makes me feel this vulnerable again. (p. 333)

A certain arrogance runs through these assumptions—that somehow we can be more than human in the face of death, that we can overcome it. To insist on our right *to* life is not enough. We appear, as well, to insist on "our right for life—and death and loss of all kinds—to 'obey' us" (p. 333).

As counselors, teachers, parents—as adults—we must do more for young people than help them acknowledge their pain. We have an obligation to help them understand their feelings and how they are involved in causing them. As Elkind (1974) has cautioned, we need to understand how young people make sense of loss.

Development and Loss

How one understands each loss is part of an ongoing evolution in the way in which meaning itself is made. The self, as a meaning-making system, undergoes regular and predictable changes in which former losses are resolved and the possibility of experiencing new ones is created. How we think about loss, in particular, is influenced greatly by how we *think*, in general. An understanding of the regularity with which thinking changes over the course of development provides a valuable framework for the study of reactions to loss.

Age, or grade in school, can serve as a practical guide in predicting an individual's level of understanding of loss through the elementary grades. Beyond ages 8 or 9, however, children's development becomes more and more variable with age. Koocher (1981) argued that *level of cognitive development* more accurately explains the changes in children's understandings of death and related losses. Beyond the problems that arise with the emergence of formal operational thought (Inhelder & Piaget, 1958) and a preoccupation with identity development (Erikson, 1968) in adolescence, there lie the additional problems of youth in living life itself (Keniston, 1970). Drawing upon the works of Erikson, Keniston, and Piaget (1952), the regular pattern of changes in children's thinking about loss can be conceptualized as falling into five overlapping periods.

1. Infancy: "All gone"

In birth, the newborn has its first encounter with death and experiences firsthand the pain of separation that comes with changes and loss.

> Consider what you might have learned about the world in this first encounter with it. Remember, you moved from a soft, warm, dark, quiet, totally nourishing place into a harsh sensory bombardment. You were physically abused, violated in a number of ways, and subjected to physical pain and insult, all of which could possibly be overcome if it weren't for one additional act of cruelty: You were isolated from your mother. (Hendricks & Weinhold, 1982, p. 51)

Recent changes (see LeBoyer, 1975; Pearce, 1977) in the practice of childbirth have directed greater attention to the impact of the trauma of birth on newborns. Klaus and Kennel (1976) reported that the first few minutes after birth are critical to the child's continued healthy development. And when the child's need to be touched and to feel go unmet, the neurotic process begins (Janov, 1970).

These first days, on into the end of the first year of the infant's experience as a "stranger in a strange land," evidence a succession of temporary separations and unanticipated reunions. They are "unanticipated" because the infant is essentially a sensory being, directing all activity toward the incorporation of objects to satisfy immediate needs. The newborn lives in "an objectless world, a world in which everything sensed is taken to be an extension of the infant, where out of sight (or touch or taste or hearing or smell) can mean out of existence" (Kegan, 1982, p. 78).

Unaware of time and without a sense of self-improvement, infants pass through states of wakefulness and sleeping that appear no more predictable to them than the parade of faces that pass over the horizon of their cribs. Yet, in their playful explorations they begin to see a regularity in the events about them and in the part they play in causing such events. When out of sight is out of mind, the child is fascinated anew each time Jack pops from his box or as playful parents pull their hands from their eyes and shout, "Peek-a-boo; I see you!" A growing awareness of objects and events leads to new experiments and new understandings.

The objectification of things as separate from the self marks an intellectual revolution in the child's thinking. No longer content to wait for Jack to appear, the child now pulls at the lid to *make* Jack come out; peek-a-boo is replaced with hide-and-seek; unwanted foods are now thrown like missiles to the far reaches of the kitchen. The child's seeming self-absorption in an undifferentiated world is evolving toward an understanding of the world as consisting of objects from which to choose. This recognition of objects in the world, Kegan (1982) explained,

> . . . is the consequence of the organism's gradual "emergence from embeddedness" (Schachtel, 1959). By differentiating itself from the world and the world from it, the organism brings into being that which is independent of its own sensing and moving. . . . But this transformation does not take place over a weekend, and it does not take place without cost to the organism, which must suffer what amounts to the loss of itself in the process. (pp. 78–79)

The concept of loss itself is born, because what can now be found can now be lost. The infant, in emerging from embeddedness in sensori-motor activity (Piaget, 1952), can now relate to self and to others as objects unto themselves. In so doing, however, the infant must give up the *me* that went before in favor of a new *me*. Thus, the process of differentiating the self creates the possibility for integrating the *self* with *other* and initiates the lifelong theme of finding and losing.

This analysis of the origins of the loss phenomenon may seem unnecessarily detailed and drawn out, but its significance lies as much in what it suggests about finding as it does about losing. The creation of objectivity involves the simultaneous loss of self as subject, but by the complimentary process the loss of oneself creates a new object. The not-me that was before is now differentiated from the new one, or even a future one, that replaces it. This re-creative cycle of lost and found underlies the basic process for the development of personality itself. To live life involves taking the risk actually to *be* alive. In daring to care for and about others, we run the risk of losing them and ourselves in the process. The other side of loss, however, is to discover new meanings for our lives and to re-create a new me out of this loss of self.

The growing recognition that objects exist apart from the self ushers in a great new development in the child's relationship with others. Because the child begins to imagine caretakers in their absence, true loss is experienced intellectually for the first time. More than the visceral reaction to changing climatic conditions, the loss of objects once known and the differentiation of *absent* from *present* give rise to the universal experience of anxiety that accompanies separation from the primary caretaker.

This transformation takes place over a period of roughly 2 to 21 months of age, during which time the child experiments with the concept of permanent loss. Toilets are flushed repeatedly, objects are tossed from car windows, and parents swallow the child's unwanted food in demonstration of the "all-gone" phenomenon. Yet, the child's anxiety is not so much about the loss of an object or another as it is about the loss of the child's very organization. Allowed to explore the permanence of some objects and the permanent disappearance of others, children during this period begin to develop the kind of healthy self that seeks out the opportunity in each crisis.

II. Pre-school: "Rest in peace"

At just the point when objects wholly exist for the child (about 21 months), separation anxiety ceases to exist. The successful child has developed the kind of self that is separate from, though not wholly independent of, others. Early in this period children begin to accept the idea of an "all-powerful force in the universe," which reflects their own egocentric understanding (Piaget, 1952).

Unable to differentiate their own thoughts from those of others, pre-school children find great difficulty in imagining things unlike themselves. Nagy (1948), for instance, found that children under age 5 regarded death as a reversible process, much as they jump up after a round of "Bang, bang—you're dead." More to the point, death is a kind of life. As one 4-year-old remarked, "After you die, you get buried, and then you have to stay there for the rest of your life." Objects, too, live on after death. For the child who believes that brooms can become horses, that wrecked cars get hurt, and that trees like to stand out in the rain, things that are lost miss us as much as we miss them. These children do not understand that their personal reactions *are* reactions.

Relying primarily on their excellent perceptual capabilities, the world for young children is something to be heard, seen, touched, tasted, and smelled. The physical properties of objects are undifferentiated from the child's subjective reaction to the object itself. Thus, divorce is perceived correctly as the parent moving away from the child, but the associated bad feelings are confused with *being bad*.

It is no wonder that statements that the child didn't *cause* the divorce make little sense at this time. Furthermore, the pre-schooler's reliance upon physical cues in definition of self make hospitalization and the possibility of death, or the loss of body parts or bodily functions, a particularly anxiety-laden situation.

Unable to accommodate the experience of others into their own thinking, these children adamantly defend the assertion, "It won't happen to me." Rather than argue with children about whether to take a favorite toy on a trip "because it might get lost," parents might suggest that Pooh Bear might like to "stay home with his family, since you are going off with yours."

In discussing loss with children during this period, one must ask for the child's understanding and gear explanations to the child's own experience. Focusing upon the intent of the child's question rather than its literal content may help in understanding the nature of the child's loss. Supportive comments should address the child's magical ("if only . . .") thinking with a balance of factual information: "I wish we could see our old friends today, too, but we live far away in a new neighborhood now and need to make new friends here." As Jewett (1982) suggested: "The clear message that you must give to children in this situation is this: *It is not your fault. It was not because you were bad in any way, because you were unlovable. There is nothing you could have done—or can do—to make things different*" (p. 8).

Finally, rehearsing the circumstances of the loss serves to reinforce its permanence. "One very important function you serve," Jewett noted, "is to give the child permission to figure out what has happened to himself, to make it real again and again" (p. 11). Children who delight in hearing the same story repeated night after night demand the same predictability in understanding the losses that take them by surprise.

III. Elementary School: "Out of control"

Sometime by the age of 7 or 8, children move on from the magical thinking of the pre-school years to the kind of thinking Piaget (1952) called *concrete*. Just as the pre-school child evolved from the infant who could not differentiate self from other, so the elementary school child evolves from the pre-schooler who cannot differentiate self from perception. The child no longer *is* his or her perceptions but, rather, now *has* perceptions. Coordinating these perceptions in a reversible cognitive movement, back and forth between perceptions, allows the child to construct groups and classes of objects and to make a changing world stand still, to make it concrete.

But elementary school children are embedded (as Kegan would say) in their own concreteness. In a new egocentrism that does not distinguish between fact and assumption, these children are thoroughly engaged in an exploration of the limits of the physical world. The newfound capacity to order things in classes is acted out in building collections and sorting things that belong to *either* X *or* Y. This either/or thinking creates their familiar interest in the good guys and bad buys, right and wrong behavior, or the establishment of clubs to separate the "in" group from the "out" group. Building a clubhouse does more than put concrete physical boundaries around those like oneself; it helps children gain a measure of control over their world.

The rule-building behavior of children at this point in their development is well established (Elkind, 1974). So much of the behavior of concrete operational children is devoted to *filling in the boxes* of life, to making predictions, ordering classes of objects, and drawing comparisons. Their inability to differentiate hypothesis from fact, however, results in their failing to understand fully that the rules are of their own making. Thus, these children are easily and constantly disappointed when what they hoped would come true doesn't. Their lives, which are made up of so much wishing and hoping, are acted out in the face of recurring disappointment. Unaware of their own part in the drama, elementary school children are often surprised by the future they worked so hard to forecast.

My father tells the story of a time when his grade school class was having a costume party:

> I had the makings of a pirate costume because some way or another I owned a *genuine* rubber dagger. This, then, got me to dress with a bandana on my head, eye patch, torn shorts, open-neck shirt, and real pirate boots. The boots were galoshes with the tops folded down so they almost covered the buckles. Into the righthand boot was thrust my 8-inch rubber dagger. This was the focal point of the entire ensemble. I would be the best of the group—a real swashbuckler. I would be able to slash and stab with my rubber dagger, scare some of my classmates, and be the envy of the rest. Off I trudged to school, and the party soon was in full swing. I reached for my dagger. It was gone! I had lost it on the way. I had nothing to fall back on, no alternate plan. I was completely abashed, devastated, and probably sulked on the sidelines. I never did find the dagger. As far as I know, it's still somewhere between home and school!

In a study involving groups of Hungarian children, Nagy (1948) found that children in this group were likely to personify death, seeing it as an angel or as an old man. Understanding that death is permanent, a fact confirmed by their perceptions, primary school children can nonetheless gain a measure of control over it through objectifying it. This helps to explain the great interest in ghost stories and Hardy Boys or Nancy Drew mysteries that children show during this period.

Although unable to confirm Nagy's findings in studies with American children, Koocher (1973) found that they wanted to know the details of death and interment, giving "concrete or stereotyped accounts of what would happen, such as detailed accounts of their funerals or explanations of what it might be like in heaven" (p. 374). Koocher (1973) speculated that they "are inclined to use specificity of detail as a means to mastery and hence 'control' over death, rather than personification" (p. 375).

Near the end of this period, children come to accept the permanency of death and the reality of loss *as a part of* the natural order of things. Unable to accept that death can come to anyone at any age, they believe that losses are governed by some set of rules. People die when they get old; automobiles fall apart after 10 years or

100,000 miles, whichever comes first; students fail when teachers don't like them; and food will spoil when left unrefrigerated.

In working with elementary school children, one must recognize their great need for order and control. This means being completely honest and accurate. Adults who don't know answers to children's questions should say they don't know and encourage children to share their own thoughts and feelings. A child's sense of order is disrupted by loss, and reactions can be overgeneralized to include any and all situations. So often, children at this age abandon an entire collection after the loss of a single piece, or they withdraw from those who love them following a loss. When an adult is involved in the loss, to regain the child's trust is particularly important.

Simply changing family plans to go on a special outing, mom changing her hair color, or dad working different hours can be as disrupting initially to the child as death or divorce. To help the child isolate the event and to begin to restore the child's trust, one must be factual and reliable: Tell children what *else,* if anything, will change, and how long and in what capacity you will continue to be around. Keep all appointments, and be prompt, minimizing immediate, future losses when possible. Make statements that apply concretely to the child's own experience, avoiding abstractions or generalities ("I know I said we'd go to the game today, but I also have a responsibility to complete my work at the office. Remember when your team rescheduled its games? Our family had to change its plans suddenly then. Let's figure out together when we will be able to go").

Children need to come to the realization that there are areas of their lives in which they have no choice. A planned family move to Tucson, or mom working, or big sister getting married are issues beyond their control. Still, learning how to protect oneself from bullies, or how to use a telephone when home alone in an emergency, or how to ask for help when lost in a shopping mall help the child to become more competent. How adults help children to deal with the little losses helps them to develop the trust in others and in themselves that will be necessary to work through the bigger losses that loom ahead.

IV. Adolescence: "I'm melting"

Beginning as early as age 9, for some, and as late as age 16, for most, American children begin to develop the capacity to reflect on their own thinking. Unlike the concrete operational children of the elementary school years, adolescents cannot only differentiate fact from hypothesis, but, too, their thinking itself is hypothetico-deductive, focused on the form of thought itself. This *formal operational thought* (Inhelder & Piaget, 1958) permits the adolescent to think about the thoughts of others. In a new egocentrism, the adolescent "fails to differentiate between the objects toward which the thoughts of others are directed and those which are the focus of his own concern. . . . He assumes that other people are as obsessed with his behavior and appearance as he is himself" (Elkind, 1974, p. 91).

Because so much of adolescence is spent in anticipating the reaction of others in social situations, "the adolescent is continually constructing, or reacting to, *an imaginary audience*. It is an audience because the adolescent believes that he will be the focus of attention, and it is imaginary because, in actual social situations, this is not usually the case" (Elkind, 1974, p. 91). Elkind's construction of the imaginary audience helps to explain much of the adolescent's reactions to loss.

Convinced of others' interest in and careful scrutiny of them, adolescents react more with shame than guilt in the context of loss. Anticipating the reactions of others to their loss, adolescents wonder more about how they will look to others following a loss than about the loss per se. Unlike the pre-schooler's fear of dismemberment that accompanies hospitalization, surgery during adolescence raises the possibility of disfigurement and, thus, rejection by one's peers. In divorce, adolescents appear preoccupied with the inevitable embarrassment that will accompany the public discovery of their parents' conflict.

The hypothesis rather than the fact is what is lost in adolescence. A young man who fails his driving test or young woman who places second in the track meet, as examples, mourn the loss of the admiration they anticipated from their friends. The victory celebrations, the congratulations in school hallways, and the adoring crowds asking to see the *trophy,* be it a driver's license or a medal, are all lost now. As Elkind (1974) offered: "One of the most common admiring audience constructions, in the adolescent, is the anticipation of how others will react to his own death. A certain bittersweet pleasure is derived from anticipating the belated recognition of his good qualities" (p. 92).

Adolescents are ambivalent about death, however, seeing in it the end of a physical world but the beginning of a better, more spiritual world. The anxiety this provokes often develops into defiance, which is evident in the risk-taking behavior so characteristic of adolescents. The longstanding appeal of death for adolescents is reflected in the success of films based on the books of Stephen King, in which teenagers are stalked by forces beyond their control. Videogames provide adolescents with an opportunity to conquer invaders from space. Cable television broadcasts Michael Jackson's *Thriller,* in which teenagers are overcome by deadly forces from within. And every year thousands of high school seniors lapse into a kind of deathly malaise in the face of their impending graduation (Hayes, 1981). In light of the current high rate of suicide among adolescents, the task of learning to differentiate between the real and the imaginary audience is especially helpful.

More than anything else, adolescence has been described as a stage transition from childhood to adulthood (Ausubel, 1977; Muuss, 1975). As I have written elsewhere (Hayes, 1981):

> It may be more than a simple metaphor to think of the adolescent's transition to adult status as the death of his or her identity as a child. A view of development based on Eriksonian theory might characterize maturation as successively more complex solutions to the problems of separation anxiety. From birth through weaning through toilet-training through going to school to leaving home, the child's growth toward adulthood involves increasing

separation from caretakers. For the adolescent, this takes the form of a separation of self from society in efforts to integrate into it. The drive toward adulthood requires emancipation from the parents and from the self of childhood. Adolescence can end only when childhood identifications have been subordinated to new identifications. (p. 370)

If adolescence is a period of identity formation, death is not so much the end of life as it is the end of existence. Death can bring a new existence in the minds of adolescents unless, of course, no one cares and they are forgotten. Like the witch in the Land of Oz, true death comes with the end of "my beautiful wickedness [as] I am melting, melting. . . ." Loss for the adolescent comes with the dissolution of one's boundaries, the loss of purpose or meaning for one's existence, and the failure of reality to live up to one's expectations. Friendships are created and destroyed as spontaneously as anticipation collides with reality. Roles are reexamined and the gods, who were our parents, become traitors, then failures, and finally just people.

This theme is captured beautifully in Miller's *Death of a Salesman* as the play traces the decay of a god—Willy Loman, Salesman-Lord of New England. The illusion of sexless godhood is destroyed when the 17-year-old Biff finds Willy with a strange woman. The tragedy lies in Biff's failure to accept his father as a sexual person and in his failure to profit from his father's example. Instead, Biff rejects his father's pleas for forgiveness and leaves home for a "couple of babes," much as his father had done before him.

More than with any other group, adolescents are influenced by the context in which their communications occur. Aware of their own thoughts and feelings about loss, adolescents need opportunities to experience their losses and to share their personal reactions in public. Reflecting their particular egocentrism, adolescents are likely to believe that others are aware of how they feel, but that others can't possibly understand their unique, personal experience. Elkind (1974) speculates that because the adolescent

. . . believes he is of importance to so many people, the imaginary audience, he comes to regard himself, and particularly his feelings, as something special and unique. . . . This belief in a personal uniqueness becomes a conviction that he will not die, that death will happen to others but not to him. This complex of beliefs in the uniqueness of his feelings and of his immortality might be called *a personal fable*, a story which he tells himself and which is not true. (p. 93)

As participant observers in their own life drama, adolescents are now witnesses to their own unmet expectations. Springer and Wallerstein (1983) noted in their work with divorced families that young adolescents "grieved not only the loss of their intact families, but also the loss of the kind of intact family they had never had and now would never attain" (p. 18). The personal fable associated with the perfect family one would have had, if only this or that hadn't happened, can present a formidable obstacle in the adolescent's successful resolution of the loss associated with divorce.

In working with adolescents, therefore, one should place them in groups with peers who may be experiencing similar losses. As the imaginary audience is progressively modified to conform to the reactions of the real audience, the adolescent can begin to form relationships that are more mutual than self-interested. Losses can be evaluated more objectively and one's reactions shared interpersonally with others whose feelings are gradually integrated with one's own.

As the adolescent is becoming well aware, parents and other "grown-ups" are not as they have seemed. The adolescent's successful transition to adulthood involves a redefinition of what it is to be an adult—the projection of a new self into which to grow. Although the outcome is "the recognition of that which before was confused with the self," growth begins with "separation and repudiation, killing off the past" (Kegan, 1982, p. 129). The old culture of childhood is thrown over and the adolescent's outmoded perspective on adulthood goes with it. Rightfully, parents feel rejected, but it is not they but, rather, their child's former understanding of them that is being rejected.

While the adolescent is busy building a new set of parents, it is vitally important that the parents hold still. Kegan (1982) explained:

> It takes a special wisdom for the family of an adolescent to understand that by remaining in place so that the adolescent can have the family there to ignore and reject, the family is providing something very important, and is still, in a new way, intimately and importantly involved in the child's development. . . . It is exactly because the newly "thrown over" culture of embeddedness is as much the old me as the not me that it must remain in place for the child herself to gradually redefine her relationship to it. For the culture to disappear at exactly the time when the child is experiencing a loss of herself is to leave the child with a kind of unrecoverable loss, a confirmation of her worst suspicions about the life project. (p. 129)

By holding still, adults help adolescents to recover the losses of childhood, for in separating from their parents, adolescents find them anew.

V. *Youth: "Don't stop me now"*

Somewhere between the struggles for identity that act themselves out in adolescence and the stability that comes with finding oneself at peace with society, there exists a stage Keniston (1970) calls *youth*. The newly evolved self of adolescence now exists in a dynamic tension with the society in which it was once embedded. Keniston explained that, "The adolescent is struggling to define who he is; the youth begins to sense who he is and thus to recognize the possibility of conflict and disparity between his emerging selfhood and his social order" (p. 636).

In youth there exists a "pervasive ambivalence" (Keniston, 1970) toward both self and society that acts itself out in potential conflicts between maintaining an autonomous self and being committed in some social involvement. The fear is that the newly developed self will be lost in a world not yet fully understood. The irony comes with the recognition that in failing to make commitments, the self is lost in not being all that it can be. Development is valued for itself, change is actively sought, and motion, in all its forms, becomes the goal.

> In youth, as in all other stages of life, *the fear of death* takes a special form. For the infant, to be deprived of maternal support, responsiveness, and care is not to exist; for the 4-year-old, non-being means loss of body intactness (dismemberment, mutilation, castration); for the adolescent, to cease to be is to fall apart, to fragment, splinter, or diffuse into nothingness. For the youth, however, to lose one's essential vitality is merely to stop. . . . To "grow up" is in some ultimate sense to cease to really be alive. (Keniston, 1970, p. 640)

The ambivalence that comes from wanting to find oneself through some commitment and the fear of losing oneself in the process make young people the loneliest people in America. Rubenstein, Shaver, and Peplau (1979) have suggested that "young people are so susceptible to loneliness because they feel more sharply the discrepancy between the search for intimacy and the failure to find it" (p. 61). The losses of youth are characterized by the *great expectations* that so often go unmet. Earlier failures to separate are echoed in the youth's reluctance to adapt to the new experiences of leaving home for college, work, marriage, or travel.

The central struggle of personality to achieve an appropriate balance between attachment and individuation, between dependence and independence, between self-absorption and a commitment to others, is acted out again on a new plane in youth. As Erikson (1968) cautioned, "It is only when identity formation is well on its way that true intimacy—which is really a counter-pointing as well as fusing of identities—is possible" (p. 135).

In earlier periods, giving up the self in the face of change was done with great reluctance. The myths that resolving loss is painful, or that it takes a long time, or that giving up the outworn means losing something important, are replaced with a new myth that change in and of itself is good (Heikkinen, 1981). For youth, who seek change as an antidote to death, a headlong leap into experimentation seems in order. For the youth who has said goodbye to childhood, leaving home brings with it the promise of new life. But whatever joyous emancipation may be associated with the adventure of leaving home *at last,* "it is a time of vulnerability and high susceptibility to depression" (Kegan, 1982, p. 185).

When working with youth, adults are cautioned to avoid cooperating in the paradox their behavior presents. Given acknowledgment of their adult status, youth often behave like children. Consider that 80% of *all* traffic fatalities involve a driver under age 25. Yet, when denied the right to think for themselves, youth demand full citizen participation in every social institution—financial, political, and the like. Youth need a bridging environment that acknowledges their efforts to make autonomous decisions without either promoting anarchy or abandoning them to fend for themselves. Adults can provide real-life examples of persons who have made choices and are living with the consequences while encouraging youth to work through the process of making their own choices.

Youth are only *provisional adults,* who require opportunities to exercise their new-found selves *in* society. They also need clear signals about the consequences of their actions for others. College students, for example, should be helped to see that failure can be positive feedback to faculty who see advisement as little more than hand holding. Kegan (1982) has offered instead that "it is a holding of the whole life enterprise" (p. 186). To be able to enter into students' efforts to make meaning of their independence without making that meaning for them is a great challenge to one's own independence.

The task that lies before youth is to separate not only self from parents but, also, self from parents as a source of judgments and expectations about the self. Working within this context, counselors and faculty must help students to clarify the basis of their own judgments without simultaneously giving in to the temptation to replace the parents as a source of new judgments and new expectations. The goal is to help youth to accept themselves as "parents"—to be in charge of themselves.

Having thrown over parents as a source of judgment and without having come to some understanding of their own self-efficacy, college students often lose their motivation. Kegan (1982) believes that in such cases "the me-I-have-been starts to look more like the expectations of *other* people, often one's parents, who are just now gradually being separated from oneself" (p. 205). This shift in the balance of self and others' expectations of self raises the question of who is in charge.

The challenge for youth is how to integrate a view of themselves as independent agents (something for which they have strived so long) who are dependent upon others (something from which they have been trying to emerge). This dilemma of youth is resolved when autonomy takes the form of self-commitment to some social activity. Political activism, religious conversion, fraternity life, or a company-sponsored athletic team can prepare the way to marriage as the most popular social vehicle for this resolution.

MEDIATING IN LOSS

If change and loss are inevitable, and if the experience associated with loss is related to one's capacity to make sense of that change, and thus to one's development, young people need to know about the changes that can affect their lives. *Development is essentially the task of mastering the facts of one's existence.*

Once the feelings associated with loss have been acknowledged, adult intervention in the lives of young people should seek to mediate *between* their experience. The loss brought on by change creates a gap between the self that is no longer me and the new self that is not yet me. To understand how someone experiences loss is to enter into that region "*between* an event and a reaction to it—the place where the event is privately composed, made sense of, the place where it actually *becomes* an event for that person" (Kegan, 1982, p. 2). In this "zone of mediation," as Kegan (1982) calls it, counselors can help their clients to make better meaning of their experience. Thus, counseling becomes a kind of *mediated learning experience* in which the interactions of counselor and client generate "the capacity of an individual to change, to modify himself in the direction of greater adaptability and higher mental processes" (Feuerstein, cited in Cordes, 1984).

Children and youth require adult guides who will encourage them to express their feelings and help them to understand their pain as a reaction to the loss they experience. In particular, adult helpers should consider the following:

- Providing honest information about hospitals, cemeteries, funerals, and the like helps children to master the facts of their existence (Bernstein, 1983) and to develop a vocabulary of feelings and thoughts about loss and its resolution (Abshier, 1984).
- News about loss is best shared by the adult to whom the young person feels closest, thus continuing the history of involvement and trust the two have shared (Jewett, 1982).
- Adults should examine their own ideas about death to avoid confusing young people with their own unresolved issues related to loss (Jewett, 1982; Nelson, 1977).
- The first thing to communicate, especially with very young children, is: "You are not alone; I am with you." This serves as a balance to magical and egocentric thinking and helps to restore some sense of control through outside support (Jewett, 1982).
- When talking about loss, the focus should be on the child's own experience. This helps to reveal the child's own understanding of the associated events and, particularly with younger children, it gives permission to trust his or her own observations and judgments about the situation. Also, drawing upon the individual's own experience makes it harder for the young person to deny the loss in the future (Jewett, 1978).
- Accurate information and an adult perspective on the facts of the loss should be provided. The facts of the loss should be conveyed in as straightforward a way as possible. This helps to relieve blame, reestablish accurate self-perception, and clarify cause-effect reasoning (Jewett, 1978).
- When approaching an impending change, children should be told how their routines and life styles will be affected, to increase their sense of control over their own lives.
- Bibliotherapy offers older children and adolescents an opportunity to identify with others and realize they are not alone. It can extend their horizons, be cathartic, lead to insight, and facilitate sharing (Bernstein, 1983).
- When working with younger children, adult helpers must listen to their questions and ask themselves what this tells them about the young person's efforts "to make sense of what has happened and to understand the hows and whys that led to the loss. This comes partially from a need to restore order and meaning to the chaotic feelings that follow loss, and partially from a need to under-

stand events leading to the loss so that further losses might be prevented" (Jewett, 1978, p. 78). Because developmental tasks are mastered sequentially, familiarity with the individual's developmental tempo can help to identify when an individual lags behind his or her own developmental pace.

When working with adolescents and youth, counselors are often confronted with helping clients to make sense of a loss that happened some time ago. Because grief is an ongoing process, losses experienced early in childhood must be reexamined and understood anew at succeeding stages of development. Old misunderstandings and confusions demand new interpretations. Anniversaries, holidays, familiar situations, and the restructuring of families give rise to old feelings. Particularly difficult is the problem of helping clients through losses that are personally distasteful. Jewett (1978) explained:

> Some of the common reasons that children lose caretakers, other than death or divorce, are abuse and abandonment; mental illness; imprisonment; incest; parental immaturity, rejection, or neglect; alcohol or drug abuse; and suicide. . . . In such cases . . . ask yourself: 1. Why would an adult do something like that? 2. What similar need or experiences has this child had in her own life? 3. How can this information be conveyed in a way that places no blame? 4. Is there anything that the child might misunderstand or feel responsible for, or any action by the parent that the child might feel compelled to repeat? (pp. 86–87)

CONCLUSION

Loss is not something that happens to us as we live. It *is* life or, rather, *living,* itself. The inevitability of change brings loss to the mind of the person who can appreciate that things are somehow different. Each loss challenges the illusion of our omnipotence and threatens to destroy our very being. In working through rather than around that loss, however, we take the risk to build a more competent self that can make better sense of the world of which we are a part.

Adults cannot protect young people from loss or make the hurt go away. Adults can help them, however, to develop the personal resources necessary to express their feelings and to discuss their fears. Each loss represents a "natural emergency" (Kegan, 1982) that creates the opportunity for growth. In learning to mourn the outgrown child that each leaves behind, young people develop the courage to become the adult that lies ahead.

REFERENCES

Abshier, E. (1984, Spring). It's O.K. to talk about death. *APGA Quarterly, 93,* 31–38.

Ausubel, D. P. (1977). *Theory and problems of adolescent development* (2nd ed.). New York: Grune & Stratton.

Bernstein, J. (1983). *Books to help children cope with separation and loss* (2nd ed.). New York: R. R. Bowker.

Bowlby, J. (1973). *Attachment and loss: Separation.* New York: Basic Books.

Cordes, C. (1984, May) Reuven Feurstein makes every child count. *APA Monitor,* pp. 18–20.

Davenport, D. (1981). A closer look at the "healthy" grieving process. *Personnel & Guidance Journal, 59,* 332–335.

Dewey, J. (1960). Theory of the moral life. In J. Dewey & H. Tufts, *Ethics* (Part 2) (rev. ed.). New York: Holt & Co. (Original work published 1932)

Elkind, D. (1974). *Children and adolescents* (2nd ed.). New York: Oxford University Press.

Erikson, E. (1968). *Identity: Youth and crisis.* New York: Norton.

Freese, A. (1977). *Help for your grief.* New York: Schoken.

Hayes, R. (1981). High school graduation: The case for identity loss. *Personnel & Guidance Journal, 59,* 369–371.

Heikkinen, C. (1981). Loss resolution for growth. *Personnel & Guidance Journal, 59,* 327–331.

Hendricks, G., & Weinhold, B. (1982). *Transpersonal approaches to counseling and psychotherapy.* Denver: Love Publishing.

Inhelder, B., & Piaget, J. (1958). *The growth of logical thinking from childhood to adolescence.* New York: Basic Books.

Janov, A. (1970). *The primal scream.* New York: Dell.

Jewett, C. (1982). *Helping children cope with separation and loss.* Harvard, MA: Harvard Common Press.

Kavanaugh, R. (1974). *Facing death.* Baltimore: Penguin Books.

Kegan, R. (1982). *The evolving self.* Cambridge, MA: Harvard University Press.

Keniston, K. (1970, Autumn). Youth: A "new" stage of life. *American Scholar, 39,* 631–641.

Klaus, M., & Kennell, J. (1976). *Maternal-infant bonding.* St. Louis: C. V. Mosby.

Koocher, G. (1973). Childhood, death, and cognitive development. *Developmental Psychology, 9,* 369–375.

Koocher, G. (1981, December). Children's conceptions of death. *New Directions for Child Development, 14,* 85–89.

Kubler-Ross, E. (1969). *On death and dying.* New York: Macmillan.

LeBoyer, F. (1975). *Birth without violence.* New York: Knopf.

Muuss, R. E. (1975). *Theories of adolescence* (3rd ed.). New York: Random House.

Nagy, M. (1948). The child's theories concerning death. *Journal of Genetic Psychology, 73,* 3–27.

Nelson, R. (1977). Counselors, teachers, and death education. *School Counselor, 24,* 322–329.

Pearce, J. (1977). *The magical child: Rediscovering nature's plan for our children.* New York: E. P. Dutton.

Piaget, J. (1952). *The origins of intelligence in children.* New York: International Universities Press. (Original work published 1936)

Rubenstein, C., Shaver, P., & Peplau, L. (1979, February). Loneliness. *Human Nature,* 58–65.

Schachtel, E. (1959). *Metamorphosis.* New York: Basic Books.

Schrank, J. (1972). *Teaching human beings.* Boston: Beacon Press.

Springer, C., & Wallerstein, J. (1983, March). Young adolescents' responses to their parents' divorces. In L. A. Kurdeck (Ed.), Children and divorce. *New Directions for Child Development, 19,* pp. 15–27.

U.S. Bureau of the Census (1983, December). *Statistical abstract of the United States: 1984* (104th ed.). Washington, DC: U.S. Government Printing Office.

Westberg, G. (1962). *Good grief.* Philadelphia: Fortress Press.

Richard Hayes is an Associate Professor, Department of Educational Leadership and Human Development, College of Education and Health Sciences, Bradley University.

TWO: FAMILY INTERVENTIONS

Jon Carlson and Judith Lewis

In our present-day civilization people are not well prepared for cooperation. Our training has been too much towards individual success, towards considering what we can get out of life rather than what we can give to it.

—Alfred Adler

The family has been called "the crucible of identity." The sense of personal integration and coherence Erikson (1981) saw as the major achievement of adolescence depends in large part on the social, intellectual, and emotional development that is fostered within family relationships.

Family life, which was once marked by gentle care and appreciation, often becomes a battleground during the teenage years. Parents who were once almost worshipped become the objects of resentment and suspicion. Teenagers are in the process of busily carving out a niche and trying to figure out where they belong, how to feel important, and how to belong. When teenagers carve out niches, parents often dig in their heels. They are determined to survive this crisis and often feel bitter, angry, and confused—on the one hand feeling like surrendering, and on the other hand feeling like creating all-out warfare. The teenage years often translate into a collision course at home.

The teen years are a time of rapid physical, psychological, cognitive, and social changes. Those changes affect parents and all family members. Teenagers begin to look at their friends more than ever before to formulate their identities and to try for feelings of belonging and worth. Those friends can either become the allies of parents or the parents' competitors as they work to influence their children in appropriate, responsible ways. Teenagers often feel uncertain on some important issues, such as identity, self-importance, self-value, sex roles, belonging, and status. Parenting is an incredible job in the teenage years, and when this becomes complicated as a result of divorce, remarriage, and marital problems, the entire situation can become chaotic and conflictual.

Often people simply think that the problem with teenagers and their parents is the generation gap. This is an oversimplification, and research seems to consistently challenge this belief. The real problem in these relationships—as with all human relationships—is the failure to talk, listen, and try to understand another's

93

point of view. Teenagers go through the turmoil of adolescence often much better than their parents do. They are anxious to make this transition to adulthood, to become independent and self-reliant. But many parents are not willing to let them go.

More than 8 of 10 teenagers report that they can talk with their parents (well, at least sometimes). Even more surprising, most adolescents really do want to share more of their lives and feelings with their parents, even though they might not know how (Dinkmeyer, McKay, Dinkmeyer, Dinkmeyer, & Carlson, 1985). Teenagers want to use their parents for sounding boards for new ideas and feelings. They don't want approval or agreement. They just want parents to listen. Teenagers want understanding and involvement. They are in the process of learning how to think for themselves. Although the process itself can be frustrating for parents, the end product—a mature, self-reliant adult—is surely worth a little agony.

The real key to communicating with young people is a readiness to listen and care about what *they* say, even when we don't agree. Listening is easy when teenagers parrot parents' beliefs. The hard part is accepting their right to argue, disagree, and speak out against parents' tightly held views. If parents want to have open communication with teenagers, they cannot belittle their opinions. Teenagers are not only testing their parents' reactions, but also their own, and the response the parent gives will determine, to a large extent, the kind of relationship they will have with their parents.

Compromise is important, to give teenagers credit for knowing something— not to lecture, judge, and criticize, but, rather, to respect. Teenagers will let others know if they need more advice or more input. Parents should try to learn to offer advice without demanding that it be followed. Although teenagers tend to prefer talking to their mothers, the power of their contacts with fathers should not be underestimated.

In the first article in this section, Jon Carlson and Dan Fullmer provide a rationale for working with families and the fundamental principles needed to intervene in the family system. The positive strengths-oriented model is the treatment of choice with adolescents. Models that emphasize criticism and exploration of weaknesses lead to resistance. Professionals who understand family dynamics and adolescent development also understand the wisdom, and in fact necessity, of a growth-centered intervention.

The second article, by Bonnie Robson, discusses the impact of changing family patterns on teenagers. She presents many interesting statistics on divorce and shows how divorce creates both positive and negative aspects for adolescents. For example, teens have increased responsibility, but they suffer many disadvantages in psychosocial, and other areas. She presents several specific methods of intervention and ways of modifying family patterns that children and teens experience. This article points out the great need for using preventive methods in these changing times.

Family mediation is an intervention that can reduce the deleterious effects of traditional adversarial divorce and other family life-cycle conflicts. In the third article, Charles Huber, Barry Mascari, and Aviva Sanders-Mascari describe family mediation as a form of negotiation and conflict resolution in which a third party aids the disputing parties in making mutual decisions. Preventive solutions to predictable universal problems allow for no situation that prevents normal development, and, specifically, does not add stress to teenagers' world of turmoil and change.

According to Richard and Bree Hayes, in the fourth article, divorce, remarriage, and stepfamilies are becoming more and more commonplace, and should be recognized as having their own unique interpersonal relationships and concerns. If not addressed, the issues unique to these families can create stress, unhappiness, and conflict. The authors offer some insight and understanding of this type of family arrangement.

In the final article, Judy Lewis discusses the unique set of difficulties posed by growing up in a home dominated by parental alcoholism. The entire family unit is affected by the alcohol problem and often must function in a framework of family secrecy. Inconsistent discipline and extreme variations in interaction, added to the confusion already present in the teen's world, make for a very challenging life. This article offers many suggestions for this once hopeless and tolerated situation.

REFERENCES

Dinkmeyer, D., McKay, G. D., Dinkmeyer, D., Dinkmeyer, J., & Carlson, J. (1985). *PREP for effective family living*. Circle Pines, MN: American Guidance Services.
Erikson, E. H. (1981). *Youth and challenge*. New York: W. W. Norton.

6

Family Counseling/ Consultation: Principles For Growth

Jon Carlson and Dan Fullmer

The national barometer of mental health seems to be dropping at an ever accelerating rate as more and more people become symptom-ridden victims of stress. Psychoses, neuroses, high blood pressure, ulcers, backaches, headaches, nervous tics and bodily discomforts are all commonplace. In today's world of emphasis on technology and change, this situation seems to be changing—for the worse. Preventive interventions are not occurring, and remedial efforts are still producing a 50% chance of recovery—the same percentage as no treatment at all. This is a time when humans must decide to live a healthy life or have a new car; to have a body or be a body; to continue to just exist or to begin to live and grow.

Typical mental health treatment (i.e., counseling, therapy, analysis) involves reducing, or *shrinking,* the symptoms of the injured, sick or identified patient. Research, however, indicates that this procedure is, for the most part, inefficient (in terms of money, resources and time usage) and largely ineffective (especially in terms of permanent rather than short-term changes). This situation need not be. Approaches to mental health that are anchored in *expanding* our educational and growth-centered perspectives produce effective, efficient, and permanent mental health. These approaches practice equality and collaboration, center upon complete systems rather than elemental analysis, and flow or work with the natural flow of living in a Tao or "Watercourse Way" (Watts & Huang, 1975).

Research indicates that the family is the prime source for the establishment of healthy and "growthful" living,* as well as the breeding ground for our pathology. Human development is a lifelong process, and growth can be facilitated or arrested

---

"Growthful" living is more than just healthy living. White (1973) claims counseling should not have chosen the metaphor or paradigm of health. The metaphor of what is the best way to live, or values advocacy paradigm, would more accurately define the counseling mission.

at any stage. The family plays a major role in personality formation and development, and we are just now realizing its lifelong importance. According to Burton
White (1976),

> 'It appears that the nuclear family is, for most children, their first and most important educa-
> tional delivery system. Yet we as a nation, for many understandable reasons . . . continue
> to fail to equip families to do the job. (p. 5)

The counseling profession has not been effective in helping people. Research
does not seem to support our traditional and current paradigms. The purpose here
is to acquaint the reader with the rationale, essential principles, and constructs of
family counseling-consultation; provide a description of a healthy and "growthful"
family; present a set of directions of how to use a strengths-oriented educational
approach with families; and discuss how school guidance counselors can use these
ideas.

RATIONALE FOR FAMILY WORK

Although family counseling has been in existence for some time, it has come
into prominence in both professional and public eyes over the past three decades or
so. Its recognition and acceptance have resulted from a growing awareness that
individuals cannot be responsible for all the problems they encounter, many of
which come from outside pressures and influences, including the family and the
social environment. Even the problems of children are typically a result of family
interaction and are best dealt with through family counseling.

There is no one model or pattern for conducting family counseling. The approach is dependent upon the problems, the conditions surrounding them, and the
counselor's theoretical orientation. But several basic universal principles are important for all family work.

General systems theory (Bertalanffy, 1968) applies the principle of synergy.*
Extending the principle to family practice, it is claimed that if one family member
changes behavior, all other family members need to change enough to cope with
the new conditions, especially the emotional climate in the family network. Fullmer's (1971) relationships theory of behavior focuses on the relationship definition
between the family members (mother-son, father-daughter, sibling peer group,
symbiotic parent-child, friendship). The basic principle is that behavior is the expression of each individual's personal experience of meaning acted out of the relationship definition perceived by each significant other in the dyad.

Adlerian, or individual, psychology has a well developed system for family
work. The primary focus for application has been on child-rearing practices. The
central principle treats the individual's behavior as goal-directed. The child's goal
is to achieve a place of importance in his or her environment. The motivation principle is a will to belong or to find a meaningful place in society. The variety of
approaches continues to grow, as does the number of counselors using the family

"Synergy is defined as "the whole is more than the sum of the parts."

network as the target for counseling. The suggested readings at the end of this article can serve as a starting place for readers desiring more theoretical background in family counseling.

PRINCIPLES USED IN FAMILY WORK

The foundation on which behavior is based can be expressed in principles that represent the key components in the family counseling-consulting model described herein. The principles incorporate motivation, needs, communication, identity, and power. The principles are given equal insight even though there may be a differential impact in any given context. The counselor, through understanding of the following principles, can learn to understand, communicate, and facilitate effectively within a family context.

Principle 1: Context is Fundamental to Meaning

The concept of "context" is simply the setting one is in. Given your behavior in an elevator, look quickly at your behavior in your bedroom. How are the two alike? How are they different? Notice your emotional response when you imagine yourself making love in the elevator! What you feel is what we refer to as "meaning." This principle can be seen within a family setting in which a child is encouraged to fight at home but not at school; where the wife is sensuous when the lights are out and frigid when the lights are on; using loose and colorful language when eating at home and being sent to the car when using these words in a public restaurant. The behaviors are the same, but the meanings or feelings are different.

Meaning has feelings because it is tied to the emotional system, the basis of the relationship system. What you feel is the way communication takes place within your family context. Processing one's own feelings is what leads to meaning. Feelings of anger, joy, sadness, elation, sorrow, and so on determine the meaning of the event. Feelings are the connection between the emotional system (myself) and the relationship system (others) (Bowen, 1971). *Your perception is what you are going to do about it.*

Principle 2: Relationships are Substance and Behavior is Form

The concept of relationship refers to the complex feelings one gets when faced with an enemy, as contrasted with a friend. The enemy relationship feels like flight or fight, but the friendship feels warm and free. Our behavior in each instance serves to express the meaning we are experiencing. The form may vary for each instance, but undoubtedly we will each display a consistent pattern of behavior with latitude for unique variation. *How you feel is how you act.* The "why" of your feeling is relationship definition.

When someone does things for someone else, the message may be "I love and care for you" or "I'll dominate and trap you," depending upon the relationship.

Relationship is substance, and behavior is form. A parent may agree to participate in family counseling (behavior) one week to placate or "butter you up" in order to *control,* and he or she may not agree to participate the next week to show you who is boss and to *control.* Although the relationship remains unchanged, the behavior is different.

Principle 3: Patterns of Behavior Repeat Themselves in Cycles

The concept of patterns of behavior is derived from the redundance in communication created by a person repeating herself or himself over and over again and receiving acceptable results. The redundant behavior can be either verbal or nonverbal, both verbal and nonverbal, or contextual-verbal/nonverbal. Take a quick imaginary trip through your past 48 hours. What do you find? It is typical for a counselor to be doing the same thing at a given moment of time each day. Nobel Prize winners Konrad Lorenz (1965) and Nikko Tinbergen (1951) have observed that much of the motor behavior of any species can be described by specifying only a few dozen fixed action patterns. Your schedule is a concrete example of redundant patterns of behavior. *What is stable is predictable. What is unstable is unpredictable. Redundance in pattern is the predictable way of life.*

One specific example of our consistent patterns can be found in the "buzz phrases" (Sperry & Hess, 1974) we frequently and automatically use in conversation. Buzz phrases are simply words, explanations, exclamations, or questions that a person uses consistently. In fact, some people actually can be identified with one or more of their buzz phrases. Researchers have found that from one half to two thirds of a person's verbalizations may be reduced to 15 to 30 buzz phrases. The buzz phrases, of course, relate to the person's dominant goal. Some possible buzz phrases associated with certain goals (Sperry, 1975, p. 24) are:

Buzz Phrase	**Goal**
"How do you like my . . ."	Attention or
"Have you ever gone to . . ."	Elevation
"I'll bet you didn't know . . ."	
"If this job's too hard for you . . ."	Power or
"I want it done *this* (my) way . . ."	Control
"Who does he think he is?"	
"Just you wait and see!"	Revenge
"It's impossible to get anything through his thick skull."	
"Well, I didn't volunteer for this job anyway."	Inadequacy
"I'll try, but I know that I can't do it."	
"Remember how things used to be . . ."	Time Wasting
"Say, what did you do over the weekend?"	

"Don't get so excited, it's nothing."   Peace Making
"There must be *something* we can do about it?"

"Wow, that's really something!"   Excitement
"I might as well try it; I've done everything else."

We take this concept into a family and quickly map the individual patterns. Frequently it becomes immediately apparent where the conflicts are likely to happen. The myriad of familial problems recurs in a predictable fashion as the same action chains or patterns are triggered. Each family is like an individual in that it has a characteristic way or pattern of generating conflict. Your action chain is another way to see how your relationships are defined.

Principle 4: Action Chains Express Definition and Relationships

The concept of an action chain (Hall, 1976) comes from observing what you do following a given cue or stimulus. All behaviors actually consist of sequences, or chains of behaviors. The links in the chains are each composed of simpler behavioral components. For example, the behavior "going to bed" can be broken down into a set of component behaviors: proceeding to the bedroom; taking off clothes; putting on sleeping attire; using bathroom and toilet facilities; saying goodnight to spouse; turning out light; getting into bed.

Each of these component behaviors could be broken down into even smaller components. Taking off clothes, for instance, may be composed of: untying right shoe; reaching down and removing shoe with hands; untying left shoe; reaching down and removing left shoe; removing right sock; removing left sock; removing pants; removing sweater; removing shirt; removing underwear; removing jewelry. *You are chained to your routine of actions.*

Chains are learned by taking simple behaviors already in the individual's repertoire and combining them into more complex behaviors. Each behavior in a chain has a dual function—serving as a reinforcer for the previous response and a stimulus for the preceding one. The action chain utilized will depend on what a situation means to the individual. For example, if someone gives you a compliment, you probably will activate an action chain that passes it on to someone else at the first opportunity. If someone gives you a put-down, you probably will activate an action chain that passes it on to someone else. The action chain will express the meaning each experience has for you, completing the communication of your definition of relationship with the sender.

Principle 5: Families From a Particular Culture Will Display Similar Behavior in a Given Context

Context is the manifestation of culture parameters or rules for the way it is supposed to be. *What I do is natural because it is culturally correct. What you do is unnatural because it is culturally incorrect.* A family teaches children the culture of which it is a part. The family is an entire culture on a small scale (microcosm). Rarely does a given family master a culture's entire rule system; thus, each family represents a particularly unique pattern in a given culture.

Because each family emphasizes unique patterns and symbols, the range of microcosm equals the number of families in the culture. Yet, each family resembles each other family within a given culture in the global dimensions such as language, values, attitudes, and basic patterns of behavior. This phenomenon provides the basic rationale for working with multiple families in groups. The healthy family is able to accommodate the wide range of differences encountered in other families without losing its own uniqueness.

Context as a concept defines meaning to an individual in any given situation. The culture's rules for "the way it is supposed to be" form the person's emotional system, complete with physiological and biochemical consequences. The way you feel in a given situation is the manifestation of the principle. The "human potential movement" claimed feelings could be the basis of behavior. The fallacy is in omission of the fact that each individual can create a new context and, therefore, new feelings by his or her own initiative.

Principle 6: People Learn Social Behaviors All at Once, in Gestalts, Not in Pieces

The context in social behavior may be more important than the specifics of what is learned. The conditions under which you come into your learning (knowledge and behavior) may be more important than the context of the learning (Loukes, 1964). *It is not what you do; it is the way you do it.*

For example, think of what is learned about sex if you are raped as your initial experience. Or think of the child who learns toilet behavior from a mother who always rewards successful execution with candy. The context may teach many values in addition to the central content of the learning experience. The counselor's attitude toward the family will set the tone for what will occur. For example, the first few minutes of contact between people, according to Zunin and Zunin (1972), usually determine whether or not a successful relationship will develop. The counselor's prejudgments in regard to prejudices, values, and attitudes influence the depth of subsequent interactions.

Principle 7: The Health Family Solves Problems Through Support and Trust from Within the Group

The power of the family bond endures because no matter when you go to your family, they will take you in. No other human group has approached that characteristic functioning in the families of the world. After more than 50 years in the kibbutz, for example, the grandparents relate to the children in much the same way as in most extended families—with a strong emotional bond.

The strong emotional bond is the base for a healthy family. The family bond helps to solve problems because it is the source of support and the essence of trust. With this emotional base, a healthy family can use the most effective means of problem solution and conflict resolution. The most effective means for solving problems is to redefine the family's relationship to the source of the problem. This can be done by stepping outside the context containing the problem. Communications experts call it *meta-communicating*. Essentially, the process requires each participant in any encounter to step outside the frame or context and look at the larger stage or picture. *The view from out here is different from the view from within.* The counseling process centers on helping families learn this method in order to become self-healing.

Principle 8: Encouragement is Fundamental to Creative Behavior

A person must gain the courage to violate his or her own rules for behaving if he or she is to achieve new behavior (Bateson, 1972). Learning is fun if the risk is manageable. If the risk is too great, the result is traumatic. Pathology in behavior frequently is generated by the anxiety or fear of failure. Failure is the deterrent to foolishness. To risk, to go beyond what you know and can predict the consequences of, requires you to violate your rules of safety. Whenever you violate your rules and survive the pathology generated, you stand to learn in significant terms or degrees.

Bateson (1972) calls this *trans-contextual learning*. You begin in context A and wind up in context B. Transpersonal experience is similar in social learning terms. You are as usual in context A; then a transformation happens (you learn something new) and find yourself changed and living in context B: I left home at age 20. Five years later I returned home to visit. Home was different, though the same people were there. My experience of home was from the perceptions in context B. I cannot go home again in terms of the old context A perceptions. Experience is altered by the new perception achieved in context B.

This process has to be anchored in a stable, secure setting. Individuals and their families gain security through understanding and accepting their assets and where they are in life. *Tell me what is right with me—not what is wrong.* Security does not result from a diagnosis of liabilities or a concentration on one's problems or weaknesses. This results in insecurity, discouragement, depression, and failure.

The counselor should model encouraging behavior, identify existing strengths in the family, and facilitate activities that increase the possibilities of future encouraging behaviors. The counselor should make frequent use of confrontation—not confronting individuals with their mistakes but, rather, with their strengths. Research has not shown much support for negative confrontation (Berenson & Mitchell, 1974) but strongly supports positive changes resulting from the use of positive confrontation (Jacobs & Spradlin, 1974; Lieberman, Yalom, & Miles, 1972).

Principle 9: Overemphasis on Individual Achievement Leads to Erosion of Basic Support within Families

A social system that produces a Howard Hughes, Albert Einstein, Henry Ford, B. F. Skinner, William Douglas, Tom Dooley, and Muhammed Ali will have a powerful emphasis upon individual achievement.

The price society pays for outstanding individual achievement is ultimate destruction of the basic social support system, the family group. Slater (1974), in *Earthwalk*, believes that this will lead to ultimate destruction of the world. You can decide for yourself if the price is right. The counselor has to be constantly aware of keeping a balance between individual and family achievement. This same balance is necessary for our survival in larger or world affairs (Slater, 1974).

Principle 10: People Do Not Change; They Become More and More Like Themselves

In a healthy environment this principle is true. In a traditional environment the principle is modified to read: People do not change; they become less and less like themselves. The shrinking, correcting, evaluating paradigm leads to reductionism, almost to zero or nothingness. The person, for example, may feel a void or nothingness and powerlessness. Contrast this unhealthy condition with the growth paradigm that encourages people to become more and more like themselves. *Happiness is finding more and more where there used to be less and less.*

COMPETENCIES NECESSARY FOR HEALTHY AND "GROWTHFUL" FAMILY LIFE

Family competencies are defined as *those vital elements responsible for maintaining the growth and health of the family unit.* To help teach people to become healthy and "growthful," we have to know what we want to teach. Imagine a math teacher teaching a unit on algebra without being too sure what equations are, or a mechanic instructing on computerization in cars without knowledge of those systems. Yet, this sometimes seems to be the situation in mental health. We previously have had little agreement on standards of growthful living for an individual, let alone a family.

The following are among the essential competencies for healthy and "growthful" family life. These are not isolated variables but, rather, form clusters, constellations, and chains that are dynamic, fluid, interrelated, and variable at different stages in a family's life cycle (Otto, 1975, p. 11):

- *Uniqueness* of each member is allowed to develop.
- The constructive use of *power* is facilitated, and each member learns to achieve intellectually, socially and emotionally.
- *Flexibility,* and *creative coping* with the ever changing environment, is a must. The ability to adapt to each other's needs creates a collaborative environment.

- Accurate *communication* among all members of the family is fostered.
- An atmosphere of *belonging* is essential to the healthy family. The family should represent a stronghold where changing needs can be met, a system in which individual problems can be resolved conjointly.
- A supportive climate that provides enough *security* for family members to attempt various endeavors is healthy for both the family and its members.
- *Democratic principles* of family management are an additional competency.
- Frequent use of *feedback* and *feedforward* helps members assess themselves and grow.
- *Problem solving* and *decision making* are needed for healthy living.
- The use of *consequences* and *consistency* in everyday family interactions is also regarded as a competency.

Otto (1975) believes there are "primary strength clusters" in a family that should be nourished, developed, and expanded throughout the life-span of a family. He thinks that these clusters have a great deal to do with a family's adaptability, resiliency, and optimum functioning. A partial list includes:

- The capacity to give love, affection and support to each other.
- Open communication and listening.
- The ability to give encouragement.
- Each helping the other to develop his or her unique potential.
- Capacity for understanding.
- Sensitivity to each other.
- Empathy.
- Fostering curiosity, creativity, and the spirit of adventure.

The family counselor-consultant can learn to encourage primary strength clusters, or positive "action chains," and facilitate their continued development through teaching family members this process. By encouraging appropriate segments of these chains, the entire chain is affected and "strength syndromes" are created. Table 1 demonstrates how to encourage specific behaviors and how these behaviors are linked to bigger action chains or clusters.

THE STRENGTHS-ORIENTED EDUCATION MODEL

The use of a strengths-oriented model in education and in family living has many ramifications. The single element most significant to behavior change for any individual is a *new life situation*. The introduction of family and group counseling has created situational changes that have led to more opportunity for new expectations and, consequently, new behavior. *Encouragement* is the second element significant to a strengths-oriented education model. New life situations create anxiety. Anxiety must be counterbalanced by *hope*. Hope comes from the encouragement to risk oneself in a new situation. In contrast to the prevailing weaknesses

TABLE 1
Encouragement of Action Chains

Positive Behavior	Positive Mental Health Principle or Larger *Action Chain*	Facilitative Response
Doing a job that is yours.	Social interest or concern for others.	"I like the way you see a job that needs to be done and do it!"
Waking up with a smile and making a nice remark (e.g., "good morning").	Encourages others and demonstrates ability and willingness to live cooperatively.	"You sure seem to know how to make me smile."
Asking for other family members' opinions.	Democratic decision making.	"It feels good to be a part of the family and to know that what I have to say matters to you."

model, the strengths model does not require one to retool. You are OK as you are—just give it a try. The task is to get the other person to try to act in a new situation. If he or she does, the public reinforcement helps maintain the new relationship definition and the new self-definition acquired. It even becomes difficult to go back to the previous behavior. As long as a situation in life does not change, the tendency is to maintain the familiar behavior. The same is true for changed behavior, but the new situation must become stable.

Weaknesses make us losers. Strengths make us winners. In the strengths-oriented model, relationships are made (tamed) and maintained over time. The rules we live by create the situation or define the relationships in which we behave. Strengths make us OK. Weaknesses make us not OK. If I am OK, I can try to imitate new behavior demonstrated in an old situation. I am free to create new behavior in a new situation. If I am not OK, none of the above is likely to happen.

To be a winner, it is necessary to have rules to live by that permit exercise or expansion and, consequently, growth. To be a loser, it is necessary to have rules to live by that require "exorcise" or shrinkage by casting out or reducing the not OK part of yourself. Win or lose, the myth of unchangeability in humans persists. Evidence is legion that the situation in which people find themselves influences their behavior more than do their inner traits of personality (Weisstein, 1970; Bakker, 1975). Cohen (1953), Milgram (1965), and Zimbardo (1971) have each concluded that the situation influences behavior beyond the personal expectations of the individual. Thus, the unpredictability of human behavior has persisted.

Counseling and education have given lip service to the idea that we should begin with a person wherever he or she is. To start where the person is constitutes the cardinal rule for a strengths-oriented education model. There will be no chance to bring the client up to grade level or put him or her back into his or her mythical group. The person must be treated as unique, and new situations must be created for him or her to learn and grow. When this was done in our Peer Counselor-Consultant Training Program (Fullmer, 1976), the new behavior the students were able to create made the significant difference in the way they saw themselves. Low self-esteem became an aspiration to post-high school training in the spirit of a winner, where prior to training, the despair of losing prevailed. *Peer counseling training* is one way to actualize a strengths-oriented *education model* in a school.

APPLICATIONS FOR SCHOOL COUNSELORS

There are two models or systems for the work of a counselor with families. The first is aimed at skill development for parents (Carlson & Faiber, 1976). And a second system or model of family counseling/consulting forms the basis for the following examples of group counseling that school counselors can use. These selected family counseling/consulting cases indicate how the 10 stated principles are applied. To change behavior, the life situation has to be changed, encouraged, and stabilized. The aim is to change the life situation or family system. Thus, individuals will behave in new ways.

Case 1

The school counselor was experienced in family counseling and consulting. The case involved the family of a seventh grade girl in a suburban setting. The presenting complaint concerned disruptive behavior and deterioration in behavior generally, especially in school achievement. Because her teachers found no obvious reasons, the counselor invited the parents to come in for an information session. During the initial session with the family, several items of information were disclosed. The most significant change in the life situation in the family was the fact that the father, 41, has just lost his job that had provided the family with a very comfortable living. A check of dates between daughter's change in behavior at school and the father's job situation confirmed that the girl's behavior change came a short time after father lost his job.

Several of the 10 principles are apparent in this case. The relationship between father and daughter was very robust (Principle 2). Principle 4 claims that action chains express definitions of behavior. The heavy emphasis on individual achievement in the family (Principle 9) seemed to have intensified the daughter's reaction.

The case was successfully handled through encouraging (Principle 8) the family members to assess their individual and family strengths and to develop ways of communicating to each other what pleases them. The family came for three additional sessions. During the family counseling, the daughter learned of resources in her family (both financial and psychological) of which she had been unaware. A new pattern of behavior was proposed to meet and stabilize the new situation. The girl's school work improved, and she modified her behavior in a new, more acceptable fashion.

Case 2

The counselor decided to try family counseling with a case referred by a teacher of a first-grade boy. The counselor had used parent conferences before, but this was the first time she tried to convene the entire family to help.

As stated in the referral, the boy was unable to handle social interaction without becoming panicky. Sometimes he would withdraw, and other times he would become hyperactive. In either mood it was difficult to reach him and to help him restore the balance of normal affect. During each event, he was unable to participate with the group in the room or on the playground. He had been removed from a private school a week earlier for similar behavior.

The public school he attends is not in his neighborhood because of the existing busing quotas in his district. Consequently, the boy, in his second month of school, has to attempt to make it under adverse conditions. The child has the additional drawbacks of being from a disadvantaged community and being ethnically different from the majority of children in his class. His new school is in an affluent neighborhood.

The counselor began by using the family counseling/consultation method of asking for help from outside resource persons. She started with the boy's mother. The boy, from a single-parent family, has older siblings and one younger brother. None of the other school-age children have any reported difficulties in school. The counselor visited the mother at home because she did not have private transportation. The counselor was welcomed into the home but experienced the impact of being out of her familiar context because of cultural "differentness" (Principle 5). She had to learn from the mother what behavior was appropriate. The mother displayed strengths and a depth of understanding that initially proved disarming to the counselor, until she realized that her first impression of the case came out of her own culture and was inappropriate.

There is a happy ending, but it didn't come easily. Time was required to bridge the cultural gap. The new learning for each participant, including the counselor, teacher, and student peers, came with application of Principle 1, that new context(s) supplied new meaning(s). Principle 2 was applied when the counselor came to the mother for help to gain understanding of the new situation. The action chain forged by the counselor defined the relationship with the mother as one of mutual trust, and the reciprocity of the helping relationship flourished. For the counselor, Principle 6 fits the learning she needed for new social behavior.

Rationale

School counselors do not always have skills to work with families, because few school counselors have permission to enter this domain. Role statements separate home and school. Professional counselors have debated the legitimacy of whether they have the right to go into the home. The real issue, however, is whether we have an obligation to help in the most effective manner available.

Most school counselors deal on the periphery of family work, however, through parent conferencing and involvement with home problems that students carry with them to school. But these marginal approaches bring marginal results, as the real issues are being overlooked. Through switching the focus to direct family work, permanent change can take place. Individuals learn to become more creative and more understanding, to communicate better with the world in general, and to learn to live and work with other people. School counselors traditionally have been noneffective because they have searched for inner traits when they should have been looking for the social context.

> Man's behavior is not primarily determined by unchangeable personality traits or other essential characteristics; on the contrary, his behavior is extremely changeable as a function of the situation in which he finds himself. Change the situation and the person's behavior will change. If one wants to predict his behavior, it is more important to know the situation than the person. (Weisstein, 1970)

Through dealing with the entire family, permanent direct change can occur. Secondary gains are felt by the community and school as their social context is changed when the "new" family ripples out.

Through family counseling/consultation, some individuals who could not be reached with other methods are helped. Individuals experience dissonance as previous behaviors no longer work when contexts are modified. Many ineffectual responses are reinforced and, though somewhat troublesome, accepted.

Methods

Counselors may choose from any or all of the following suggested interventions.

Family Education

A family education program is a formal learning experience that teaches families in a didactic setting how to live in a healthy fashion. Topics might include communication, family planning and decision making, conflict resolution, family activities and recreation, vacations, stages of family development, encouragement, sex, and birth order.

Family Demonstration Model

Each week a different family volunteers to receive counseling on normal problems in front of an audience. The counselor uses this format to teach or educate all present. From any given group about 80% to 90% of the parents can make direct use of the information that the family in focus receives (Christensen, 1972, p. 129).

Family Involvement Communication System (FICS)

The FICS model provides a human relations "umbrella" approach for parent and teacher input and participation in a school guidance program. This system uses a variety of strategies to enhance the educational growth of children by providing information and assistance to families who are experiencing normal and problematic growth (Shelton & Dobson, 1973).

Multiple-Family Group Counseling (MFGC)

MFGC is a short-term, relatively new form of treatment in which several families are brought together in weekly group sessions. MFGC combines the advantages of group therapy and family counseling, and increases the counselor's effectiveness and the size of the population reached (Sauber, 1971)

Family Counseling

Assisting families with normal or abnormal problems is an important counselor function. Treatment involving the family unit directly affects the situation in which an individual lives rather than dealing with the "identified patient." Treating the living unit rather than the "symptom bearer" has proven effective for problems of different types and magnitudes.

Others

Among additional strategies available to counselors:

- Refer to outside sources—psychologists, mental health centers, clergy.
- Establish a community-wide family clinic where several professionals volunteer their services on a minimal or no-fee basis. Lay people, paraprofessionals, or graduate students may intern under a professional's supervision.
- Offer family life education courses for junior and senior high school students.
- Prepare newsletters and other printed materials that provide information and activities to help families with "normal" problems (e.g., caring, sharing, thinking positively, communicating, recreation, finances).

- Provide parent and couples counseling and education to develop strong relationship and management skills.
- Give group counseling and education for mothers (Carlson & Golding, 1976).

School counselors who choose to do family work are initially confronted with the problem of *when*. Once the importance of doing family work is clearly understood by the counselor and communicated to administrators, alternatives become available. Scheduling conferences during lunch time, early morning hours, evenings, and weekends offers more options for working parents. Some counselors arrange for the school to be open during evenings and weekends to conduct family work.

SUMMARY

Family counseling/consulting is an effective process that counselors should utilize. A wide variety of theoretical approaches and techniques is available. Procedures that focus on strengths and encouragement are the most successful.

REFERENCES

Bakker, C. B. (1975). Why people don't change. *Psychotherapy, 12(2),* 164–172.

Bateson, G. (1972). *Steps to an ecology of mind.* New York: Ballantine.

Berenson, B. G., & Mitchell, K. M. (1974). *Confrontation for better or worse.* Amherst, MA: HRD Press.

Bernard, H. W., & Fullmer, D. W. (1977). *Principles of guidance: A basic text* (2nd ed.) New York: T. Y. Crowell.

Bertalanffy, L. Von. (1968). *General system theory: Foundations, development, application.* New York: Braziller.

Bowen, M. (1971). The use of family therapy in clinical practice. In J. Haley (Ed.),*Changing families* (pp. 159–192). New York: Grune & Stratton, 159–192.

Carlson, J., & Faiber, B. R. (1976). Necessary skills for parenting. *Focus on Guidance, 8(7),* 1–12.

Carlson, J., & Golding, G. (1976). A school initiated group counseling program for mothers. Available from Human Resources Development Center, 1110 University Ave., Suite 308, Honolulu, HI 96814. (mimeo).

Christensen, O. C. (1972). Family education: A model for consultation. *Elementary School Guidance & Counseling, 7(2),* 121–129.

Cohen, E. A. (1953). *Human behavior in the concentration camp.* New York: Grosset & Dunlap.

Fullmer, D. W. (1971). *Counseling: Group theory and system.* Scranton, PA: Intext.

Fullmer, D. W. (1976). *Peer counselor-consultant training manual.* Honolulu: Department of Education.

Fullmer, D. W. (1976). Family consultation. In Gazda, G. (Ed.), *Theories and methods of group counseling in the schools.* Springfield, IL: Charles C Thomas.

Hall, E. T. (1976). *Beyond culture.* Garden City, NY: Anchor Press/Doubleday.

Jacobs, A., & Spradlin, W. (1974). *The group as agent of change.* New York: Behavioral Publications.

Lieberman, M. A., Yalom, I. D., & Miles, M. B. (1972). *Encounter groups: First facts.* New York: Basic Books.

Lorenz, K (1965). *Evaluation and modification of behavior.* Chicago: University of Chicago Press.

Loukes, H. (1964). Passport to maturity. *Phi Delta Kappan, 46,* 54–57.

Milgram, S. (1965). Liberating effects of group pressure. *Journal of Personality & Social Psychology, 1,* 127–134.

Otto, H. A. (1975). *The use of family strengths concepts and methods in family life education.* Beverly Hills, CA: Holistic Press.

Sauber, S. R. (1971). Multiple family group counseling. *Personnel & Guidance Journal, 49*(6), 459–465.

Shelton, J. E., & Dobson, R. L. (1973). FICS: An expanded view of counselor-consultation. *Elementary School Guidance & Counseling, 7*(3), 210–215.

Slater, P. (1974). *Earthwalk.* New York: Bantam.

Sperry, L. (1975). *Developing skills in contact counseling: A workbook.* Reading, MA: Addison-Wesley.

Sperry, L., & Hess, L. R. (1974). *Contact counseling: A workbook.* Reading, MA: Addison-Wesley.

Tinbergen, N. (1951). *The study of instinct.* Fairlawn, NJ: Oxford University Press.

Watts, A. & Huang, A. C-H. (1975). *Tao: The watercourse way.* New York: Pantheon.

Weisstein, N., (1970). Kinder, kuche, kinche as scientific law: Psychology constructs in the female. In R. Morgan (Ed.), *Sisterhood is powerful.* New York: Vintage Books.

White, B. (1976). Exploring the origins of human competence. *APA Monitor, 7*(4), 4–5.

White, R. (1973). The concept of a healthy personality: What do we really mean? *Counseling Psychologist, 4*(2), 3–12.

Zimbardo, P. G. (1971, October 25). *The psychological power and pathology of imprisonment.* Statement prepared for the U.S. House of Representatives Committee on the Judiciary (Subcommittee No. 3, R. Kastenmeier, Chairman: Hearings on Prison Reform).

Zunin, L., & Zunin, N. (1972). *Contact: The first four minutes.* Los Angeles: Nash.

CHECKLIST OF HEALTHY FAMILY CHAINS OR STRENGTHS

	Never				Repeatedly
1. Regular periods of relaxation, recreation, and rest are scheduled.	1	2	3	4	5
2. Positive feedback and encouragement are noted frequently.	1	2	3	4	5
3. In daily conversation, assets are included more than liabilities.	1	2	3	4	5
4. Family activities are frequently scheduled, and family has a lot of fun together (many common interests).	1	2	3	4	5
5. Decision making is done in a democratic fashion.	1	2	3	4	5
6. Communication among family members is accurate (includes facts and feelings).	1	2	3	4	5
7. Family problems are dealt with as they come up—never staying at odds long (willing to forgive) or burying problems.	1	2	3	4	5
8. Family work responsibilities are divided in a fair and equitable fashion.	1	2	3	4	5
9. Sharing daily experiences is done on a regular basis and with respect.	1	2	3	4	5
10. Rules are made cooperatively.	1	2	3	4	5
11. Personal goals and family goals are interfaced in an agreeable fashion (a sense of mission).	1	2	3	4	5
12. The family's physical needs are provided for.	1	2	3	4	5
13. The family's spiritual needs are provided for.	1	2	3	4	5
14. The family's emotional needs are provided for.	1	2	3	4	5

15.	Support of family members and security are ever present—a liking/loving caring for each other, freedom of expression.	1	2	3	4	5
16.	Growth-producing relationships and experiences are initiated and maintained both within and without the family.	1	2	3	4	5
17.	Constructive and responsible community involvement is created and maintained.	1	2	3	4	5
18.	Growth is evidenced through and with children.	1	2	3	4	5
19.	The family has the ability for self-help, as well as to accept outside help when appropriate.	1	2	3	4	5
20.	The family uses "injuries" and "crises" from which to grow.	1	2	3	4	5
21.	Family members have time together and time alone.	1	2	3	4	5
22.	The family has a good circle of friends.	1	2	3	4	5
23.	Good humor is valued.	1	2	3	4	5
24.	Family finances are understood and agreed upon.	1	2	3	4	5
25.	The family has good food and nutrition patterns.	1	2	3	4	5
26.	Family traditions and celebrations are celebrated.	1	2	3	4	5
27.	Family members share respect for self and each other and are sensitive to each other's needs.	1	2	3	4	5
28.	The family has the ability to plan ahead rather than react.	1	2	3	4	5

SUGGESTED READINGS

Ackerman, N. J. (1984). *A theory for family systems*. New York: Gardner Press.

Ackerman, N. W. (1958). *The pschodynamics of family life: Diagnosis and treatment of family relationships*. New York: Basic Books.

Ackerman, N. W. (1966). *Treating the troubled family*. New York: Basic Books.

Allred, G. H. (1974). *On the level: With self, family and society*. Provo, UT: Brigham Young University Press.

Andreozzi, L. L. (1985). *Integrating research and clinical practice*. Rockville, MD: Aspen Systems Corp.

Andrews, E. E. (1974). *The emotionally disturbed family*. New York: Jason Aronson.

Ault-Riché, M. (1986). *Women and family therapy*. Rockville, MD: Aspen Systems Corp.

Bagarozzi, D., Jurich, A., & Jackson, R. W. (1983). *Marital and family therapy: New perspectives in theory, research and practice*. New York: Human Sciences Press.

Baruth, L. G., & Huber, C. H. (1984). *An introduction to marital theory and therapy*. Monterey: Brooks/Cole.

Bentovin, A., Barnes, G. G., & Cooklin, A. (1982). *Family therapy: Complementary frameworks of theory and practice* (Vols. 1 & 2). New York: Grune & Stratton.

Bjorksten, O. J. W. (1985). *New clinical concepts in marital therapy*. Washington, DC: American Psychiatric Association Press.

Block, D. A. (1973). *Techniques of family therapy: A primer*. New York: Grune & Stratton.

Bowen, M. (1971). The use of family theory in clinical practice. In J. Haley (Ed.), *Changing families*. New York: Grune & Stratton.

Breunlin, D. C. (1985). *Stages: Patterns of change over time*. Rockville, MD: Aspen Systems Corp.

Campbell, D., & Draper, R. (1985). *Applications of systemic family therapy: The Milan approach*. Orlando, FL: Grune & Stratton.

Coleman, S. B. (1985). *Failures in family therapy*. New York: Guilford Press.

Curran, D. (1985). *Stress and the healthy family*. Minneapolis: Winston Press.

Dreikurs, R., Gould, S., & Corsini, R. J. (1974). *Family council*. Chicago: Henry Regenery.

Einstein, E. (1985). *The step-family: Living, loving and learning.* Boulder, CO: Shambhala Publications.

Feldman, H., & Feldman, M. (1985). *Current controversy in marriage and family.* Beverly Hills: Sage Publications.

Fishman, H. C., & Rosman, B. L. (1985). *Evolving models for family change.* New York: Guilford Press.

Foley, V. D. (1986). *An introduction to family therapy (2nd ed.).* Orlando, FL: Grune & Stratton.

Framo, J. L. (Ed.). (1972). *Family interaction: A dialogue between family researchers and family therapists.* New York: Springer.

Friesen, J. D. (1985). *Structural-strategic marital and family therapy.* New York: Gardner Press.

Fullmer, D. W., & Bernard, H. E. (1968). *Family consultation.* Boston: Houghton Mifflin.

Galvin, K. M., & Brommel, B. J. (1986). *Family communication: Cohesion and change (2nd ed.).* Glenview, IL: Scott, Foresman.

Geismar, L. L., & Wood, K. (1986). *Family and delinquency: Resocializing the young offender.* New York: Human Sciences Press.

Gelles, R. J., & Cornell, C. P. (1985). *Intimate violence in families.* Beverly Hills, CA: Sage Publications.

Glick, I. D., & Kessler, D. R. (1974). *Marital and family therapy.* New York: Grune & Stratton.

Goldenberg, I., & Goldenberg, H. (1985). *Family therapy: An overview (2nd ed.).* Monterey, CA: Brooks/Cole.

Grebe, S. C. (1985). *Divorce and family mediation.* Rockville, MD: Aspen Systems Corp.

Grunwald, B. B., & McAbee, H. V. (1985). *Guiding the family: Practical counseling techniques.* Muncie, IN: Accelerated Development.

Gullotta, T. P., Adams, G. R., & Alexander, S. J. (1986). *Today's marriages and families: A wellness approach.* Monterey, CA: Brooks/Cole.

Gurman, A. S. (1985). *Casebook of marital therapy.* New York: Guilford Press.

Haley, J. (1969). *The power tactics of Jesus Christ and other essays.* New York: Avon.

Haley, J. (1971). *Changing families.* New York: Grune & Stratton.

Haley, J. (1973). *Uncommon therapy.* New York: Ballantine.

Haley, J., & Hoffman, L. (Eds.). (1967). *Techniques of family therapy.* New York: Basic Books.

Handel, G. (1985). *The psychosocial interior of the family (3rd ed.).* Hawthorne, NY: Aldine Publishing Co.

Horne, A. M., & Ohlsen, M. M. (1982). *Family counseling and therapy.* Itasca, IL: F. E. Peacock Publishers.

Howells, J. G., & Guirguis, W. R. (1985). *The family and schizophrenia.* Madison, CT: International Universities Press.

Howells, J. G., & Lickorish, J. R. (1984). *Family relations indicator.* Madison, CT: International Universities Press.

Jackson, D. D. (Ed.). (1968). *Communication, family and marriage.* Palo Alto, CA: Science & Behavior Books.

Kantor, D., & Lehr, W. (1975). *Inside the family.* San Francisco: Jossey-Bass.

Kaufman, E. (1985). *Substance abuse and family therapy.* Orlando, FL: Grune & Stratton.

Koledzon, M. S., & Green, R. G. (1985). *Family therapy models of convergence and divergence.* New York: Springer.

L'Abate, L. (1985). *The handbook of family psychology and therapy (Vols. 1 & 2).* Homewood, IL: Dorsey Press.

L'Abate, L., Ganahl, G., & Hansen, J. C. (1986). *Methods of family therapy.* Englewood Cliffs, NJ: Prentice-Hall.

L'Abate, L., & McHenery, S. (1983). *Handbook of marital interventions.* New York: Grune & Stratton.

Laing, R. D. (1969). *The politics of the family and other essays.* New York: Pantheon.

Laing, R., & Esterson, A. (1964). *Sanity, madness and the family.* Baltimore: Penguin.

Lansky, M. R. (1985). *Family approaches to major psychiatric disorders.* Washington, DC: American Psychiatric Press.

Lansky, M. R. (1981). *Family therapy and major psychopathology.* New York: Grune & Stratton.

Levant, R. F. (1936). *Psychoeducational approaches to family therapy and counseling.* New York: Springer.

Luthman, S. G., & Kirschenbaum, M. (1974). *The dynamic family.* Palo Alto, CA: Science & Behavior Books.

McGoldrick, M., Pearce, J. K., & Giordano, J. (1982). *Ethnicity and family therapy*. New York: Guilford Press.

Miller, S., Nunnally, E. W., & Wackman, D. B. (1975). *Alive and aware: Improving communications in relationships*. Minneapolis: Interpersonal Communication Programs.

Minuchin, S. (1974). *Families and family therapy*. Cambridge, MA: Harvard University Press.

Moynihan, D. P. (1986). *Family and nation: The Godkin lectures, Harvard University*. Orlando, FL: Harcourt Brace Jovanovich.

Nerin, W. F. (1986). *Family reconstruction: A long day's journey into light*. New York: W. W. Norton & Co.

Newberger, E. H., & Bourne, R. (1985). *Unhappy families*. Littleton, MA: PSG Publishing Co.

Otto, H. A. (1975). *The use of family strengths concepts and methods in family life education*. Beverly Hills, CA: Holistic Press.

Papp, P. (1983). *The process of change*. New York: Guilford Press.

Patterson, G. R. (1975). *Families: Applications of social learning to family life*. Champaign, IL: Research Press.

Patterson, G. R., Reid, J. B., Jones, R. R., & Conger, R. E. (1975). *A social learning approach to family intervention*. Eugene, OR: Castalia.

Peseschkian, N. (1986). *Positive family therapy: The family as therapy*. New York: Springer-Verlag.

Richman, J. (1985). *Family therapy with suicidal people*. New York: Springer.

Roy, R. (1985). *The family and chronic pain*. New York: Human Sciences Press.

Sager, C. J., & Kaplan, H. S. (Eds.). (1972). *Progress in group and family therapy*. New York: Brunner/Mazel.

Satir, V. (1967). *Conjoint family therapy* (rev. ed.). Palo Alto, CA: Science & Behavior Books.

Satir, V. (1972). *Peoplemaking*. Palo Alto, CA: Science & Behavior Books.

Sauber, S. R., L'Abate, L., & Weeks, G. R. (1985). *Family therapy: Basic concepts and terms*. Rockville, MD: Aspen Systems Corp.

Sherman, R., & Fredman, N. (1986). *Handbook of structured techniques in family therapy*. New York: Brunner/Mazel.

Speck, R. and Atteneave, C. (1973). *Family networks*. New York: Pantheon.

Springer, J. R., & Woody, R. H. (1985). *Healthy promotion in family therapy*. Rockville, MD: Aspen Systems Corp.

Sugarman, S. (1986). *The interface of individual and family therapy*. Rockville, MD: Aspen Systems Corp.

Turk, D. C., & Kerns, R. D. (1985). *Health, illness and family: A life-span perspective*. New York: Wiley-Interscience.

Umbarber, C. C. (1983). *Structural family therapy*. New York: Grune & Stratton.

Wahllroos, S. (1974). *Family communication*. New York: Macmillan.

Will, D., & Wrate, R. M. (1986). *Integrated family therapy*. New York: Methuen.

Ziffer, R. L. (1985). *Adjunctive techniques in family therapy*. Orlando, FL: Grune & Stratton.

Zuk, G. H. (1971). *Family therapy: A triadic-based approach*. New York: Behavioral Publications.

Zuk, G. H. (1974). *Process and practice in family therapy*. Haverford, PA: Psychiatry & Behavioral Science Books.

Jon Carlson is a Psychologist with the Lake Geneva (Wisconsin) Wellness Clinic. Dan Fullmer is Professor of Educational Psychology, University of Hawaii.

7

Changing Family Patterns: Developmental Impacts On Children

Bonnie E. Robson

Today, children are likely to grow up experiencing more than one family pattern. The traditional structure of a family unit or household as a set of parents and children and possibly other blood relatives has been replaced by a multitude of possible family patterns. These include single parents, widowed, separated, divorced, adoptive, or selective families, and blended or remarried families, as well as the adoptive or biological two-parent families with intact first marriages.

Recently the interest of researchers, counselors, and the general public has focused on the effects of various patterns on individuals within the family. This article explores the impact of the change from one type of family structure to another on the development of children. It focuses on which developmental styles or coping strategies and which environmental supports potentiate healthy adaptation to a change in family pattern. Using this knowledge, counselors can exert a positive influence on the process of normal development in ameliorating or preventing maladaptive responses.

THE PROBABILITY OF CHANGE IN FAMILY PATTERN

Most children who have lived in more than one family pattern have experienced parental separation or divorce (Bane, 1979; Norton & Glick, 1979). Since 1972, in the United States, more than one million children under age 18 have been affected each year by their parents' divorce (Carter & Glick, 1976) (although not all marital separations end in legal divorce proceedings). An estimated 40%-50% of children born in the 1980s will spend some time in a single-parent home (Hetherington, 1979; Statistics Canada, 1983).

By the end of the 1980s, almost half of Canadian families and 45% of American families will be of the remarried form (Visher & Visher, 1982). This prediction is not surprising given that 80% of divorced men and 75% of divorced women remarry (widowed persons are much less likely to remarry) (Morrison & Thompson-Guppy, 1985). These statistics suggest that 25% of all children will be part of a remarried family; others will live with parents who are in a blended common-law union. Although the latter is not remarriage, the children will be required to form a relationship with an adult in the stepparent role. Even this readjustment is not the end of the divorce process for some children, as 47% of second marriages eventually dissolve (Morrison & Thompson-Guppy, 1985) and the children of these parents must adapt once more.

PARENTAL MARITAL STATUS EFFECTS

That children of divorce are over-represented in psychiatric populations has been known for almost two decades (Kalter, 1977; McDermott, 1970). These children show higher rates of delinquency and antisocial behavior, more neurotic symptoms, depression, conduct disorders, and habit formations such as sleep disturbances than do children in intact homes (McDermott, 1970; Morrison, 1974; Schoettle & Cantwell, 1980). In non-clinic populations the reported maladaptations are numerous. The children are more dependent, disobedient, aggressive, whining, demanding, and unaffectionate (McDermott, 1970). Hetherington, Cox, and Cox (1978) reported that children with divorced parents have generalized feelings of anxiety and helplessness and lower self-esteem. They perform less well on a variety of social and adjustment indices (Guidubaldi & Perry, 1985).

In interviewing 703 children from separated, divorced, and remarried families, Brady, Bray, and Zeeb (1986) found that they differed in both type and degree of problems. Although differences between children with separated parents and children with divorced parents were not significant, the children with separated parents showed more immature behavior, tensions, hyperactivity, and sleep disturbances. Children from remarried families "were found to demonstrate more behavior problems as characterized by conduct problems and hyperactive behavior" (p. 409).

DEMOGRAPHIC VARIABLES

In a 6-year follow-up of 60 children of divorcing parents who were compared with 64 children of non-divorcing parents, Hetherington, Cox, and Cox (1985) found that divorce had more adverse long-term effects on boys. Remarriage of the custodial parent was found to be associated with an increase in behavioral problems for girls and a decrease in problems for boys. Further, stability of the problem behaviors was found to be related to the gender of the children. "Early aggressive and antisocial behavior is more predictive of later behavior problems and lack of

social competence than is early withdrawal and anxiety. Moreover, early external-
izing behavior in girls, perhaps because it is less frequent and viewed as less sex
appropriate, is the best predictor of later socially inept behavior" (p. 529). They
suggested that these gender differences may be more prominent in younger
children.

Brady, Bray, and Zeeb (1986) failed to find any significant interaction among
parental marital status and the child's age and sex. Similarly, other studies have not
found gender to be correlated significantly with divorce adjustment (Kalter, 1977;
Kurdek, Blisk, & Siesky, 1981; Saucier & Ambert, 1986). In a psychiatric population McDermott (1970) found that the proportion of male to female patients was
generally equivalent.

Firstborn children, who might feel more responsible for their parents and
younger siblings, may experience more stress. The youngest child may have difficulty in later adolescence in identity formation and leaving home to pursue a career
if leaving home means abandoning his or her single parent.

Studies of non-clinic populations have suggested that the child's age or specific developmental phase at the time of parental separation is related to the quality
as well as the severity of the reaction (Kalter & Rembar, 1981; Wallerstein & Kelly,
1980). Further, the child's age appears to be related to adjustment to the divorce
(Kurdek, Blisk, & Siesky, 1981; McDermott, 1970). Generally the younger the
child is, the more vulnerable he or she appears to be, because younger children
show the most behavioral disturbance (Brady, Bray, & Zeeb, 1986; Hetherington,
Cox, & Cox, 1978; Kalter, 1977; Wallerstein & Kelly, 1980).

DEVELOPMENTAL REACTIONS

The child's developmental stage at the time of parental separation appears to
be related to the reaction (Hetherington, Cox, & Cox, 1985; Wallerstein & Kelly,
1980; Robson, 1980, 1985). Thus, the following descriptions of the common reactions are divided into age-related (but not age-specific) groupings.

Infants and Preschool Children (0–5)

Following parental separation children under age 5 tend to regress in their development, showing feeding difficulties, toileting problems including soiling,
smearing, and enuresis, and frequently disturbed sleeping patterns. Preschool and
kindergarten children show, among other symptoms, intense separation anxiety
manifested as fear that they will be left alone or abandoned by both parents.

The intensity of this reaction has two possible explanations. These children
understand, albeit simplistically, that their parents no longer love each other; they
are no longer living together. They reason that if this can happen to their parents,
they, too, can be abandoned. An alternate explanation is that having lost one
parent, they already have experienced abandonment. Fearing that they will be

abandoned by the other parent, they regress to more childish behavior, recalling that when they were babies, they were loved and cared for and in close proximity to both of their parents.

Early responses of anger, fear, depression, and guilt are common in children in this age group. Preschoolers repeatedly state that they miss the non-resident parent. Although these statements may anger the custodial parent, he or she should be helped to realize that this expression of loss does not mean the child loves the resident parent any less—rather, that the child wishes for both parents to be together again.

A child in this age group can develop an attachment to other parental figures and may come to view a resident stepparent as a psychological parent. This result can lead to ongoing discord between the biological parents, with subsequent negative effects on the child.

School-Age Children: Younger (6–8), Older (9–11)

Open denial of the separation or of any difficulties with the separation are frequent findings in early school-aged children. Initially, parents may report that the child is adjusting well, but underlying feelings may not be readily apparent. As one illustration, Virginia, while drawing a picture of her father on the playroom blackboard, announced, "When he's not home, I pretend he's at work and it's okay. When I see him, then I'm sad." Thus, despite the denial, they view the separation as a profound loss. If these children are symptomatic, they appear depressed with anxious mood. They may be extremely hard to control and often have temper tantrums.

To differentiate the vulnerable from the invulnerable in this age group may be difficult for the counselor. The high-risk group appears to express more of a sense of guilt for having caused the separation. Nightmares are common. In addition, refusal to go to school, school failure, and unexplained illnesses are not uncommon.

School refusal may indicate a child who, in the intermediate phase of the divorce process, 6 months to a year after the initial separation, is attempting to get the parents back together. Parents who are concerned about their child's sudden change in behavior sometimes meet to discuss what should be done. This, however, reinforces the behavior and confirms for the child that his or her actions can bring the parents back together. Hence, negative behavior patterns may escalate. Despite the remarriage of one or both parents, children of 7 or 8 remain hopeful that their parents will reunite. For some children these fantasies persist as long as 10 years after the separation (Wallerstein, 1984).

Shock, surprise, denial, incredulity, and disbelief are characteristic of children within the older school-age group. This makes sense when we recall that these children adhere strongly to a sense of fair play. Rules are based on a strong identification with parental guidelines. When parents separate, the image of an all-knowing, all-good, ideal parent is destroyed, and children in this developmental phase can become intensely angry—usually at the non-resident parent. Once their initial anger subsides, they may assume that their parents are still angry with each other. Thus, they are vulnerable to a propaganda game in which they will accept, without question, bitter or false statements by one parent about the other.

Children in this developmental stage experience loyalty conflicts but fail to express them openly. They may attempt to resolve the conflict by becoming excessively dependent on one parent while completely rejecting the other. Susan, who is 9 years old, is unable to go out without her mother. She does not play with friends after school, preferring her mother's company. When the mother and daughter were interviewed, they sat huddled together on a coach. To pry them apart—even to get them to sit in separate chairs—was difficult at first.

These children frequently become enmeshed of their own volition in the custody struggle, and some hang on for years to the image of one parent as all good and the other parent as all bad. Some children engaged in the custody battle are permitted to read court transcripts and even testify on behalf of one parent. They are forced into a position of rejecting not only the other parent's behavior but also all those parts of that parent with which they had previously identified.

Shortly after his parent's separation, Kurt, who previously had shared an interest in soccer with his father, dropped the team despite his obvious enjoyment of the sport. This perceived need to reject all parts of one's life that were associated with the "other" parent can result in a lowered self-image and a concomitant decrease in level of functioning, both socially and academically.

Children in this age group may show anger at the time of a parent's remarriage. Anger that may have been directed at the non-custodial parent may be displaced onto the new marital partner. This can severely disrupt integration of the new family unit (Weiss, 1975).

Adolescents (13–18)

Parental divorce in adolescence can accelerate growth toward maturity, with many adolescents taking on more responsibility than their peers (Robson, 1980). This observation led many people to assert that the adolescent personality was minimally affected by divorce (Reinhard, 1977). If the spurt comes too early, however, it can intensify normal adolescent developmental conflicts and result in a premature attempt at mastery or a pseudo-adolescence (Wallerstein & Kelly, 1980).

Hetherington (1972) has found that adolescent girls, fatherless through separation, tend to change in their interactions with males. They seek attention from men and demonstrate early heterosexual behavior, as compared with the daughters of widows, who tend to be more inhibited around men.

After surveying 1,519 high school students from three different districts, Saucier and Ambert (1986) found that adolescents from divorced families were most disadvantaged on a wide range of psychosocial variables. These included mental health, subjective reporting of their school performance, and perceptions of their life in the future, their parents, and their environment. Those authors also found that boys of widowed parents were more disadvantaged than girls but found no striking difference between boys and girls with divorced parents.

Without conventional support systems and parental guidance, the independent capacity to make judgments and to establish interpersonal relationships is weakened. Lack of parental discipline, which is perceived as emotional withdrawal, is often a crucial factor constituting a further loss and an increased sense of abandonment.

College Students (18–22)

Only recently have young adults been considered when taking a developmental approach to the reactions of offspring to their parents' divorce or remarriage. Cooney, Smyer, Gunhild, Hagestad, and Klock (1986) studied 18 male and 21 female university students whose parents had been divorced 3 years or less. The authors found that in this age group the girls were more likely to experience the divorce as initially stressful.

The students appeared to lack networks, both formal and informal, and only 14% sought formal counseling. This low utilization rate may have been because of a lack of services or a lack of awareness of the availability of services. Entry into a university, with the loss of former peer support systems accompanied by the stress of an unfamiliar environment, is reported to delay adjustment to the parental separation. "The occurrence of multiple transitions was an important issue in the divorce experience in this age group" (Cooney et al., 1986, p. 473). The authors reported that this does not apply to all of the students because some found that living away from home provided protection from enmeshment in the family crisis.

Fifty percent of males and 62% of females reported a change in their relationship with their parents (Cooney et al., 1986). The women seemed more polarized in their post-separation parental relationships and experienced a deteriorating relationship with their fathers.

These are extremely important findings because the quality of relationships cannot be accounted for by custody decisions, as they might be with younger children. Although two-thirds of the college students experienced anger directed at one or both parents, they were equally worried about their parents' future. More students reported being worried about their mothers' ability to cope with independent living situations.

A study of 400 18- and 19-year-old college students revealed that those with divorced or separated parents were anxious about their own future marriages (Robson, 1985). They were less likely to want children. If they planned to marry, they thought they should delay it until they were older—perhaps in their late 20s. More of the students reported that they planned to live with their partners prior to marriage because of their anxiety that their own marriage might end in divorce. Wallerstein and Kelly (1980) reported similar concerns in their interviews with younger adolescents.

ROLE OF THE COUNSELOR

From the preceding discussion of the severity and extent of typical reactions of children to their parents' separation, one can readily agree with Hetherington, Cox, and Cox, (1978) that every family breakdown has its victim or victims. The results of Wallerstein's (1980) study are troubling. It revealed that one-third of the children were still distressed and intensely unhappy 5 years after their parents' separation. Of course, two-thirds of the children were coping well and described as emotionally healthy.

Thus, some children cope, and some do not. Viewing divorce as an inevitable disaster may be only one perspective; the divorce process might encourage healthy development for some children. This is not to suggest that these "invulnerable" children have escaped unscathed but, rather, that they may experience the divorce as a growth enhancing process albeit a painful and initially distressing event.

Primary Prevention

Education

Educational programs designed to enhance adjustment fit well with Caplan's (1964) definition of primary prevention as a ". . . community concept. It involves lowering the rate of new cases of mental disorder in a population over a certain period by counteracting harmful circumstances before they have had a chance to produce illness. It seeks to reduce the risk for a whole population" (p. 26). In this instance the population at risk consists of children who are exposed to parental separation and divorce. In discussing children's adjustment, Kurdek, Blisk, and Siesky (1981) stated that:

> Adjustment involves cultural beliefs, values and attitudes surrounding modern family life (the macro system), both the stability of the post divorce environment and the social supports available to the restructured single parent family (the exo system), the nature of the family interaction in the pre and post separation periods (the micro system), and the child's individual psychological competencies for dealing with stress (the ontogenic system). (p. 569)

The literature contains few reports of community intervention strategies designed to correct cultural misperceptions and attitudes (which might be stated as programming directed at the macro system). Educational programming may be in the forms of *bibliotherapy, programs, public forums, information events, individual parent education groups, group education for children, formal school curriculum,* and *education for professionals.* Gardner (1979) strongly advocated that educators be involved in all aspects of the divorce process.

Rubin and Price (1979) have recommended education within the school system as a preventive measure that can counteract the perpetuation of divorce in families. This type of intervention is especially important for married teenagers, because we know that this group is at high risk for marriage dissolution. By actively working with this population to further knowledge and problem-solving skills, a higher marital success rate may be ensured.

Warren and Amara (1984) found that parenting groups for custodial parents that begin after legal divorce proceedings are more effective than groups offered immediately after the separation. They further reported that participants in these 6-week groups who benefited most were the parents who had reported the greatest post-divorce stress.

Structured, educationally oriented groups exclusively for children of separated and divorced parents, either within the nursery or primary schools or within community centers and public libraries, have been recommended (Boren, 1983; Fine, 1982; Kurdek, Blisk, & Siesky, 1981; Nevins, 1981; Robson, 1982; Tableman, 1981). These community or non-clinic groups appear to be more effective when they are highly structured and when they adhere to a specific curriculum. Many organizations offer family-oriented parallel group programs similar to the program proposed by Isaacs and Levin (1984).

Freeman (1984) stated that children who participated in an 8-week semistructured educational group were significantly better adjusted than their waitlisted controls. They showed improved in-classroom behavior, and their parents reported that they were more achievement-oriented. They had developed more specific coping repertoires and responses to stress.

In one unique program Crossman and Adams (1980) used crisis theory and social facilitation programs with preschool children. This intervention was based on the assumption that children of divorce need adult-child interaction in addition to that provided by the mother, to mediate the negative consequences of having only one parent available. In a carefully designed double control study, preschool children with separated parents made marked gains in locus of control and intelligence testing.

Legislation

Most recommendations for legislative changes advocate uniform state laws to avoid child snatching by a non-custodial parent. Others suggest changes to involve children in determining custody and visitation and to promote the concept of no-fault divorce (Atwell, Moore, Nielsen, & Levite, 1984; Payne & Dimock, 1983).

Conciliation counseling may assist families through the legal procedures surrounding a divorce and can help reduce adverse effects (Cleveland & Irvin, 1982; Lebowitz, 1983). Similarly, family mediation can simplify the procedures by proper preparation of the couple for the legalities. A full description of the place of family mediation in the divorce process is described by Haber, Mascari, and Sanders-Mascari (1983).

Much has been written about the best arrangements for custody and visitation of children. In recent years several states have followed the example of California in awarding joint custody as the preferred mode of custody. Joint custody acknowledges the continuation of parenting rights, responsibility, and duties of both parents but does not dictate place of residence or visiting and access practices. Wallerstein and Kelly (1980), Clingempeel and Reppucci (1982), and Steinman (1981) recommend joint custody, while Nehls and Morsenbesser (1980) and Goldstein, Freud, and Solnit (1973) caution against its overuse.

In examining 414 consecutive cases of divorce Ilfeld, Ilfeld, and Alexander (1982) found a significant decrease in relitigation rates when joint custody was awarded. This is not surprising when one considers that a requirement for successful joint custody is the ability to negotiate. In 18 cases the joint custody award was made over the opposition of both parents, and their relitigation rate was the same as when sole custody was awarded.

Is joint custody the best alternative? Certainly some children find a joint custody arrangement that requires frequent changes of residence unsettling and anxiety provoking (Steinman, 1981). In conclusion, joint custody can work, but it is not effective in all cases.

Direct Intervention

Early Identification

To be most effective, programs should be provided first for children and adolescents who are at high risk for maladaptive responses to their parents' separation. The previously described research indicated that the children more at risk are boys (Hetherington, Cox, & Cox, 1985), children with poor academic achievement (Rutter, 1979), first-born children (Despert, 1962), and children whose parents are only recently separated (Wallerstein, 1980).

Several researchers (Chess, Thomas, Korn, Mittleman, & Cohen, 1983; Ellison, 1983; Rutter, 1971) have implicated ongoing parental discord as a high risk factor for maladaptive patterns. Alternatively, children and adolescents who had a supportive peer group and were able to rely on their custodial parent and siblings were less vulnerable (Kalter, 1977; Robson, Homatidis, Johnson, & Orlando, 1986).

The quality and availability of support services, both before and after the separation, appear to differentiate the vulnerable and the invulnerable. Because vulnerable children make less use of their families for support and rely more heavily on fewer friends who also are more likely to have separated parents, peer support groups for these children would seen to be an efficacious preventive program.

School-Based Supportive Group Programs

The education of teachers, administrative personnel, and parents can provide a firm basis for the success of school-based group programs. Supportive groups that are moderately structured and time-limited seem to constitute ideal programming for adolescence and late latency (ages ± 10–12) children for the reasons indicated earlier (Rubin & Price, 1979). During these group sessions, children often project and portray their parents as mean, selfish, abusive, and violent. Ultimately, the parents do emerge as having strengths as well as weaknesses.

Children's divorce groups led by elementary school counselors have been found to be extremely successful (Wilkinson & Bleck, 1976). This type of group, which is based on a developmental model of counseling and includes play activities and crafts, is synopsized by developmental phase in Table 1. From personal experience, common themes of these groups are loneliness, fears of separation or abandonment, and feelings of guilt.

While acknowledging that preventive programs based on a crisis intervention model can be effective initially, Kalter, Pickar, and Lesowitz (1984) believe that children go through a reworking of "nodal developmental points." They caution that divorce should be viewed not as a single life event but, rather, as a process. Thus, they recommend that groups within the school setting should assist children "to negotiate more effectively the developmental tasks associated with both divorce and post-divorce experiences" (p. 614). Although they worked with students in grades 5 and 6, they also recommend groups for students at other nodal developmental points and possibly at the point of entry or leaving junior or senior high school and as preparation for college or university entrance.

Themes that emerge for students of about 10–12 years are anxiety over parental fighting, loyalty conflicts, worry about custody decisions, loss of family and loss or partial loss of the father, worry and anger about parents' dating, and concern about stepparents' discipline (Kalter et al., 1984). In adolescent school-based groups, anxiety-charged issues include marital infidelity and family violence. Teens express fear about parents' dating—and about parents who are not socially active. Adolescents feel an increased sense of responsibility and guilt if the parent is not socially active, but when the parent expresses a wish to remarry, the adolescent is concerned about having to revert from the adult position that he or she currently occupies back into a child role.

In addition, anxieties about homosexuality are increased during adolescence. Although this is a normal developmental fear during adolescence, it appears to be increased among students with divorced parents. They express fears about disturbed gender identity formation as a result of living with only one parent—particularly if that parent has preferred an opposite-sex child. Not being of the preferred gender is an issue for both males and females.

Discussion of loyalties is prominent in group sessions when holidays and vacations are imminent—especially summer and Christmas. Girls' groups tend to confirm research demonstrating lower self-concept among girls whose parents are separated (Parish & Taylor, 1979). A persistent theme in girls' groups was that they felt deprived of a normal teenage life and that they felt abnormal and unlike their peers.

An advantage of students participating in school-based groups is the opportunity to observe participants more closely in peer interactions. Close observation can enable the counselor to select students who might benefit from a more individualized approach or who might warrant referral to a clinical setting for treatment.

School-based groups, compared with community-based groups, are less likely to require parallel parent groups. Adolescent groups prefer not to have par-

TABLE 1
School-Based Groups for Children of Separation or Divorce

Developmental Phase	Early School Age (6-8)	Latency (8-12, 9-11)	Early Adolescent (13-15)	Middle and Late Adolescent (15-18) (18-22)
Symptoms	Pervasive sadness, crying, suffering, experience loss. Fearful nightmares. Guilt. Reconciliation desired.	Shock and surprise. Intense anger. Blaming and rejecting one parent. Dependency conflicts.	Shock, not surprise. Pain, "loss of family." Anger at loss. Pseudo-maturity. Acting-out, delinquency, promiscuity.	
Group Size	5-6	5-7	5-6	6-8
Sex	Both sexes	Same sex	Same sex	Both sexes
Length of Time	1 hour	1 - 1½ hours	1 hour	1 - 1½ hours
Setting	One room. Table, chairs around it. Carpeted floor space.	Two rooms — group room and activity space. Sturdy chairs.	Group room. Video playback and taping. Sturdy chairs.	Group room. Avoid swivel chairs. Lamps, pictures. Regular seating, coffee tables.
Equipment, Supplies, and Materials	Pillows, craft supplies, paper, scissors, glue, crayons, etc. Simple games— Bingo, Twister, ET, Simon Says, Star Wars, Candyland. Plasticine, Polaroid camera, display area. Juice, milk, cookies.	Indoor/outdoor sports— floor hockey, soccer, softballs. Film. Dress-up materials, hats, belts, make-up. Polaroid camera, craft supplies, string, paper, cooking supplies. Juice, milk, cookies.	Suggestion box. Paper, pens. Films. Simple dress-up props, collage materials. Soda pop.	Pop, coffee, tea. (15-18) No refreshments. (18-22)
Activities	Individual—crafts or games (2 per session) plus refreshment time (start with snack).	One per session— alternate large motor with quieter. End with refreshment.	Films, guest speakers, videodrama, discussion. Refreshments available at outset.	Discussion. Refreshments available at outset. (15-18)
Counselor Activity	Group preparation. Interpretation of positive transference. Avoid splitting. Modeling. Individual in group. Structure, rules, boundaries. Coaching. Rules—listen when someone is talking, stay in room, keep hands off others and others' work.	Coaching approach. Interpret group process during planning. Define boundaries. Provide security. Stimulate ideas, topics. Promote group cohesion, psychodrama.	Focus on group process. Define boundaries. Assist in maintaining structure and focus. Role play. Participate. Relate group to reality.	Group as whole. Use reasoning. Use events to develop group insights. Use modeling. Allow for verbal confrontation with adult. Relate group to reality.

TABLE 1 (continued)

Developmental Phase	Early School Age (6-8)	Latency (8-12, 9-11)	Early Adolescent (13-15)	Middle and Late Adolescent (15-18) (18-22)
Parent Involvement	Regular contact (once a week/ once a month).	Group meetings irregular, discussed with group. Parents available to transport and wait for children if necessary. Parent groups.	Initially 6-8 weeks.	As indicated; not necessary.
Goals	Have peer support. Reduce anxiety. Reduce unrealistic or catastrophic expectations of adults. Link feelings with language. Help child focus on individual needs. Improve concentration and school motivation through improved self-image.	Have peer support. Reduce guilt. See both sides of parents. Gain insight. Improve behavior. Control, reduce impulsiveness. Improve self-image. Improve interpersonal skills.	See both sides of parents. Tolerate ambivalence. Not use alcohol and drugs for loneliness. Improve self-image. Gain insight.	Share and care. Foster cohesion and confrontation in supportive environment. Develop capacity to resolve conflicts in school and family. Develop hope for future. Improve self-esteem.
Themes	Loneliness. Guilt. Being left out. Abandonment.	Anger. Blame. Rights and fair play. Intolerance of mistakes. Sadness linked with anger.	Hostility. Violence. Rejection. Too much responsibility too soon. Hunger and pain.	Loneliness. Fear of future. Existential anxiety. Loss of adolescence. Sexuality.

ents regularly involved, and groups may be more productive when they are free from direct parental interference. To participate actively and openly, adolescents need to be reassured about confidentiality.

Family or Individual Counseling

Reviewing the literature that deals with disruption of the family unit, there are few reports advocating a family approach. Beal (1979) has recommended family counseling as a preventive measure. Multiple family group therapy, as employed by Messinger, Walters, and Freeman (1978), promotes change and realignment with the family.

Parental *support,* not education, is recommended to assist very young children in adapting to separation and divorce of their parents. As Rutter (1971) pointed out, a good relationship with one parent can be highly preventive of later difficulties. Parents who participate in parent support groups report improved self-esteem as they acquire better parental coping skills (Kessler, 1978; Thiessen, Avery, & Joanning, 1980). And if they feel more positive about their own skills, they are likely to have improved relationships with their children.

Parents of preschoolers need support in maintaining appropriate limits in the face of their child's often extreme regression. Parents who already are stressed may become intensely angry and displace their anger at the failure of the marriage onto their preschoolers. If the child is encopretic and smearing or crying and stating repeatedly that he or she wants the absent parent, the resident parent is likely to get even angrier. Preschoolers need to cope with the separation cognitively, but 80% of them are given no explanation for the loss or partial loss of one parent (Waller-stein, 1980).

When parent counseling alone is insufficient to promote security and reassurance, filial therapy, in which the parent is trained to interact in a therapeutic-like play session with the child, is recommended. Filial therapy is especially helpful when a child appears to have an ambivalent attachment to the resident parent and an anxious avoidant attachment to the non-resident parent (Robson, 1982).

Individual secondary prevention or treatment programs should be oriented to the child's developmental phase. Individually oriented programs usually are reserved for secondary prevention or treatment of symptomatic children. One exception is the specific high-risk population of children "kidnapped" by their non-custodial parent. Individual counseling is recommended with these children to avoid post-traumatic stress syndrome, which is specific to this group (Terr, 1983).

Early school-aged children seem to respond extremely well to individual play therapy sessions in which issues of the "neurosis of abandonment," as defined by Anthony (1974), can be represented symbolically. Play therapy assists the child in achieving mastery of the stressful situation by repetition of the feared event in the play situation. Short-term play therapy, supported by frequent visiting with the non-resident father, has been extremely effective in reducing boys' anxiety symptoms such as nightmares or fears of robbers, murderers, or monsters.

Clinical Group Counseling Programs

More symptomatic older children and adolescents in clinic settings similar to those in school-based programs appear to respond well to group therapy. Older school-aged children have a tendency to take sides and become embroiled in parental conflict and intractable custody disputes (Robson, 1982). In this situation, family counseling with the unfavored parent and the child or children is imperative. Separate individual counseling for the favored (usually the custodial) parent is recommended in conjunction with family counseling. The custodial parent must be helped to overcome his or her own anger and resentment at the situation and to support the children in a more reality-oriented approach to visitation.

Adolescents who show more severe reactions, such as acting-out through delinquent behavior or promiscuity or marked withdrawal, can benefit from an intensive psychotherapeutic group experience, which may protect them from developing a personality disorder. The creative drama and videotape playback employed in these groups increases the individual's awareness, facilitates expression of fantasy and feelings, and promotes problem solving (Stirtzinger & Robson, 1985).

The video playback technique is unique in that it allows the adolescent to both invest in the process and maintain a safe distance. In light of these adolescents' loss of alliance with parents and their difficulty in forming a treatment alliance, video playback allows each group member to maintain a sense of control. It allows the adolescent to be an active participant either as part of the audience or as the director of a drama. Thus, the individual is permitted to identify with the group in a role function rather than as a dependent patient.

Creative drama can be viewed as a complex form of play. The adolescent is developmentally intermediate between needing the discharge of play and the ability to bind and delay inherent in talking therapy. Creative drama is intermediate between concrete, symbolic play with toys and personal revelation. It permits displacement on the characters.

In my experience with early adolescent clinic groups, family violence seems to be portrayed with increasing frequency. In client dramatizations fathers set themselves on fire and threaten the family with guns, while mothers take overdoses or suddenly abandon the family. There is much sex stereotyping, often linked with violence and anger (Robson, 1986).

Confusion over the cause of separation and the need to blame is captured in plays about family conflicts. In these plays parents frequently are portrayed as fighting over their adolescent's behavior—such as failing to clean up his or her room or not finishing homework or getting into trouble at school. Portrayal of the parents' continued fighting may represent an ambivalent wish to have the parents reunite. Fathers usually are blamed for the break-up; mothers are viewed as stupid and inadequate. Stepmothers typically are seen in the classic Cinderella sense. Parents who remarry often bear another child, so expression of the theme of being "replaced" by an infant also is common in these groups.

The older adolescent clinic groups, in my experience, tend to be more metaphorical. Through discussion these adolescents rework their understanding of their parents' separation, issues of dating, or the loss of a boyfriend or girlfriend. These themes may reflect a greater sense of parents as individuals with needs of their own. Dramatized solutions to the dilemmas, however, are at times magical and childish, with the main character suddenly becoming a famous rock star, lawyer, or journalist—an individual who goes into the world successfully, needing help from no one.

Families sometimes are portrayed as arguing endlessly with no resolution, but later themes frequently involve asking for and receiving help. A loss of discipline may represent the loss of the family as a unit. The adolescent's strivings for independence and identity can be intensified in an attempt to seek the appropriate discipline. A struggle that extends beyond the family unit into the community suggests that the parent (or both parents) needs support and guidance in providing consistency and structure. Individual counseling for the single custodial parent or separate counseling with the same counselor for both the resident and the non-resident parent may be indicated.

CONCLUSION

The percentage of students in elementary, secondary, and even postsecondary schools who recently have experienced a change in their family pattern is increasing. This demands the development of more innovative, preventive programming for the students affected. This programming is vital if counselors are to ward off maladaptive responses in later years and help both adults and children cope with changing family patterns.

REFERENCES

Anthony, E. J. (1974). Children at risk from divorce: A review. In E. J. Anthony & C. Koupernik, *The child in his family* (pp.461–477). New York: Wiley.

Atwell, A. E., Moore, U. S., Nielsen, E., & Levite, Z. (1984). Effects of joint custody on children. *Bulletin of American Academy of Psychiatric Law, 12,* 149–157.

Bane, M. J. (1979). Marital disruption and the lives of children. In G. Levinger & O. C. Moles (Eds.), *Divorce and separation* (pp. 276–286). New York: Basic Books.

Beal, E. W. (1979). Children of divorce: A family systems perspective. *Journal of Social Issues, 35,* 140–154.

Boren, R. (1983). The therapeutic effects of a school-based intervention program for children of the divorced. *Dissertation Abstracts International, 43* (12-A), 3811–3812.

Brady, C. P., Bray, J. H., & Zeeb, L. (1986). Behavior problems of clinic children: Relation to parental marital status, age and sex of child. *American Journal of Orthopsychiatry, 56,* 399–412.

Caplan, G. (1964). *Principles of preventive psychiatry.* New York: Basic Books.

Carter, H., & Glick, P. E. (1976). *Marriage and divorce: A social and economic study.* Cambridge, MA: Harvard University Press.

Chess, S., Thomas, A., Korn, S., Mittleman, M., & Cohen, J. (1983). Early parental attitudes, divorce and separation and adult outcomes: Findings of a longitudinal study. *Journal of American Academy of Child Psychiatry, 22*(1), 47–51.

Cleveland, M., & Irvin, K. (1982). Custody resolution counselling: An alternative intervention. *Journal of Marital & Family Therapy, 8,* 105–111.

Clingempeel, G. W., & Reppucci, N. D. (1982). Joint custody after divorce: Major issues and goals for research. *Psychology Bulletin, 92,* 102–127.

Cooney, T. M., Smyer, M. A., Hagestad, G. O., & Klock, R. (1986). Parental divorce in young adulthood: Some preliminary findings. *American Journal of Orthopsychiatry, 56,* 470–477.

Crossman, S. M., & Adams, G. R. (1980). Divorce, single parenting and child development, *Journal of Psychology, 106,* 205–217.

Despert, J. (1962). *Children of divorce.* New York: Doubleday.

Ellison, E. S. (1983). Issues concerning parental harmony and children's psychosocial adjustment. *American Journal of Orthopsychiatry, 53*(1), 73–80.

Fine, S. (1982). Children in divorce, custody and access situations: The contribution of the mental health professional. *Journal of Child Psychology & Psychiatry, 21,* 353–361.

Freeman, R. (1984). *Children in families experiencing separation and divorce: An investigation of the effects of brief intervention.* Toronto: Family Service Association of Metropolitan Toronto Press.

Gardner, R. A. (1979). Social, legal and therapeutic changes that should lessen the traumatic effects of divorce on children. *Journal of the American Academy of Psychoanalysis, 6,* 231–247.

Goldstein, J., Freud, A., & Solnit, A. J. (1973). *Beyond the best interest of the child.* New York: Free Press.

Guidubaldi, J., & Perry, J. D. (1985). Divorce and mental health sequelae for children: A two year follow-up of a nationwide sample. *Journal of American Academy of Child Psychiatry, 24,* 531–537.

Haber, C. H., Mascari, J. B., & Sanders-Mascari, A. (1983). Family mediation: An idea whose time has come. *Counseling & Human Development, 16*(3), 1–16.

Hetherington, E. M. (1972). Effects of father absence on the personality development in adolescent daughters. *Developmental Psychology, 7,* 313–326.

Hetherington, E. M. (1979). Divorce: A child's perspective. *American Journal of Psychiatry, 34,* 851–858.

Hetherington, E. M., Cox, M., & Cox, R. (1978). The aftermath of divorce. In J. Stevens & M. Mathews (Eds.), *Mother-child relations.* Washington, DC: National Association for the Education of Young Children.

Hetherington, E. M., Cox, M., & Cox, R. (1985). Long term effects of divorce and remarriage on the adjustment of children. *Journal of American Academy of Child Psychiatry, 24,* 518–530.

Ilfeld, F. W., Jr., Ilfeld, H. Z., & Alexander, J. R. (1982). Does joint custody work? A first look at outcome data of relitigation. *American Journal of Psychiatry, 139,* 62–66.

Isaacs, M. B., & Levin, I. R. (1984). Who's in my family? A longitudinal study of drawings of children of divorce. *Journal of Divorce, 7,* 1–20.

Kalter, N. (1977). Children of divorce in an out-patient psychiatric population. *American Journal of Orthopsychiatry, 47,* 40–51.

Kalter, N., Pickar, J., & Lesowitz, M. (1984). School-based developmental facilitation groups for children of divorce: A preventive intervention. *American Journal of Orthopsychiatry, 54,* 613–623.

Kalter, N., & Rembar, J. (1981). The significance of child's age at the time of parental divorce. *American Journal of Orthopsychiatry, 51,* 85–100.

Kessler, S. (1978). Building skills in divorce adjustment groups. *Journal of Divorce, 2,* 209–216.

Kurdek, L. A., Blisk, D., & Siesky, A. (1981). Correlates of children's long-term adjustment to their parents' divorce. *Developmental Psychology, 17,* 565–579.

Lebowitz, M. L. (1983). The organization and utilization of child-focused facility for divorcing, · single-parent and remarried families. *Conciliation Courses Review, 21,* 99–104.

McDermott, J. R. (1970). Divorce and its psychiatric sequelae in children. *Archives of General Psychiatry, 23,* 421–427.

Messinger, L., Walters, K. N., & Freeman, S. J. J. (1978). Preparation for remarriage following divorce: The use of group technique. *American Journal of Orthopsychiatry, 48,* 263–272.

Morrison, J. (1974). Parental divorce as a factor in childhood psychiatric illness. *Comprehensive Psychiatry, 15,* 95–102.

Morrison, K., & Thompson-Guppy, A. (1985). *Stepmothers: Exploring the myth.* Ottawa: Canadian Council on Social Development.

Nehls, N., & Morsenbesser, M. (1980). Joint custody: An exploration of the issues. *Family Process, 19,* 117–125.

Nevins, V. J. (1981). Evaluation of effectiveness of a group treatment intervention with children of divorce. *Dissertation Abstracts International 42* (2-B), 781.

Norton, A. M., & Glick, P. S. (1979). Marital instability in America. In G. Levinger & O. C. Moles (Eds.), *Divorce and separation* (pp.6–19). New York: Basic Books.

Parish, T. S., & Taylor, J. C. (1979). The impact of divorce and subsequent father absence on children's and adolescents' self concepts. *Journal of Youth & Adolescence, 8,* 427–432.

Payne, J. D., & Dimock, J. L. (1983). Legal and psychiatric approaches to marriage breakdown or divorce. *Psychiatric Journal University of Ottawa, 8,* 189–197.

Reinhard, D. (1977). The reaction of adolescent boys and girls to the divorce of their parents. *Journal of Clinical Child Psychology, 6,* 21–23.

Robson, B. (1980). *My parents are divorced, too.* New York: Everest House.

Robson, B. E. (1982). A developmental approach to the treatment of children of divorcing families. In L. Messinger (Ed.), *Therapy with remarriage families* (pp. 59–78). Rockville, MD: Aspen Systems Corp.

Robson, B. (1985). Marriage concepts of older adolescents. *Canadian Journal of Psychiatry, 30,* 169–172.

Robson, B. E. (1986). School-based groups for children and adolescents of divorce. *Canadian Home Economics Journal, 36,* 13–22.

Robson, B., Homatides, G., Johnson, L., & Orlando, F. (1986). *Toronto family study.* Toronto: Toronto Board of Education Publication.

Rubin, L. D., & Price, J. H. (1979). Divorce and its effects on children. *Journal of School Health, 49,* 552–559.

Rutter, M. (1971). Parent-child separation: Psychological effects on the children. *Journal of Child Psychology & Psychology, 12,* 233–260.

Rutter, M. (1979). Invulnerability or why some children are not damaged by stress. In S. J. Shamsie (Ed.), *New directions in children's mental health* (pp. 53–75). New York: Spectrum.

Saucier, J., & Ambert, A. (1986). Adolescents' perception of self and of immediate environment by parental marital status: A controlled study. *Canadian Journal of Psychiatry, 31,* 505–512.

Schoettle, J. C., & Cantwell, D. P. (1980). Children of divorce: Demographic variables, symptoms and diagnoses. *Journal of American Academy of Child Psychiatry, 9,* 453–476.

Statistics Canada. (1983). *Divorce: Law and the family in Canada.* Ottawa: Ministry of Supply & Services.

Steinman, S. (1981). The experience of children in joint custody arrangement: A reprint of a study. *American Journal of Orthopsychiatry, 51,* 403–414.

Stirtzinger, R., & Robson, B. (1985). Videodrama and the observing ego. *Journal of Small Group Behaviour, 16*(4), 539–548.

Tableman, B. (1981). Overview of programs to prevent mental health problems of children. *Public Health Reports, 96,* 38–44.

Terr, L. C. (1983). Childsnatching: A new epidemic of an ancient malady. *Journal of Pediatrics, 103,* 151–156.

Thiessen, J. D., Avery, A. W., & Joanning, H. (1980). Facilitating post divorce adjustment among women: A communication skills training approach. *Journal of Divorce, 4,* 4–22.

Visher, E. B., & Visher, J. S. (1982). Step families in the 1980's. In L. Messinger (Ed)., *Therapy with remarriage families* (pp. 105–119). Rockville, MD: Aspen Systems Corp.

Wallerstein, J. S. (1980). The impact of divorce on children. *Psychiatric Clinics of North America, 3,* 455–468.

Wallerstein, J. S. (1984). Children of divorce: Preliminary report of a ten year follow-up of young children. *American Journal of Orthopsychiatry, 54,* 444–458.

Wallerstein, J. S., & Kelly, J. B. (1980). *Surviving the breakup: How children and parents cope with divorce.* New York: Basic Books.

Warren, N. J., & Amara, I. A. (1984). Educational groups for single parents: The parenting after divorce programs. *Journal of Divorce, 8*(2), 79–96.

Weiss, R. S. (1975). *Marital separation.* New York: Basic Books.

Wilkinson, G. S., & Bleck, R. T. (1976). Children's divorce groups. *Elementary School Guidance & Counseling, 11,* 205–213.

Bonnie Robson, M. D., is affiliated with the C. M. Hincks Treatment Centre, a psychiatric service for children and adolescents, in Toronto, Ontario.

8

Family Mediation: An Idea Whose Time Has Come

Charles H. Huber, J. Barry Mascari, and Aviva Sanders-Mascari

Family mediation is one of the most rapidly growing movements today for facilitating more favorable family relations. Its growth may parallel society's search for a new sense of community where the healthy survival of the family, in whatever form, takes precedence over the search for individual satisfaction. Or perhaps the increased use of legal action in recent years accompanied by the seemingly constant display of intimate family concerns in the public arena has pushed society too far (Vroom, Fassett, & Wakefield, 1982). Whatever the basis, professionals and the public alike have a growing realization that family mediation can resolve family conflicts in an equitable and more sensitive manner.

Mediation is a form of negotiation and conflict resolution in which the disputing parties are aided by a third party in making mutual decisions. The mediator does not exert decision-making power on the issue(s) in dispute. As such, family mediation maintains decision-making power with those it most directly affects— the family members themselves. It fosters a cooperative sharing of power that results in positively transformed rather than negatively severed relationships. The attraction of the mediation process for settling family disputes is obvious and is being applied to a wide range of issues throughout the family life cycle. Some of these issues are briefly identified and illustrated in Figure 1.

THEORETICAL FOUNDATIONS

Family mediation draws practitioners from a wide spectrum of professional backgrounds. Each has contributed somewhat differently to the practice of family mediation as it exists today. Coogler (1978) described family mediation as "an art in its early stages of development" (p. 79). The greater portion of research efforts on conflict resolution have been carried out only in the last 15 years, and family mediation is still somewhat of a pioneering application of that research.

FIGURE 1 Some Issues in Family Mediation

Mediation Along the Family Life Cycle

Pre-Marital Mediation
Mediators are helping couples draw up marriage agreements prior to the ceremony. This "ounce of prevention" can help ensure a more stable marriage.

Disabled and Handicapped
Stress often occurs in families caring for disabled or handicapped members. Counselors are using mediation to resolve some of the resulting conflicts.

Teenage Pregnancy
Struggles often arise over situations involving unmarried pregnant teenagers. Mediation can assist in resolving the conflicts between parents and child.

Homosexuals
Gay couples ending a relationship often have many of the same conflicts that divorcing couples do. The legal system does not necessarily provide a forum, so mediation can be valuable in resolving disputes.

Unmarried Cohabitants
At least one campus mediation service handles disputes between nonmarried couples who live together and seek a solution other than separation.

Teenagers and Parents
Numerous conflicts arise between parents and their adolescent children. Parent-teenager disputes often involve power struggles, and mediation can help restore relative peace to these households.

Runaways
Mediation is being used to bring together runaways and their families, and to resolve their conflicts out of court. Mediators are also helping to resolve family differences caused by juvenile drug abusers.

Relocation

New comprehensive relocation services use mediation to resolve the conflicts brought to the surface by a family move, such as problems related to dual careers, care of dependents, adolescent anxieties and emotional problems.

Domestic Violence

Mediation is helpful in the area of spouse abuse, particularly with first-time abusers.

Separation and Divorce

Property settlements and support payments are often the two areas of greatest contention in separation and divorce disputes. Mediation helps the couple to separate emotional issues from financial decisions.

Custody and Visitation

Mediation allows for more flexible and finely tailored child custody arrangements than those resulting from the adversarial process. Couples often reach cooperative joint custody agreements.

Retirement

Mediation services can help settle disputes at retirement time, such as when a husband might want to move to Florida just when his wife is embarking on a new career.

The Elderly vs. Their Middle-Aged Children

With the elderly population increasing, more and more conflicts are arising when older people can no longer care for themselves. Mediators help families to reach decisions about institutional versus home care.

Wills and Estate Planning

Mediation is useful when families disagree over estate plans. It also cuts costs when family members are contesting the execution of a relative's will.

Although family mediation as an identifiable professional practice is a relatively new phenomenon, many mental health and legal professionals claim that they have been doing it for some time. To a certain extent, they are correct. Therapists who assist families in restructuring during times of change, conflict, or crisis may be involved in a form of mediation. Those utilizing problem-solving strategies or task-oriented interventions are especially likely to crisscross the seemingly ambiguous boundary between therapy and mediation.

Court judges in pre-trial conferences often actively advocate that adversary family members and their attorneys attempt to arrive at a mutually amicable agreement outside of court, if possible. Lawyers may be operating in a mediating capacity when they agree that a proposed settlement is fair and each believes it to be in the best interest of his or her client. In these contexts, however, the professional has a role that takes precedence over his or her role as a mediator, and the mediating process is simply a tactic to further the goals of another process (Girdner, 1983). The actual dynamics of family mediation are specific unto themselves when a professional is engaged as a mediator for the sole purpose of mediation.

Conflict Resolution vs. Conflict Cessation

Mediation involves the resolution of conflict, not merely the cessation of it. Cessation of conflict is frequently mistaken for conflict resolution. Consider the following example:

> Sarah, 15 years old and pregnant, had strong personal convictions about abortion and believed it to be morally wrong. Her parents—actually more concerned about what the community would think of *them* as Sarah's condition became increasingly evident—provided her with many reasons why an abortion was the "best" alternative. Sarah, dependent and unassertive, followed their advice. Not really agreeing with that course of action, she later underwent a long period of therapy to deal with the guilt and depression she experienced as a result.

Without full and mutual participation in the decision-making process by all involved, actual resolution of a dispute may not be achieved. Some family members, like Sarah, are overwhelmed by others' seemingly more powerful positions. Often, finding themselves in a disadvantageous position, individuals simply withdraw—but fully intend to resume the controversy when conditions are more favorable. Others respond by passively accepting whatever terms are thrust upon them, with absolutely no expectation of complying with them. In none of these instances is resolution reached.

Decision making can be viewed as an unequal, superior-inferior relationship wherein one party (the superior) decides, while another (the inferior) is given little or no role in the process—only the outcome; or, alternatively, as a mutual venture in which all concerned contribute to the process and take responsibility in any outcome decided upon (Huber, 1981). Mediation seeks to make decision making "mutual" and its results mutually acceptable. This has a dramatic impact upon the way in which decisions are made and adhered to, as well as the emotional after-effects experienced.

Coogler (1978) proposed that six conditions be present for true conflict resolution to occur:

1. The physical well-being of each party involved is maintained during negotiations and in the resolution reached.
2. Each party maintains its feelings of self-worth during the negotiating process and in the resolution itself.
3. All involved parties are respected and tolerated as persons, but with the understanding that this need not imply approval of others' morals or values.
4. All relevant facts, available options, and technical information are considered and used in reaching any resolution.
5. The consequences of each available option are considered by all parties before any resolution is agreed upon.
6. The resolution that is reached is agreed to by all parties even though other choices were available.

The Structures of Family Mediation

Coogler further proposed that these six conditions suggest a specific structure that fosters resolution of conflict rather than merely controlling or ending it. He identified a coherent integration of three separate structures as being the essence of family mediation (Coogler, 1978): the procedural structure, the value structure, and the psychological structure.

The Procedural Structure

The procedural structure gives order to the mediation process. It presents all involved with a clear and common framework from which to function. It provides the means by which the factual and technical information needed for assessing alternatives becomes available to family members. The procedural structure identifies issues to be considered, schedules regular times for negotiations, establishes a neutral territory in which mediation is conducted, and gives the mediator the power to see that all parties follow agreed-to rules. Coogler (1978) cautioned that the procedural structure be kept simple so that family members need not devote excessive efforts to understanding it or, conversely, be encouraged by its complexity and resulting confusion to manipulate it to their advantage.

The Value Structure

The value structure establishes basic ethical standards of fairness to be followed during mediation. Family members should be told that these standards constitute the framework of an elementary sense of fairness. The standards cannot be expected to satisfy everyone's personal idiosyncratic conceptualizations of what is just. The intent is to project a common value structure that can be comprehended by all concerned and seen as fairly applicable to them rather than to try to provide a procedure for meeting every test of fairness—which would be fruitless.

The Psychological Structure

The psychological structure creates a setting wherein the physical and emotional needs of family members are sufficiently met so they can make optimal use of their decision-making capabilities. The mediator's understanding of group and family dynamics, and accompanying skills for creating a favorable working environment, provide the basis for the psychological structure. The procedural and value structures also contribute significantly to an appropriate psychological structure by creating a context that facilitates a fair and equitable resolution of conflict.

Mediation Models

Mediation as a means of conflict resolution has been employed since the earliest recorded history. Traditionally, the extended family has been the primary mediating institution. Similarly, the church has played a large role in helping families deal with internal conflicts. The local minister, rabbi, or parish priest has been called upon frequently to help family members mutually resolve problems. Family friends likewise have often been a source of objective advice and support.

Although these and similar forms of mediation have been present, their informal character has facilitated little objective evaluation and scientific development of the process. Examination of the professional literature reveals surprisingly little information. In an analytic review of research on the process of mediation, Wall (1981) stated that "mediation remains understudied, less than understood, and unrefined" (p. 157). The emphasis has been on the characteristics and techniques of mediators and on the content of disputes rather than on the process itself (Girdner, 1983).

In most forms of mediation, practices have been established largely by the "unwritten law" of custom rather than specified procedures. Most mediators have learned by "on-the-job experience," and most have come to mediation from another field quite by accident. Mediators who have developed their own style have written about their experience in an anecdotal fashion, but research still lags (Coogler, Weber, & McKenny, 1979).

Gulliver (1979) proposed a cyclical and developmental model for understanding the process of mutual decision making in negotiated settlements. This model provides one concentrated focus that ties together the common threads used to define varying forms of interaction as being mediation. The cyclical aspects of Gulliver's model refer to the information sharing and learning that take place during the course of family mediation. The developmental aspects illustrate an overview of the family mediation process as it progresses from the time at which a disagreement becomes a dispute to its final outcome.

Family members come to mediation with often vague and inconsistent expectations that must be continually revised throughout the course of mediation efforts. Each member is expected to convey information about his or her demands, desires, strengths, and weaknesses, as well as to process similar forms of data from the other members and the mediator. Throughout this repetitive process of information exchange, family members and the mediator must learn to progressively adjust their expectations and preferences in order to make clearly understood and common choices. Thus, *mediation is a dynamic interactive process that facilitates change through clarification and discovery* (Girdner, 1983). This cycle repeats itself over and over as mediation proceeds from beginning to end.

A Typical Sequence of Mediation

When family members elect to come to mediation, they are mutually recognizing some dispute they need to work on together to resolve. Shortly, however, a shift from coordinated to antagonistic positions occurs as family members move from agreeing on mediation to disagreeing about the issues in dispute. This can involve disagreement about the issues themselves or the order in which they are to be considered. With the mediator's assistance the family members seek agreement regarding the boundaries of their dispute and the agenda to be followed. The mediator explains that it is his or her responsibility to give them information about various options so they can make more informed decisions. The mediator stresses, however, that the final outcomes will be of their own making.

Agreement on the agenda is normally followed by an antagonistic phase wherein family members communicate, often in rather extreme terms, their preferences and present positions. This is not a period during which solutions are considered but, rather, a phase in which symbolic issues and declarations are used to emphasize personally held positions. These can include open or veiled threats, or absolutistic statements about what one is willing to accept. The mediator's interventions are critically important in this phase. He or she must identify underlying overlapping interests and points of agreement. Otherwise family members may reach an impasse, refusing to move from an entrenched position.

For example, the mediator might acknowledge family members' mutual concern about constant arguing and fighting and ask them if they would like to know more about the potential future effects of their continuing conflict and possibly consider the types of arrangements that have created more cooperative circumstances for other families. In this manner, the emphasis is shifted from individual personalities and positions to the shared problem. Specific potential outcomes are raised and discussed. As family members are helped to further clarify their preferences and positions, they revise them and begin brainstorming various possibilities. Family members are urged to consider options in terms of what they would perceive to be realistically workable for them. *The mediator clarifies communication, identifies overlapping interests, and reinforces cooperative interactions.*

Frequently, the mediator may have to refocus a problem. Before actual agreement can be reached, family members, with the mediator's assistance, must establish a range of acceptable outcomes, further clarify the more difficult issues, and examine possible trade-offs. During the final bargaining, the mediator proposes suggestions that would lead to an integrated outcome. A positive momentum evolves as successful coordination and agreements accumulate, leading family members to see that a mutually acceptable resolution is possible. The final agreement is followed by closure to the mediation process.

Throughout this process the mediator's role is that of "an advocate of the process of discussion and bargaining rather than an advocate of a particular settlement" (Trombetta, 1982, p. 69). The mediation process seeks to facilitate the orientation of family members and their efforts toward one another in arriving at a mutual solution. It helps them "achieve a new and shared perception of their relationship, a perception that will redirect their attitudes and dispositions toward one another" (Fuller, 1971, p. 325).

PREPARING TO MEDIATE—CHANGING HATS

Mediation is not psychotherapy. It may, of course, be therapeutic in many ways, but it should have no pretense of providing therapy. The mediator must learn to "change hats" from his or her primary function (as psychologist, counselor, family therapist, police officer, etc.) to that of mediator. Unlike clinical counseling or psychotherapy, *mediation is a nonexploratory process.* The mediator's role is not to change a family relationship but, rather, to help members resolve the concrete issues that have brought them to mediation (Vroom, 1983).

The mediator should keep in mind that his or her goal is to help family members reach *their* goal. Irrational beliefs, minor pathology, or neurotic behavior may become obvious, but these must be left alone unless they are interfering in the mediation process. The subtle art of intervening in disruptive interchanges among family members as a mediator and not as, for example, a trained mental health professional often takes time to master. Without this competency, mediators can get lost in issues and never facilitate family members in achieving a solution.

Circumstances calling for therapeutic intervention are best approached through referral for concurrent treatment by a mental health professional. Thus, the mediator might share the following with the family members:

"My role is that of a mediator and not a therapist. It is my responsibility, however, to provide you with objective feedback that might be helpful to you during this mediation as well as in your future. For some reason, you all are having a great deal of difficulty objectively hearing what each other is saying. Emotions seem too often to be getting out of control. It might be best to seek the additional assistance of a mental health or family counselor."

Before seeking to mediate any family dispute, acquiring some formal training is advisable. The effective mediator must be competent in many skills. The mediator must be able to train and facilitate family members in negotiation—focusing, clarifying, bargaining, and compromising on important issues. Being able to create open, receptive communication channels is critical. Family members also must be aided in identifying general principles rather than simply specifying their demands.

Allowing family members to state fixed demands without understanding the general principles or underlying motives behind the demands results in "blind bargaining." In contrast, *principled negotiation* helps all sides see and understand others' positions and viewpoints and the real issues involved. These real issues are usually not what family members are actually disputing but, rather, an underlying principle of personal involvement on each participant's part—who is right, who is being treated unfairly, the desire to win, threats to personal status, prestige, or superiority (Huber, 1981). Increased give-and-take and real resolution can take place only if these principles are brought to awareness and considered. *Getting to Yes* (Fisher & Ury, 1982) is an excellent source explaining the key points of principled negotiation.

Family members are often heard to say, "Why do we need to mediate with you? It seems like a simple enough process." In a gentle way, family members should be told that if they had the skills to work out their differences on their own, they would not need formal mediation assistance. The mediator should stress to the family that mediation is not only an isolated problem-solving experience but also a training program in which skills are being learned for future use. In one research investigation of family mediation efforts, the conclusion noted as most critical was "participants' increased confidence about their ability to solve problems given a new orientation for resolving future concerns on their own" (Pearson & Thoennes, 1982).

An initial contact with a family is not the time to consider "changing hats." Advanced preparation in both attitude and skills application is necessary before taking on the role of a mediator. Readings, workshops, association with an experienced mentor, and participation in a peer supervision group are ideal ways of acquiring the knowledge base and mind set to facilitate the family mediation process.

THE MEDIATION PROCESS

The mediation process we follow in our work with families has 10 steps:

1. Referral.
2. Orientation and clarification.
3. Identification of principles and prioritization of demands.
4. Negotiations: Initial demands.
5. Negotiations: Early bargaining.
6. Negotiations: Investigating options.

7. Negotiations: Narrowing differences and trading.
8. Tentative agreement and revisions.
9. Memorandum of understanding.
10. Termination and follow-up.

Mediation is a fluid process, and the steps presented here can represent, but do not necessarily correspond to, specific sessions. Normally, more than one step of the process is accomplished at a session, depending upon the specific portion of the mediation involved. Also, the chronology of the process may be changed occasionally to meet the individual needs of certain families. Although a universal process of mediation can be described, the process should be applied idiosyncratically to individual families as it will be affected by the particular needs of a specific family (Haynes, 1982).

Referral

The typical mediation case is normally referred from the court, an involved community agency, or knowledgeable professional colleague. The initial contact with a family is usually by telephone. The mediator should be prepared to provide a brief overview of mediation without going into great depth—especially if only one family member is initiating the contact. If this occurs, the mediator should request to speak to all involved parties *before* the intake meeting. In this way, the idea of mutuality and balance is established at the very onset (Haynes, 1982). An initial screening should be conducted by telephone so that a more relevant referral, if indicated, can be made immediately. If mediation appears appropriate, the first appointment is set.

Orientation and Clarification

Orientation and clarification take place in the initial intake session. The mediator's responsibility in this session focuses on a number of tasks: establishing his or her credibility, setting a positive tone, explaining the process and the mediator's role, clarifying family members' expectations, establishing empathy, and determining participants' readiness for mediation efforts (Haynes, 1981).

Family mediation is still relatively new to referring professionals and the public alike. Therefore, the mediator must fully educate family members about the mediation process. After sharing the scope, function, goals, and other pertinent details of the mediation process before it formally begins, the mediator should request that family members sign an "Engagement Letter" outlining the parameters of the process, as well as arrangements relating to fees, co-mediators, and the like. Copies should be distributed to all concerned parties to further ensure everyone's understanding of the process.

After introducing the Engagement Letter, the mediator must help family members become aware of the family issues that have heretofore gone unaddressed.

This ability to help the family "focus" is an important skill that enables family members to interpret their current conflict as a potential reflection or symptom of more serious dysfunction. Often, families come to mediation as a "premature referral." Too much dysfunction is present for mediation to effectively proceed. In cases like this, the mediator should recommend that the family seek therapeutic assistance either concurrently with, or prior to, beginning mediation efforts.

Engaging reluctant family members can create another issue that must be addressed in the intake session. The mediator must "sell" the positive and immediate, as well as the long-term problem-solving potential that mediation can have. Many persons entering mediation have a history of poor or ineffective experiences with professional "helpers." The family members have been termed resistant, blamed for lack of progress, or led to feel responsible and guilty for not achieving any concrete solutions to their problems. Providing a positive connotation through reframing the current conflict ("This crisis is a sure signal that your family wants positive change to take place") often helps to draw in all the family members.

> Marie and her mother were reluctant to participate in mediation—very angry and hostile toward each other—knowing that nothing up to this time had worked for them. Both expected further failure and felt helpless. Getting basic information and identifying each party's beliefs about what was happening was impossible because the other would openly disagree and begin yelling. The mediator met with each of them individually and suggested that the conflict and their responses to it were most helpful in calling attention to the problems at hand. The mediator also "joined" empathically with each of them, explaining that "it must be difficult to live with (Mom/Marie), and you have done an admirable job. . . . "
>
> This family had experienced extreme conflict, with Marie throwing scissors at her mother just prior to the session. Development of "ground rules" was imperative. Using the leverage of the Juvenile Justice System (and lock-up), a simple agreement for no violence, with built-in options such as punching the bed, was created. The mediator placed the demand for no violence, and the parties agreed. They were relieved of the sense of losing that they would have felt from giving in to one another. The mediator accomplished this by going from room to room, meeting with Marie and her mother, separately, shuttling information back and forth.

During the intake session the mediator also must elicit initial clarification of issues. The mediator should listen carefully to all the family members and actively question the relevant information presented. For example, in working with Marie and her mother, the mother had a series of complaints about Marie coming home late, swearing, staying on the telephone, and other "smaller" issues. If the mediator were to similarly focus on these smaller events, the major issues would be missed. In this case, these issues related to the disregard of rules and basic challenges to the mother's power.

Successful orientation and clarification in the intake session will therefore establish:

—a win-win atmosphere with no "bad guy."
—an atmosphere of equality, but with a clear sense of the mediator's power to prevent imbalance in the participants' bargaining abilities.

—a sense that the mediator emphasized and believes that *each* family member has valid, legitimate demands.

—the belief that resolution is possible.

—a clearer understanding of the major issues involved.

—a summary of agreements or beliefs common to all parties.

Identification of Principles and Prioritization of Demands

During the intake session specific issues were identified. If these were to remain the focus of mediation, a stalemate would likely occur quickly. Basic principles underlying these issues must be brought to awareness if any movement is to occur when negotiations begin in the next step of the process. In addition, each family member must develop a sense of priorities. Frequently, family members employ a linear priority system in which every action carries the same weight.

> Marie's mother would seek to ground Marie or even call the police if Marie came in late, played her stereo too loud, or visited a friend whom her mother disapproved of. Whatever the offense, the mother's reaction was the same.

In identifying principles, the mediator seeks to facilitate family members' comprehension of their basic belief systems and the principles that guide them. Before beginning any in-depth discussion of demands, the mediator assists family members in formulating principled demands. Initial complaints are reconsidered with a goal of identifying general principles underlying them—the result being more relevant, pointed demands. Table 1 illustrates this process, as experienced in part by Marie and her mother.

TABLE 1
The Formulation of Principled Demands

From Complaints ➡️	To Principles ➡️	To Demands
Mrs. S.: I want Marie to stop disobeying me. She totally disregards every rule I establish. I want her to come in early, clean her room, do what I say . . .	What is most important is that Marie is safe. Also, it is important that she know that I am her parent. Her room is not really that significant to me.	Marie should call me if she will be late. I want her to acknowledge that I am her parent and she must listen to me.
Marie: I hate my mother. All she wants to do is put restrictions on me and not allow me to grow up and have my own friends. I want to make my own rules.	I think I'm old enough to participate in making my own rules and should be allowed to pick my friends.	Mom should let me discuss rules instead of assuming that I have to agree with her because she is older and is my mother.

When specific demands based on principles have been adequately identified, each party must rank them. This prioritization is done individually and in private, although the mediator's assistance is strongly urged. The list of initial demands can be substantial. It may present a picture so imposing to other family members (in the upcoming step of the process) that they immediately feel a sense of defeat. The mediator might help by discussing with each family member the issues being prioritized—before their presentation—making sure that only major issues are noted, with a focus on underlying general principles.

Family members who have a prioritized list of principled demands will be better able to negotiate. They can enter negotiations with a clearer sense of what is important to them, what they *must* have to be satisfied, and what they are willing to give up. This knowledge encourages active participation and increases the probability that individual family members will be satisfied with their final agreement.

Negotiations: Initial Demands

"Negotiations" as an overall descriptor constitutes the next four steps of the mediation process, beginning with negotiations regarding initial demands. The various components are difficult to separate in terms of actual time and number of sessions. These portions of the process may repeat themselves throughout the entire process until the Memorandum of Understanding is firmly agreed to.

Before beginning each session—during the negotiations' portions of the process especially—the mediator must summarize and recap for family members the events of the preceding session and highlight any agreements made. Following this opening ritual, movement directly into specific negotiations' concerns flows much easier.

> "During our previous session, Mrs. S., you said that you wanted ___ from Marie and, Marie, you said you believed that. . . . " (An agreement was reached during that session, so the mediator also highlights the points of agreement, providing a sense of positive movement and accomplishment.) "In addition, Marie acknowledged that she realizes you (Mrs. S.) do worry about her and agreed with you that she will make a telephone call when she is going to be late."

In considering initial demands, each family member is given a limited time to present his or her list of demands that have been compiled privately (usually with the mediator's assistance) in the previous step. Even though each party knows his or her own priority order, the demands should be presented with equal importance. During this period, the mediator should request clarification of any demands that generate puzzled looks from fellow family members, prevent immediate discussion of any demand at this point in time, and block "put downs" by one party toward another's demands. For reference purposes, the mediator might list the demands, in simplified form as they are presented, on a blackboard or large newsprint so all can look at them simultaneously.

After the demands are presented and listed for all to see, the mediator should help family members take note of similar demands or common areas of concern. Different views about the same issue will present conflicts that must be addressed. By focusing on the principles of each family member underlying his or her demands, greater movement and flexibility can be attained. In the case of initial demands presented by Marie and her mother, the mediator rearranged the initial list of demands, placing similar issues across from each other to better focus on the degree of difference between Marie and her mother on the same issue. Relevant principles motivating Marie and her mother in their demands were also requested and noted at this time. This revised list is illustrated in Table 2.

In the case of parent-child conflicts, the process of identifying accompanying principles often has a remarkably positive effect on each party. Children, especially, gain from hearing the beliefs their parents hold about issues or demands that

TABLE 2
Initial Demands and Underlying Principles

Mrs. S.	Marie
• Stay away from "undesirable" friend. (An adult friend might sway your opinion/ challenge my authority; *I* want to be your friend.)	• Visit friend Mom dislikes. (An adult friend can give me different ideas about areas I'm uncomfortable talking about with Mom.)
• Call if you are going to be late. (I worry that something might have happened to you.)	
• Follow *my* rules. (Mothers are supposed to be the ultimate authority; kids should listen.)	• Participate in making rules. (I'm old enough to have a say in rules that apply to me.)
• Keep your room clean. (Sloppy rooms are not good; you need to learn to be clean as a kid.)	
• No telephone calls after 10 p.m. (Late calls wake up the rest of the family.)	• Telephone use any time. (I like to talk to my friends about dates, etc. If I have to be in for curfew, at least I can use the phone.)
• Go to school every day and get good grades. (Marie oversleeps; if she keeps going this way, she won't amount to anything.)	• Stop being nagged about grades and school. (No matter what I do, it isn't good enough; I like school but hate to get up.)
• Come in at stated times: 9 p.m. weekdays and 10 p.m. weekends. (I'm responsible for your safety; something might happen at night. I worry.)	• Come in 10 p.m. weekdays and be allowed out later on weekends and special occasions. (When my brother was my age, he had later hours; my friends stay out until this time.)

have been longstanding areas of conflict. Frequently, this simple sharing in itself can unlock a diehard dispute by "demystifying" the importance of calling home or getting good grades in school.

Once the initial list of demands is prepared, recorded, and rearranged by the mediator, if appropriate, family members are ready to bargain, based on the priorities that were individually established in the previous step of the mediation process.

Negotiations: Early Bargaining

Although family members are called upon to "bargain" daily, they surprisingly are often ill prepared to do so with each other. Children bargain with their friends over what games they will play and activities they will mutually participate in. Parents commonly bargain at the local fruit and vegetable stand or discuss what is a fair price for a used car in a give-and-take process similar to mediation. Yet, this procedure within the family is frequently "foreign."

At this point in the mediation, the mediator may have to demonstrate how to bargain. Especially in families with intense conflict or longstanding mistrust on the part of all parties, some "leading" must be done. Borrowing a technique from labor mediation, the mediator meets with each party separately. During these individually oriented sessions, the mediator plays each party off the other(s) by "speculating" about what the other side might accept, remembering, of course, to not influence family members toward a direction they may truly not want. The major function of this phase of the mediation process is to create enough movement and reference to specific principles that family members will develop their own suggestions as to how and what they will proceed to bargain.

Negotiations: Investigating Options

All through the mediation process, the mediator has actually been helping family members focus on potential options available to solve their concerns. Now that family members have identified the items of most importance and the personal principles behind them, made their initial demands, and begun to consider how they will bargain, they have effectively narrowed their own options. They are now locked into working around specific problems and finding solutions that have previously eluded them. At this point, potential options are investigated in a way that will enable family members to narrow their differences and trade, using the options available to them.

A common deficiency among families in conflict is their failure to investigate or create different options for resolving mutual problems. One means mediators have for preparing family members to expand their outlook is to instill the belief that what has not worked in the past will not work now. Parents, in particular, hold on to methods that are ineffective or inappropriate with their children. The mediator can demonstrate, through questioning, that their present mode of interacting is not working; otherwise they would not be here. Staying with that mode will only continue to undermine cooperative family relationships and lead to further disagreements on additional issues.

New options for resolving differences must be developed and explored. If family members describe themselves as being stuck or continue to consider only one or two ideas, the mediator must tactfully probe these blockages. Questions that focus back on the principle behind the demand often lead family members to their own discovery of new options; for example, "Are you telling me that this is the *only* way to solve this problem?" The mediator should encourage family members to create a long list of options, no matter how ridiculous. "Brainstorming"—simply listing potential options to be evaluated later—can be valuable in leading to mutually acceptable ideas.

Many times family members stop themselves from creating options—not because they do not exist or cannot be identified but because members would rather not see these options exist. Confronting family members who withdraw into a "turtle-in-the-shell" style of problem solving will encourage them to consider new options even if they don't like them. For example, with reference to Table 2, Marie's mother originally acted as if the only option available to prevent late-night calls from Marie's friends from interrupting the family's sleep were to make a rule: "No phone use after 10 p.m." She was unwilling to come up with alternative solutions. The mediator confronted her inflexible stance. The list eventually developed (see Table 3) might contain a number of presently unacceptable alternatives, but it did encourage her toward more creative thinking.

This creativeness often is translated into a willingness to develop increased flexibility, and it frequently gives rise to humor stemming from the absurd possibilities available. Embroiled in conflict, many family members take everything,

TABLE 3
Some Brainstorming Options For Phone Use

Problem	Current Option	Creative Options
Late telephone calls interrupt family's sleep.	No phone use after 10 p.m.	1. Make only outgoing calls. 2. Put phone in Marie's room. 3. Get bell silencer on phone. 4. Store phone in insulated bag. 5. Remove phone from home. 6. Put light instead of bell on phone. 7. Buy family members headsets to block sound.

regardless of how insignificant or minor, with great seriousness. Being able to laugh at what they previously saw as serious can indicate real progress.

When an impasse exists regarding options, the mediator can utilize self-disclosure and appropriately mention similar situations that he or she has worked with in the past: "One family I mediated with had a similar stalemate and came up with. . . . " Showing how other families have resolved their disputes makes family members feel that they are not alone. Framed properly, suggestions of this nature can facilitate identification with the case example and learning by modeling. If the mediator cannot think of a relevant previous example to propose, a hypothetical one created to fit the situation is appropriate.

Homework assignments can be another helpful tool for investigating options. Assigning family members the task of writing at least five options each for solving a particular problem usually results in a list that did not exist before. If family members decide to work together to create options, this is most facilitative to the mediation. Other family members have consulted friends or other relatives in search of options. These interchanges, too, facilitate cooperative problem-solving interactions. The mediator must emphasize that homework is *required*. By forcing family members to consider doing something they may find distasteful, they are not choosing to do it; the mediator is "directing" them to do it. Participants may use this as an excuse to give up some of their responsibility. But they can regain it when they complete their assignment.

Negotiations: Narrowing Differences and Trading

Family members usually want to achieve their objectives without giving up anything. The work of the previous steps of the process—setting priorities, early bargaining considerations, and investigating options—should have caused participants to begin to think that if any agreement is to be realized, they must give up some things or, at the very least, change their expectations. Now is the time to make these necessary concessions.

For example, parents often expect their children to change while they themselves refuse to give ground on issues. Gentle reminders such as, "You've been living in less than desirable conditions with your daughter, and I'm sure you're ready to try something new" can help create a more positive mind set. In more difficult cases, the mediator can meet individually with family members, encouraging movement by carrying options back and forth and suggesting a "deal" for them. Although this is a "gamey" technique, it is often quite successful.

With Marie and her mother, neither would budge unless the major objectives of both were met. It was suggested alternatively to both mother and daughter that if they were to accept one of the other's first-priority items, the other would be willing to give in on a demand.

Most trading is done, and resultant trade-offs made and accepted, in "package" form. In focusing on singular areas of disagreement, settling a dispute is often much more difficult than considering total packages. The package that Marie and her mother arrived at is illustrated in Table 4.

Tentative Agreement and Revisions

Once family members agree to a tentative package, a rough draft of the areas of agreement can be set forth. Presenting the family members with a typewritten draft on which they can make corrections, and eventually sign, is preferable to simply summarizing the agreement by reading it to them. (Younger children, too, should be given a written copy even though they may need the mediator's assistance in reviewing it.)

Having tangible evidence of their efforts to review and critique provides participants with a sense of accomplishment and power. They are now taking responsibility for refining what their agreement will actually be like. Any concerns raised in this step of the process are dealt with by recycling to relevant previous procedures. Once this step is completed, the formal Memorandum of Understanding can be prepared.

Memorandum of Understanding

Preparing a written document of what the family members have already agreed to is relatively easy. The Memorandum of Understanding should be written in simple, clear language and at a level that all family members can readily understand. They will likely have to refer to the agreement in the future and ought to be able to understand it completely without assistance. Incorporating the language the family members themselves have used to characterize their problems and solutions is usually best. This is especially important for keeping children involved in

TABLE 4
A Trading Package

Mrs. S.'s Priorities	Marie's Priorities
1. Follow my rules.	1. Visit friend Mom dislikes.
2. Call if you'll be late.	2. Use telephone anytime.
3. Go to school every day.	3. Stop being nagged about school.
4. Don't be late; come in at stated times.	4. Revised curfew: Weekends.

Concessions by Mrs. S.	Concessions by Marie
— Stay away from friend.	— Participate in making rules.
— Keep room clean.	— 10 p.m. curfew weekdays.
— No telephone calls after 10 p.m.	
— 10 p.m. curfew on weekends.	

understanding and maintaining the agreement (Wixted, 1982). Also, by keeping language plain and simple and items behaviorally oriented, family members have a yardstick by which to measure compliance and, ultimately, the success of their agreement.

Although the mediator and the family members know that the document is an *agreement,* the mediator is advised to use the term "Memorandum of Understanding." Family members tend to see the final agreement more significantly when it has this formalized title. In addition, if the mediation is part of a court-sanctioned program or agency, this is the preferred descriptor for the document presented to a judge for approval.

Figure 2 gives an example of a Memorandum of Understanding. Note that a re-mediation clause is added to the basic agreement. This simple clause can prevent future disputes from adding to an already clogged court calendar or overwhelmed social service agency client load. Reentry into mediation efforts forms a preventive first step.

Termination and Follow-up

Family members who have signed the Memorandum of Understanding have worked out with the mediator and each other a most significant agreement—to seek new paths of conflict resolution. As noted earlier, the most important part of this process might simply be learning and experiencing the process itself. Agreements are only as good as the family members' willingness to adhere to them. The mediator should monitor agreements for a time, by telephone, brief follow-up "progress" sessions, or mail, as a gentle reminder that the mediator (and system) is watching and really cares about the ultimate outcome of the mediation.

ETHICS AND ETHICAL ISSUES

Even though family mediation services are becoming increasingly available, certain basic questions remain (Vroom, 1983). How does a consumer find a qualified mediator? How do members of the mental health or legal profession refer a family to a mediator they know is competent? Currently, no licensing or certification requirements for family mediators are in force to provide any objective clues to a mediator's skill level.

Without any organized certifying procedure, both consumers and professionals making referrals would do well to consider a code of ethics to which a mediator might subscribe. Codification of principles of ethics is an important benchmark in the development of any professional field. It speaks to the willingness of professionals to take responsibility for protecting their clientele and, equally important, it defines the boundaries, standards, and legitimate purposes of any endeavors entered into (Margulies, 1982). We adhere to a code adapted from the Canons of Ethics developed by the New Jersey Council on Divorce Mediation (Margulies,

FIGURE 2   *Memorandum of Understanding*

MEMORANDUM OF UNDERSTANDING

This agreement by and between Mrs. S. and her daughter, Marie, was developed with full knowledge and participation by both of us on May 19, 1983. We have developed this agreement as outlined below to reduce conflict and continue to enjoy the good parts of our relationship. We agree to the following:

1. Marie will be allowed to choose and visit her own friends. Mrs. S's prior approval is required for overnight stays with friends.

2. Marie agrees to discourage her friends from calling her at home after 10 pm and before 7 am. She will be allowed to make outgoing calls during these times.

3. Marie agrees to call home if she will be late. If she does not call, her curfew will be shortened for the following night, at a ratio of two (2) minutes for every one (1) minute she was late.

4. Mrs. S. agrees not to be responsible for waking Marie up on school days and Marie will wake up on her own and attend school regularly.

5. The established curfew will be 9 pm weekdays and 11 pm weekends for Marie as long as she informs Mrs. S. of her destination.

6. A subsequent set of rules will be appended to this agreement.

In the event of any dispute arising out of this agreement, we agree that prior to directing the problem to the Court, we will first attempt to settle the dispute through the use of mediation services.

Signed this 19 Day of May, 1983.

_____   _____
                                        Aviva Sanders-Mascari, Mediator

_____

cc: Juvenile Court Clerk
    Mrs. S.
    Marie
    File

1982) and applied to our practice of family mediation. This code, with accompanying explanatory comments, is presented in the appendix.

The ethical principles identified here are only a beginning. As the field of family mediation continues to grow as a professional practice, these basic principles will have to be expanded, and additional principles will have to be developed.

FUTURE IMPLICATIONS

Forecasting the future course of family mediation suggests some obvious trends already under way and some others representing our "crystal ball gazing."

As family mediation becomes increasingly recognized as an effective alternative for resolving family conflicts, referrals will increase. This will undoubtedly swell the ranks of mediators in independent practice, as well as increase the number of agencies that include family mediation as a core service. Many professionals are already beginning to identify family mediation as their area of speciality.

Professional schools have begun to offer courses, as well as degree programs, in family mediation. For example, Vroom (1983) has reported that courses in family mediation are being offered at the University of Illinois and the University of Iowa; a curriculum in family mediation has been developed in the Department of Human Development at the University of Maryland's College of Education; and a 2-year graduate certification in family mediation is being contemplated at Catholic University in Washington, DC.

Although family mediation will likely not be a cure-all for society's ills, it has the potential to drastically influence the way Americans interact. The influence of mediation on the American family, if popularly embraced, will undoubtedly serve to further democratize and encourage egalitarian family relationships and, with that, the skills and understandings to create a more egalitarian society. Small, formerly powerless groups and persons will be able to truly be heard, and thus, realistically negotiate with powerful groups, individuals, and institutions.

More research will be done to answer the questions that are now beginning to be asked. What is required to be an effective family mediator? Who is best suited to mediate family disputes? What form of training and how much is necessary to produce effective family mediators? Ethical questions that are now in the gray areas will become clearer and resolved.

What was once said about banks could one day be said about family mediators—that "there is one on every street corner." Only time will tell. One thing is clearly affirmable: Family mediation is not another fad; it is an idea whose time has come. And American families are benefiting from it.

A CAVEAT: DIVORCE MEDIATION

One of the major areas of practice currently within the family mediation movement is divorce mediation. All the components identified and discussed in this article are similar in divorce mediation, with one notable addition necessary. Mediators facilitating divorce mediations must have specific technical and legal knowledge and resources at their command to a degree not needed for most family mediation efforts. Consultation with attorneys, accountants, and similar professionals relevant to a divorce settlement are an integral part of the former. The interface of law and mediation, especially, must be clearly understood. State domestic relations laws must be fully comprehended, because agreements reached by a divorcing couple through mediation eventually will be translated into a formal legal document drawn up by a relevant professional.

Readers who are interested in investigating divorce mediation are referred to

Structured Mediation in Divorce Settlements (Coogler, 1978) and *Divorce Mediation: A Practical Guide for Therapists and Counselors* (Haynes, 1981), two seminal works on the intricacies of this particular process.

REFERENCES

Coogler, O. J. (1978). *Structured mediation in divorce settlements*. Lexington, MA: Lexington Books.

Coogler, O. J., Weber, R. E., & McKenny, F. C. (1979). Divorce mediation: A means of facilitating divorce and adjustment. *Family Coordinator, 28,* 255–259.

Fisher, R., & Ury, W. (1982). *Getting to yes*. Boston: Houghton-Mifflin.

Fuller, L. (1971). Mediation: Its forms and functions. *Southern California Law Review, 44,* 305–339.

Girdner, L. K. (1983, March). *Adjudication and mediation: A comparison of custody decision-making processes involving third parties*. Paper presented at the National Conference on Peacemaking and Conflict Resolution, Athens, GA.

Gulliver, P. H. (1979). *Disputes and negotiations: A cross-cultural perspective*. New York: Academic Press.

Haynes, J. (1981). *Divorce mediation: A practical guide for therapists and counselors*. New York: Springer.

Haynes, J. (1982). A conceptual model of the process of family mediation: Implications for training. *American Journal of Family Therapy, 10,* 5–16.

Huber, C. H. (1981). An Adlerian approach to marital counseling. *Counseling & Human Development, 14,* 1–16.

Margulies, S. L. (1982). *Ethical principles of divorce mediation*. Montclair, NJ: New Jersey Council on Divorce Mediation.

Pearson, J., & Thoennes, N. (1982). Divorce mediation: Strengths and weaknesses over time. In H. Davidson, L. Ray, & R. Horowitz (Eds.), *Alternative means of family dispute resolution*. Washington, DC: American Bar Association.

Trombetta, D. (1982). Custody evaluation and custody mediation: A comparison of two dispute interventions. *Journal of Divorce, 6,* 65–75.

Vroom, P. (1983). The anomalous profession: Some bumpy going for the divorce mediation movement. *Family Therapy Networker, 7,* 38–42.

Vroom, P., Fassett, D., & Wakefield, R. A. (1982). Winning through mediation: Divorce without losers. *Futurist, 16,* 28–34.

Wall, J. (1981). Mediation: An analysis, review and proposed research. *Journal of Conflict Resolution, 25,* 157–180.

Wixted, S. (1982). The children's hearings project: A mediation program for children and families. In H. Davidson, L. Ray, & R. Horowitz (Eds.), *Alternative means of family dispute resolution*. Washington, DC: American Bar Association.

APPENDIX

Ethical Principles of Family Mediation

I. Within the mediation process, the mediator shall remain impartial at all times and not represent any one party.

This Principle is the basis for the impartiality a mediator must bring to the process, as well as the basis for the integrity of mediation as mediation, not legal representation, not therapy, not arbitration, not anything else.

Mediators may, and at times should, share generic information based upon objective facts of which they are aware. Mediators may share this information with clients in order to inform clients about the consequences of proposals as an aid to informed decision making. The essence of this Principle is to protect and emphasize the mediator's stance as an impartial facilitator with a role to play that is discrete from those taken by professionals engaged in traditional modes of dispute resolution.

II. The mediator shall not mediate in instances where he or she has previously treated, counseled, or represented one or more of the clients.

This Principle is an outgrowth of the strict necessity of impartiality on the part of mediators, and their avoidance of conflict or the appearance of conflict. By elevating this requirement to the status of an Ethical Principle, the absolute independence and impartiality of mediators, both in substance and in appearance, are promoted.

III. The mediator shall use an Engagement Letter in connection with each mediation.

Mediation is a process still new enough to professionals and the public at large that mediators have an educative responsibility to state clearly and in plain language the scope, function and goals, and other pertinent details of the mediation process before it begins, and in writing. Clients shall sign, and each keep a copy of, the Engagement Letter so that there will be no question regarding each person's understanding of the process. In the letter, any fee arrangements shall be clearly stated, including fee arrangements respecting co-mediators.

IV. The mediator shall encourage the parties to consult with outside experts whenever appropriate during the mediation process.

The mediator shall be alert to the necessity for accurate answers to any questions that arise during the mediation process by encouraging clients to seek the service of relevant professionals who can provide information germane to informed decision making. The mediator shall stay apprised of available professionals by maintaining an ongoing list of competent persons in appropriate disciplines.

V. Subject to the requirements of law, the mediator shall retain confidentiality of the clients.

Any testimonial privilege attached to mediation, whether under the statutes, rules of evidence, or judicial opinion, is unknown. Notwithstanding, the mediator has an ethical obligation to preserve client confidentiality at all times within his or her control.

As a corollary, the mediator shall undertake to maintain confidentiality in the storage and disposal of records accumulated in the course of mediation.

Further, to the extent that the mediator intends to refer to particular cases in published material or lectures, he or she shall expressly refrain from revealing any information that will identify individual clients, and shall obtain any appropriate releases.

VI. The mediator shall maintain knowledge of current professional information related to the services he or she provides.

The mediator has a serious responsibility, expressly recognized by this Principle, to engage in continuing education relevant to legal and societal changes and developments affecting the mediation process. The mediator shall participate in appropriate ongoing professional education such as seminars, workshops, and peer supervision (where possible), and shall keep current his or her professional affiliations and adhere generally to a high standard of competence.

Adapted from "Ethical Principles of Divorce Mediation" by S. L. Margulies (Montclair, NJ: New Jersey Council on Divorce Mediation, 1982).

Charles H. Huber is Director of Psychological Services, The Samaritan Center, Jacksonville, Florida. J. Barry Mascari is Special Assistant to Superintendent of Schools, Clifton, New Jersey. Aviva Sanders-Mascari is with North Valley Regional High School District, Demarest, New Jersey.

9

Remarriage Families: Counseling Parents, Stepparents, and Their Children

Richard L. Hayes and Bree A. Hayes

By the year 1990 one of every three children under the age of 18 in the United States is projected to spend a portion of his or her life living with a single parent (Glick, 1979). Given that 80% of divorced persons remarry within 4 to 5 years, and that 60% of them have children, single-parent and remarriage families will comprise nearly 45% of all families (Visher & Visher, 1982). As a consequence of these changes, more people are expected to be living in a second marriage than in a first marriage by the end of this century (Duberman, 1975). Recognizing that these figures represent large amounts of loss and pain—much of which will go : unresolved—one can easily understand why 40% of second marriages end in divorce in the first four years, with the likelihood of another divorce increasing when children from a previous marriage are present (Becker, Landes, & Michael, 1977).

This statistical picture suggests that most of us will have close contact with persons who have divorced (at least once) *and* remarried. Moreover, these persons are likely to be living with children other than their own, or with a person some of whose children will be living with someone else. Yet, despite the prevalence of this family structure, the portrait of the American family continues to present Mom, Dad, and *their* children as living together in marital bliss. One might say that the nuclear family remains the standard but not the norm.

What will be required during the remainder of this century is to develop new traditions that set more realistic standards for families to follow. Counselors can play an important role in the development of these new traditions. This article presents an overview of the unique challenges that face remarriage families, and suggestions as to how counselors can help these parents and their children deal more realistically with the challenges facing them.

WHAT DO WE MEAN BY REMARRIAGE FAMILIES?

Despite calls from some researchers for counselors to broaden their views of acceptable family structures (Ahrons, 1981), the rapid increase in families resulting from the merger of two preexisting families has left the profession without a common vocabulary to describe the phenomenon. Traditionally, these families had been called *stepfamilies,* but many writers have abandoned the term in reaction to its long historical use as what Bernard (1956) has called a "smear word." *Blended, recoupled, reconstituted, merged, reorganized,* and *restructured* have emerged as more sympathetic and descriptive titles.

Although the term *restructured* captures an essential element of these families, it describes single-parent, foster-parent, and adoptive-parent families as well. For purposes of this article, we have used the term *remarriage family* to refer to families that are formed as the result of a marriage between two partners, at least one of whom has been previously married. This type of family is considered a specific type of restructured family. Even though remarriage families may and do arise without children, the concern here will be with remarriage families that include at least one child from the outset.

A PRESENT BORN OF THE PAST

To point out that one must first have been married before one can be remarried may seem so obvious as to be unworthy of mention. Nonetheless, critical to understanding the remarriage family is to recognize its origins in the losses of prior marital relationships. Unresolved losses play significant roles in the lives of remarriage family members and can profoundly limit subsequent developmental progress (Hayes, 1984). Members of remarriage families must each resolve the losses associated with dissolution of previous family structures as a prelude to creating a successful remarriage family.

Parents must resolve the losses associated not only with the old marriage, but also with their *expectations* for marriage, and then with the passing of their single-parent status. As Garfield (1980) has pointed out, those who divorce must attend to a number of developmental tasks in dealing with resolution of loss. These include self-acceptance, acceptance of new roles and responsibilities, renegotiating roles and relationships with family and friends, and transforming the relationship with the former spouse.

Unlike death or abandonment, only the relationship—not the person—is lost through divorce. Often, former spouses continue to influence the lives of those who remarry, especially when children are involved. Spouses who have resolved former marital losses appear better prepared for remarriage than those who have not (Messinger, Walker, & Freeman, 1978).

Counselors working with remarriage families must evaluate the extent to which unresolved mourning is exerting an influence on the current situation. Clients then must be encouraged to work through, rather than around, previous losses and to accept the reality of former losses. Bowlby (1980) noted that widowed spouses were healthier if they continued to speak with their spouses in fantasy rather than to let go of the relationship. This method for resolving mourning suggests that remarriage clients may do better to transform existing relationships to more productive ones rather than to deny the loss, especially when those former spouses are living and in frequent contact with the client. Because clients may be reluctant to raise these issues in front of the current spouse, counselors should be sensitive to and aware of the need to schedule some sessions with spouses individually.

As complicated as divorce and remarriage appear to an adult, to the child these changes present "a cognitive puzzle [that brings] dissonance and inconsistency to the child's social and affective world. To deal with loss and to rearrange the disrupted perceptions demand time and energy that must be withdrawn from the work of the schoolroom and from social interaction with peers" (Hess & Camara, 1979, p. 82). The cycle of attachments and losses that attends the history of a remarriage family disrupts the child's normal developmental progress. Familiar schemes of family and the social order must be reconstructed as the child attempts to form workable solutions to the problem of forming attachments to many different people.

In working with families, Huntington (1982, pp. 27–28) encouraged counselors to consider a number of transactional factors associated with attachment, divorce, and remarriage:

1. For the child:
   - the child's cognitive and emotional assimilation and understanding of the divorce and the subsequent remarriage.
   - personality traits, flexibility, temperament, tolerance for stress, handling of affect, adaptive behaviors, and areas of competence.
   - developmental level and prior developmental tasks accomplished.
   - the sex of the child and siblings.
2. For the parent:
   - each parent's emotional health or relative narcissistic injury.
   - the effects of being a single parent: in terms of the economy, on discipline and order, emotionally, and practically, in terms of child-care arrangements and the like.
   - the remaining bonds with the ex-spouse; the desire to continue the battle or to resolve it.

- remarriage and the quality of that new relationship; the dynamics are very different for the cases in which both parents remain single, either custodial parent remarries, or both remarry.
3. For the parent-child relationship:
   - quality of total family interrelationships, prior to and after divorce.
   - parental needs for the child for emotional support.
   - loyalty conflicts.
   - custody and visitation battles and agreements.
   - the effects of parental absence directly on the child and indirectly via the impact on the remaining parent.
4. For the context:
   - the life event changes that coincide with divorce.
   - outside supports and support networks—social groups, extended family, and so on.
   - economic realities.
   - prior and current levels of discord—conflict prior to and after divorce.
   - the changes over time; divorce does not set people in concrete—the outcome is not predetermined.

MYTHS AND EXPECTATIONS

Myths serve as powerful half-truths that crystallize our thinking and actions around important social issues, the most important of which may be the family (see Capaldi & McRae, 1979; Coleman & Ganong, 1985; Einstein, 1982; Lewis, 1980; Schulman, 1972; Visher & Visher, 1979). Early in their lives children are introduced to the folklore about stepfamilies as hostile environments. Taking heed of the warning to avoid these entanglements, children are sent happily to bed, secure in the knowledge that they are safe in the care of their natural and biological parents. As Mead (cited in Thies, 1977) noted, "Each American child learns, early and in terror, that his whole security depends on that single set of parents" (p. 60).

This notion—that to love anyone else as your mother or father means that you are being disloyal to them—has been called the *loyalty myth* (Lewis, 1980). Not infrequently, children in remarriage families believe, and often rightfully, that their biological parent will be angry or hurt if the children express any affection toward the stepparent. The frightening experiences of Snow White, Cinderella, and Hansel and Gretel serve as cogent remainders of the importance attached to keeping the family intact and avoiding contact with persons who would presume to take the place of one's parents.

The term *step* actually comes from the Anglo-Saxon *āstēpan,* "to deprive," from which came *stepchild,* "a bereaved child or orphan" (Simon, 1964, p. 19). Despite their prevalence, remarriage families continue to be the object of popular derision, viewed as led by parents who have deprived their children of a *normal* family life and who are somehow *out of step* with the natural order of things.

The myth of the *wicked stepparent* is balanced by the myth of *instant love*. Because two adults love one another and choose to become marriage partners is no guarantee they will love each other's children or that the children will love them in return. Yet this expectation, perhaps more than any other, is the source of a substantial amount of the stress generated in remarriage families. More to the point is the realization that love takes time to grow and must be nurtured. Parents and children do have a right to expect that they will be treated with respect; they must not expect, however, that this will be easy or instantaneous.

The modern antidote to the fairy tale presentation is the equally engaging myth that remarriage families are really no different than nuclear families. Television's "Brady Bunch" blissfully combined a father and his three sons with a mother and her three daughters with the housekeeper Alice. Together they encountered the problems common to original families but met few of the problems encountered by remarriage families.

The major difference between original and remarriage families is in the structure of their relationships (Capaldi & McRae, 1979; Jones, 1978; Kompara, 1980; Nelson & Nelson, 1982). Consider that two people can have one relationship with each other. Add another person, and three people now have a system characterized by three relationships (see Figure 1). It is little wonder that a new baby in the home creates stress in a previously stabilized relationship. Add another child, and the number of relationships doubles to six—confirming many parents' observation that two children are far more work than they had originally anticipated. Using the formula $[n^2 - n]/2 = R$ (where n equals the number of people and R equals the number of relationships between them), the Brady Bunch, with its 9 members (including Alice), has 36 relationships ($[81 - 9]/2$) with which to contend.

Beyond the obvious note that members of remarriage families are not necessarily related biologically, stress is created by the division of loyalties between separate but related nuclear families (Ahrons & Perlmutter, 1982). The presence of

**FIGURE 1   Relationships Between Family Members
In Selected Family Structures**

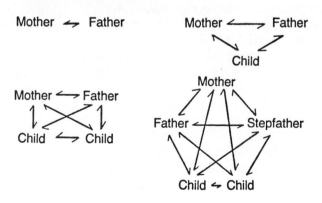

other parents and grandparents, as well as stepgrandparents, and unresolved feelings from the past, continue to remind family members of their previous family history. Add these members to the 9 above and the number swells to 19, if all parents and grandparents are living, neither absent spouse remarries or has other children, and Alice's parents stay out of the family. (Actually we never hear about these people on "The Brady Bunch.") The number of relationships that this not-so-unusual remarriage family must form is an overwhelming 171!

Remarriage families, at least at first, have a family but no history. More than any single thing remarriage families need, but don't yet have, is time together. Clearly love is not something that stepparents ought to expect instantly.

A final myth that characterizes the expectations of remarriage families is the *take away myth* (Lewis, 1980), so-called because those who accept it believe that the stepparent will take away the love of the child or the parent. So, too, the custodial parent may see the continued involvement of absent parents with their children as undermining the stepparent's relationship with the children. Of course, love is not a fixed pie to be divided among those who want a share, but the significance of a myth is its power to shape the believer's reality.

CONCERNS OF REMARRIAGE FAMILIES

In our experience in working with remarriage families, not the least important of which has been our own, we have found a set of concerns that arise recurrently in our discussions. These concerns, which have been described in varying detail by other authors (Brady & Ambler, 1982; Crohn, Sager, Brown, Rodstein, & Walker, 1982; Skeen, Covi, & Robinson, 1985; Visher & Visher, 1978), can be grouped under four general categories: roles and relationships, feelings and fantasies, rules and regulations, and external forces.

Roles and Relationships

The instability of remarriage families is exacerbated by the lack of positive, institutionalized roles for each of the members to play. Because more than one half of remarriage families formed after divorce include stepfathers (Rallings, 1976), the task of dealing with the spouse's children more often falls to men than to women. Socialized to be in charge, men find themselves in the awkward position of enforcing discipline when they have no apparent authority. In remarriage families wherein stepfathers set consistent limits, however, and when the mother welcomed his support, the stepchildren (especially boys) generally functioned better than did children in single-parent families or conflicted, non-divorced families (Hetherington, Cox, & Cox, 1982). Stern (cited in Skeen, Covi, & Robinson, 1985) suggested that "stepfathers are more likely to be successful disciplinarians when taking a slow, gentle, flexible approach and develop a friendship to foster the child's participation, instead of trying to control the child through authoritarian means" (p. 122).

Women, on the other hand, have been socialized toward fulfilling the needs of others as their primary obligation in life. Placed in the role of stepmother, the woman often tries to take on the burdens of the entire family and finds herself rearing his children. Duberman (1975) reported that women were far less likely than men to achieve a good relationship with their stepchildren. Although reports are mixed on whether older or younger women have less difficulty as stepmothers, there is agreement that younger children have better relationships with their stepmothers than do adolescents (Draughton, 1975; Duberman, 1973; Wallerstein & Kelly, 1980). In general, the younger the child is at the time of divorce, the more likely the child is to accept the stepparent (Hetherington et al., 1982; Santrock, 1972; Wallerstein & Kelly, 1980).

A final difficulty that stepparents encounter is their ambiguous legal status. Although stepparents are considered in loco parentis—and thereby have all the rights, duties, and obligations of the biological parents—their assumption of the role is voluntary and may be terminated at will (Wald, 1981). As well, the rights of the stepparent toward the stepchild, regardless of whether that parent provides support for the child, are unclear and vary from one court ruling to another (Kargman, 1983).

Sibling rivalries are typical in any family. In families with a common history, territorial battles often are resolved on the basis of privilege of age. In remarriage families, however, each dispute provides an occasion for rekindling old memories.

After an extensive review of the literature, Skeen, Covi, and Robinson (1985) concluded that "stepsibling relationships are crucial to the success of stepfamilies . . . [and although] in most cases the presence of stepsiblings makes the marriage much more complex . . . the better the relationships between stepsiblings, the better the total family integration" (p. 122). In addition, when couples choose to have children of their own following the remarriage, relationships among all the children are more likely to be harmonious, although some children from former marriages may feel left out of the new relationship (Brooks, cited in Skeen, Covi, & Robinson, 1985, p. 122). As remarriage families grow in their relationships with one another, the children report feelings of divided loyalties—uncomfortable feelings that often are vented as anger directed at the stepparent (Einstein, 1982)—as each move toward the "new" family threatens to separate them from the "old."

Perlmutter, Engel, and Sage (1982) have suggested that sexual boundaries loosen in remarriage families. Without the usual time to develop deeper parent-child relationships, and devoid of the customary biological and legal prescriptions against sexual contact, stepfamilies become stimulating places sexually, especially for adolescents (Visher & Visher, 1979). "In biological families, children often consider their parents as nonsexual beings" (Visher & Visher, 1982, p. 117), while in remarriage families sexual desires can be heightened, increasing anxiety and disrupting already fragile relationships. Anger may mask attempts to cope with the situation, further compounding the difficulties in developing meaningful relationships. Although sexual abuse by males accounts for more than 80% of reported cases (Berliner cited in Skeen, Covi, & Robinson, 1985), no clear data support the notion that stepfathers are any more or less involved in incestuous relationships with their stepdaughters than are biological parents (Meiselman, 1978).

Feelings and Fantasies

As noted earlier, myths play an important role in the lives of remarriage families, especially to the extent to which those families are dysfunctional. Because the remarriage family begins with children and without a history, these myths provide an instant history that projects at least a sort of reality to which the members can react. The inevitable disappointments that result are a direct consequence of the experience of the remarriage family to live up (or down) to the various members' expectations. For example, the wicked stepmother turns out to be less wicked and more likeable (if not loveable) than expected by the children, while the stepmother comes to grips with the reality that she is less perfect and her stepchildren less adoring than she had thought they might be.

The consequence of members' failed expectations are feelings of disappointment. Some turn this feeling outward in anger or resentment directed at any convenient target. Disappointment turned inward becomes guilt. Although these expectations remain unidentified, they continue to go unmet and set up a recurring cycle of guilt and resentment (Einstein, 1982).

Rules and Regulations

Stepparents appear to take one of three approaches to the discipline issue (Capaldi & McRae, 1979; Skeen, Covi, & Robinson, 1985). Some remain inattentive and disengaged from the relationship, giving the natural parent little support or encouragement. Others become very actively involved, tending to be overly restrictive—especially stepfathers with stepsons. And some remain tentative, as if "walking on eggshells," paralyzed by the anticipation of feeling guilty if they do or don't do this or that just right.

Of course, none of these strategies is particularly successful because each acts to inhibit the development of an open and trusting relationship between the stepparent and the stepchild. Instead, the struggle degenerates into a series of contests in which neither participant emerges with the respect each attempts to get from the other. Remarriage couples do not have the luxury of time to develop shared ideas on discipline as they did in their original families before the children were born. Because these couples must develop a relationship with each other and with their children at the same time, Capaldi and McRae (1979) advocate a cooperative approach to discipline that acknowledges the rights of all parties.

External Forces

Because parents divorce each other and not their children (Duncan & Duncan, 1979), the degree to which the absent parent accepts the fact of the remarriage family has a significant impact on its chances for success. Research indicates that the greater is the amount of contact between the absent parent and the child, the less is the disruption in the parent-child relationship, and thus less stress in the remarriage family (Greif, 1982). The more limited is the contact between absent parents and their children, the more precious does that time become, such that both parties are reluctant to say goodbye as they court one another to extend the visit.

Despite the "common assumption that diminishing a child's relationship with a biological parent promotes the development of a relationship with the same-sexed parent, . . . children often feel as though an unequal distribution of their time with each parent is reflective of their having been made to choose the step-parent over the absent biological parent" (Greif, 1982, p. 53). Instead, Greif suggested that shared parenting after divorce may protect the remarriage family system by decreasing the experience of loss, blunting the potential for conflicting loyalties, and mitigating competition between adults.

Beyond the instability introduced by the relative involvement of the absent parent in the affairs of the remarriage family, persons whom Bohannan (1970) called *quasi-kin* are present. These relatives of relatives, so to speak, create an extended network of additional expectations that complicate an already ambiguous social structure. As Clingempeel (cited in Skeen, Covi, & Robinson, 1985) reported, people from remarriage families in which only the wife had children from a previous marriage showed higher marital quality than did people from more complex families. Further, people who maintained only moderate, as opposed to high or low, contact with quasi-kin showed better marital quality.

Given that the predominant proportion of children affected by divorce and remarriage is of school age, the school, its policies, and the people who work there have a substantial effect on the success of remarriage families. Visher and Visher (1979) believe that effect is largely negative, serving to reinforce stereotypes and exacerbate conflicts in the family. In particular, the school's role in observing customs such as Mother's Day or Father's Day, holding father-son banquets, limiting seating at school functions or graduations to selected family members, and sending notices and report cards to only one set of parents all serve to increase stress and miscommunication between parents.

DEVELOPMENTAL TASKS OF REMARRIAGE FAMILIES

More than anything, remarriage families appear to be characterized by a greater reliance on fantasy and hopes in their interactions (Schulman, 1972), greater expectations for themselves and acknowledgment by their stepchildren (Visher & Visher, 1979), and the lack of a commonly shared history (Goldner, 1982) than is the case with natural parents in original families. Because remarriage families start with children and yet have had no time to build a history, the family must deal with the tasks required of more mature families while possessing the skills of a family just starting out. Because they lack a common set of experiences, remarriage families hold limited or unrealistic expectations that paralyze them into inaction or galvanize them into a reaction against people or events they little understand.

Developmental tasks that are important for remarriage families to accomplish include clarifying roles and developing realistic expectations, setting reasonable limits and establishing a pattern of appropriate discipline, and liberalizing the boundaries between families by acknowledging the nature of shifting alliances. Most importantly, the family must begin to shape its own traditions and to acknowledge the development of its own history. Turnbull and Turnbull (1983) have suggested 10 guidelines that parents in remarriage families might follow in resolving some of their inevitable conflicts:

1. Provide neutral territory.
2. Don't try to fit a preconceived role.
3. Set limits and enforce them.
4. Allow an outlet for feelings by the children for natural parents.
5. Expect ambivalence.
6. Avoid mealtime misery.
7. Don't expect love.
. 8. Don't take all the responsibility. The child has some, too.
9. Be patient.
10. Maintain the primacy of the marital relationship.

WHAT CAN COUNSELORS DO?

Counselors working with remarriage families can help by:

—encouraging family members to relinquish myths they may hold about the remarriage family.
—helping members to understand the entire family system, its differences from their past families, and the involvement of non-family members in the system.
—teaching members more effective communication skills.
—helping members, especially children, to mourn the loss of previous relationships and encouraging the development of new relationships.
—providing a forum in which members can work out their relationships with one another and with quasi-kin, especially the absent parent.
—offering structured programs of parent training and lists of readings that family members can use as self-instructional devices.
—informing members of the latest research findings and clinical evidence that may be helpful to them in the reorganization process.
—identifying the tasks of parenting and the relationships that are necessary to enact those roles.
—running groups for remarriage parents in the community or for stepchildren in the schools.

In closing this section, these questions by Kirby (1979) are offered for remarriage families:

- What evidence is present to indicate that each family member will feel secure in the merged family?
- What are illustrations of how the merged family will gain strength from the usual cultural conditions imposed?
- Under what conditions have the merged family members demonstrated open family discussions?
- When have we as parents cooperatively reinforced predictable consequences in the children?
- What are our attitudes toward seeking professional help in working with the children?
- What are the role expectations of the various merged family members?

THE FUTURE FOR REMARRIAGE FAMILIES

Remarriage is coming to be recognized as a normal developmental phase in an increasingly complex family life cycle (Goldner, 1982). As such, remarriage families represent a normal adaptation to changing social conditions. Recognizing that more complex internal organizations are better able to withstand the threats posed to them by outside forces, remarriage families may provide just the family structure necessary to prepare members for survival in the multicultural, interdependent, global society of the future. Indeed, its differences from the nuclear family of recent American tradition may be the very strength of the remarriage family.

Certainly members of remarriage families have made notable contributions to our history. Unlike the remarriage families of fable, those of George Washington, Abraham Lincoln, Nancy Reagan, and Jacqueline Onassis are all reported to have been nurturing environments that encouraged greatness in their members. In a nation where some fear that the family may be failing, it just may be that the society around it fails to appreciate the vitality of the family's evolution in this period of transition.

REFERENCES

Ahrons, C. R. (1981). The continuing coparental relationship between divorced spouses. *American Journal of Orthopsychiatry, 51*, 415–428.

Ahrons, C. R., & Perlmutter, M. S. (1982). The relationship between former spouses: A fundamental subsystem in the remarriage family. In L. Messinger (Ed.), *Therapy with remarriage families* (pp. 31–47). Rockville, MD: Aspen Systems Corp.

Becker, G. S., Landes, E. M., & Michael, R. T. (1977). An economic analysis of marital instability. *Journal of Political Economy, 85*, 1141–1187.

Bernard, J. (1956). *Remarriage: A study of marriage.* New York: Dryden.

Bohannan, P. (Ed.) (1970). *Divorce and after.* New York: Doubleday.

Bowlby, J. (1980). *Attachment and loss* (Vol. 3). New York: Basic Books.

Brady, C. A., & Ambler, J. (1982). Use of group educational techniques with remarried couples. In L. Messinger (Ed.), *Therapy with remarriage families* (pp. 145–157). Rockville, MD: Aspen Systems Corp.

Capaldi, F., & McRae, B. (1979). *Stepfamilies: A cooperative responsibility.* New York: New Viewpoints/Vision Books.

Coleman, M., & Ganong, L. (1985). Remarriage myths: Implications for the helping professions. *Journal of Counseling & Development, 64,* 116–120.

Crohn, H., Sager, C., Brown, H., Rodstein, E., & Walker, L. (1982). A basis for understanding and treating the remarried family. In L. Messinger (Ed.), *Therapy with remarriage families* (pp. 159–186). Rockville, MD: Aspen Systems Corp.

Draughton, M. (1975). Step-mother's model of identification in relation to mourning in the child. *Psychological Reports, 36,* 183–189.

Duberman, L. (1973). Step-kin relationships. *Journal of Marriage & The Family, 35,* 283–292.

Duberman, L. (1975). *The reconstituted family: A study of remarried couples and their children.* Chicago: Nelson-Hall.

Duncan, T. R., & Duncan, D. (1979). *You're divorced, but your children aren't.* Englewood Cliffs, NJ: Prentice-Hall.

Einstein, E. (1982). *The stepfamily.* New York: Macmillan.

Garfield, R. (1980). The decision to remarry. *Journal of Divorce, 4,* 1–10.

Glick, P. C. (1979). Children of divorced parents in demographic perspective. *Journal of Social Issues, 35,* 170–182.

Goldner, V. (1982). Remarriage family: Structure, system, future. In L. Messinger (Ed.), *Therapy with remarriage families* (pp. 187–206). Rockville, MD: Aspen Systems Corp.

Greif, J. B. (1982). The father-child relationship subsequent to divorce. In L. Messinger (Ed.), *Therapy with remarriage families* (pp. 47–57). Rockville, MD: Aspen Systems Corp.

Hayes, R. (1984, November). Coping with loss: A developmental approach to helping children and youth. *Counseling & Human Development, 17*(3), 1–12.

Hess, R., & Camara, K. A. (1980). Post-divorce relationships as mediating factors in the consequences of divorce for children. *Journal of Social Issues, 35*(4), 79–96.

Hetherington, E. M., Cox, M., & Cox, R. (1982). Effects of divorce on parents and children. In M. E. Lamb (Ed.), *Non-traditional families* (pp. 233–288). Hillside, NJ: Erlbaum.

Huntington, D. S. (1982). Attachment loss and divorce: A reconsideration of the concepts. In L. Messinger (Ed.), *Therapy with remarriage families* (pp. 17–29). Rockville, MD: Aspen Systems Corp.

Jones, S. M. (1978). Divorce and remarriage: A new beginning; a new set of problems. *Journal of Divorce, 2,* 217–227.

Kargman, M. W. (1983). Stepchild support obligations of stepparents. *Family Relations, 32,* 321–328.

Kirby, J. (1979). *Second family.* Muncie, IN: Accelerated Development.

Kompara, D. R. (1980). Difficulties in the socialization process of stepparenting. *Family Relations, 20,* 69–73.

Lewis, H. C. (1980). *All about families: The second time around.* Atlanta: Peachtree Publishers.

Meiselman, K. (1978). *Incest.* San Francisco: Jossey-Bass.

Messinger, L., Walker, K. N., & Freeman, S. J. (1978). Preparation for remarriage following divorce. *American Journal of Orthopsychiatry, 48,* 263–272.

Nelson, M., & Nelson, G. (1982). Problems of equity in a reconstituted family: A social exchange analysis. *Family Relations, 31,* 223–231.

Perlmutter, L. H., Engel, T., & Sage, C. J. (1982). The incest taboo: Loosened sexual boundaries in remarried families. *Journal of Sex & Marital Therapy, 8,* 83–96.

Rallings, E. M. (1976). The special role of stepfather. *Family Coordinator, 25,* 445–449.

Santrock, J. W. (1972). The relations of type and onset of father absence to cognitive development. *Child Development, 43,* 455–469.

Schulman, G. L. (1972). Myths that intrude on the adaptation of the stepfamily. *Social Casework, 53,* 131–139.

Simon, A. W. (1964). *Stepchild in the family.* New York: Odyssey Press.

Skeen, P., Covi, R., & Robinson, B. (1985). Stepfamilies: A review of the literature with suggestions for practitioners. *Journal of Counseling & Development, 64,* 121–125.

Thies, J. M. (1977, Summer). Beyond divorce: The impact of remarriage on children. *Journal of Clinical Child Psychology, 6,* 59–61.

Turnbull, S. K., & Turnbull, J. M. (1983, April). To dream the impossible dream: An agenda for discussion with stepparents. *Family Relations,* 227–230.

Visher, E. B., & Visher, J. S. (1978). Major areas of difficulty for stepparent couples. *International Journal of Family Counseling, 6,* 70–80.

Visher, E. B., & Visher, J. S. (1979). *Stepfamilies: A guide to working with stepparents and stepchildren.* New York: Brunner/Mazel.

Visher, E. B., & Visher, J. S. (1982). Stepfamilies in the 1980s. In L. Messinger (Ed.), *Therapy with remarriage families* (pp. 105–119). Rockville, MD: Aspen Systems Corp.

Wald, E. (1981). *The remarried family: Challenge and promise.* New York: Family Service Association of America.

Wallerstein, J. S., & Kelly, J. B. (1980). *Surviving the break-up: How children actually cope with divorce.* New York: Basic Books.

Richard Hayes is affiliated with the College of Education and Health Sciences, Bradley University, and Bree Hayes is president of Resource Management Services, Peoria Heights, IL. The authors, who met while pursuing doctoral study in counseling psychology at Boston University, have been married nearly 10 years. At the time this article was written, Richard had an 11-year-old daughter by a previous marriage, who lived with her mother. Bree had a 17-year-old son by a previous marriage, who lived with foster parents, and a 14-year-old daughter by a previous marriage, who lived with them. They had a 7-year-old daughter, who lived with them. Both of their former spouses have remarried and have or were expecting children of their own.

10

Children of Alcoholics

Judith A. Lewis

As Hastings and Typpo (1984) have pointed out, "Living in a family where drinking is a problem is a lot like living with an elephant in the living room." In a workbook designed for use by pre-adolescent children of alcoholics, they suggest that children imagine the "elephant's" role as follows:

> People have to go through the living room many times a day and you watch as they walk through it very . . . carefully . . . around . . . the . . . ELEPHANT. No one ever says anything about the ELEPHANT. They avoid the swinging trunk and just walk around it. Since no one ever talks about the ELEPHANT, you know that you're not supposed to talk about it either. And you don't.
>
> But sometimes you wonder why nobody is saying anything or why no one is doing anything to move the ELEPHANT . . . You wonder if maybe there is something wrong with *you*. But you just keep wondering, keep walking around it, keep worrying and wishing that there was somebody to talk to about the ELEPHANT.

Growing up in a home dominated by the huge, gray elephant of parental alcoholism places an obvious strain on children. Not only must they spend their pre-adolescent and adolescent years attempting to cope with a unique set of difficulties, but they also are frequently forced to address these problems within a framework of family secrecy. The functioning of the entire family unit is likely to be affected by the alcohol problem of one member, and the issues presented by the alcoholic family system have important implications for the psychological, social, and even physical development of each child.

THE FAMILY AS A SYSTEM

Any discussion of alcohol's impact on family dynamics and child development must begin with the recognition that the family is an ongoing system characterized by consistent modes of interaction. The notion of the family as a system

173

depends on general systems theory (von Bertalanffy, 1968), an epistemology that can be contrasted with the reductionistic thinking underlying Newtonian science. Traditional Newtonian thinking was reductionistic in its attempt to break down complex phenomena into the smallest possible parts, and linear in its attempt to understand these parts as a series of less complex cause-and-effect relationships.

Systems theory represents an entirely different mode of thought, viewing all living things as open systems best understood by examining their interrelationships and organizing principles. Attention is paid not to linear, causal relationships but, rather, to consistent, if circular, patterns of interaction.

> If a *system* is defined as a set of units or elements standing in some consistent relationship or interactional stance with each other, then the first concept is the notion that any system is composed of elements that are *organized* by the consistent nature of the relationship between these elements. Consistency is the key; consistent elements are related to each other in a consistently describable or predictable fashion. (Steinglass, 1978, p. 305)

Living organisms are *open systems* in that they interact with their environments, taking in and discharging information or energy through boundaries that are sufficiently permeable to allow these interactions to take place. The system itself also encompasses *subsystems*, which interact in a predictable manner within the context of the larger system. Clearly, the family unit as we know it conforms to these principles.

> The human family is a social system that operates through transactional patterns. These are repeated interactions which establish patterns of how, when, and to whom to relate. . . . Repeated operations build patterns, and these patterns underpin the family system. The patterns which evolve become familiar and preferred. The system maintains itself within a preferred range, and deviations which pass the system's threshold of tolerance usually elicit counterdeviation mechanisms which reestablish the accustomed range. (Minuchin, 1979, p. 7)

Thus, each family has its own *homeostasis,* or preferred steady state, which may or may not be "healthy" but is monitored through feedback and control mechanisms and protected by the system as a whole. Each family has a set of rules that governs its interactions and makes them predictable. Each includes subsystems (e.g., spousal, parental, sibling) that have specialized functions and attempt to preserve the integrity of the overall system. Each is an organized whole, making intervention in one part impossible to consider without taking the other parts into account.

As family therapists have learned, one cannot legitimately separate the individual from the family, the "sick" from the "well," the cause of a dysfunction from the effect. "Rather than seeing the source of problems or the appearance of symptoms as emanating from a single 'sick' individual, the . . . approach views that person simply as a symptom bearer—the identified patient—expressing a family's disequilibrium" (Goldenberg & Goldenberg, 1985, p. 7).

THE ALCOHOLIC FAMILY SYSTEM

In a family characterized by the alcohol dependence of one or more members, the disequilibrium makes individual adjustment difficult.

> Trapped (or at least thinking they are trapped) in this highly disordered system, how do family members adjust? The only healthy response would be not to adjust to it but to open it up by voicing honestly their practical problems, their mental confusion, and their emotional pain and frustration. This course would protect their own psychological well-being and offer the best hope of bringing the [alcohol] Dependent [person] to treatment as well. But few family members choose it, for they risk losing the whole matrix of their lives. Instead, they opt for preserving the family system at whatever cost. Left with only unhealthy alternatives, they choose . . . the same defense as the Dependent: they hide their true feelings behind an artificial behavior pattern, a supporting role in the alcoholic drama, which seems to promise some kind of reward in a system that offers few. (Wegscheider, 1981, p. 84)

Thus, each family member plays his or her role in an ongoing system patterned around the alcohol or drug use of one member. Substance abuse, like any other presenting problem, can be seen as a "systems-maintaining and a systems-maintained device" (Kaufman, 1985, p. 37). Abusive substance use is often central to a family's functioning—becoming a primary organizing factor in the system's structure. A family with an alcoholic member learns to maintain its homeostasis around the continued drinking of the alcohol-dependent individual.

Alcohol may even be a stabilizing factor, producing "patterned, predictable and rigid sets of interactions which reduce uncertainties" (Steinglass, 1979, p. 163). A number of families studied by Steinglass (1978) and his associates seemed to use, the alcoholic's intoxicated state as a way of dealing with conflict and re-stabilizing their interactions.

> The transition from sober to intoxicated behavior appeared to serve a specific functional role for . . . marital couples, a role that was felt to be primarily problem-solving in nature. Although it was felt that three different types of problem-solving activities were associated with alcoholism (problem-solving associated with individual psychopathology, intra-familial conflict, or conflict between the family and the external environment), in each case the emergence of the intoxicated interactional state appeared to temporarily restabilize the marital system. (Steinglass, 1978, pp. 357–358)

These findings do not mean that unstable family dynamics "cause" alcohol problems or that the homeostasis found by alcohol-affected families should be considered a healthy or positive state. What they do imply is that families develop consistent, predictable methods for adapting to alcoholism, just as they create rules and interactional styles for dealing with other kinds of problems. At the same time, alcohol or drug abuse may also be one method—if a spectacularly ineffective one—for coping with the stresses of a family system.

> Drinking behavior interrupts normal family tasks, causes conflict, shifts roles, and demands adjustive and adaptive responses from family members who do not know how to appropriately respond. A converse dynamic also occurs: marital and family styles, rules, and con-

flict may evoke, support, and maintain alcoholism as a symptom of family system dysfunction or as a coping mechanism to deal with family anxiety. (Kaufman, 1985, pp. 30–31)

EFFECTS ON CHILDREN

The problems inherent in the alcoholic family system have important implications for the development of children who must learn to adjust. Although families affected by substance abuse obviously vary, they do tend toward some common patterns, at least as far as child rearing is concerned.

In a family affected by parental alcoholism, at least one parent is likely to be somewhat impaired in the ability to provide consistency in child rearing practices. Interactions with the alcoholic parent may have extreme variations, with the parent being effective or ineffective, warm or cold, distant or affectionate, depending on alcohol consumption at the time. The non-alcoholic parent also may show variations in parenting as a result of his or her focus on the partner's drinking. Thus, in some alcoholic families neither parent is truly available to the child on a consistent basis.

The structure and boundaries of the alcoholic family system also may be problematic. Within the family unit, boundaries between subsystems may be weak, with the unity of the parental subsystem broken and children taking on what should be adult responsibilities. At the same time, boundaries between the family and its environment may be overly rigid as the family tries to maintain secrecy about the alcohol problem. Children who are unable to count on solid support from their parents also may be prevented from reaching out beyond the family for fear of breaking the family's rule of silence. The delicate homeostasis of the alcoholic family system is maintained—but at high cost to the development and self-esteem of individual family members.

Children reared in these circumstances may need to work to provide consistency and order that otherwise are lacking in their home lives.

> Children need consistency and structure. As an alcoholic progresses into alcoholism, and the co-alcoholic becomes more and more preoccupied with the alcoholic, children experience decreasing consistency and structure in the family unit, and their lives become less and less predictable. Some days, when dad is drinking, no disruption or tension occurs, but on *other* days when he is drinking, he becomes loud, opinionated and demanding in his expectations of the children. Mom, at times, reacts to this disrupting behavior by being passive and ignoring it; and other times, she makes arrangements for the children to go the neighbors until dad goes to bed, or tells them to go outside and play until she calls for them. The children don't know what to expect from dad when he drinks, nor do they know what to expect from mom when dad drinks. When structure and consistency are not provided by the parents, children will find ways to provide it for themselves. (Black, 1981, pp. 17–18)

Individual children differ in the mechanisms they use to adjust to their family situations. Some writers and counselors believe that children of alcoholics play a limited number of identifiable roles that give their family systems a semblance of order. Wegscheider (1981) identified four basic roles that children may adopt in alcoholic families: (a) the family hero, (b) the scapegoat, (c) the lost child, and (d) the family mascot.

The "family hero" takes over many functions that normally would be carried out by adults, assuming responsibility for solving family problems and providing stability for himself or herself and for other children in the family. This leadership is carried over into other childhood situations, including school, and into adulthood, making the family hero a success at most tasks attempted. The "scapegoat" is identified as the troublemaker in the family and tends to receive attention for his or her misbehavior. The "lost child," in contrast, remains in the background and seems to need little in the way of attention from the family. The "mascot" becomes the focus of attention as a way of lessening anxiety; he or she uses clowning as a way of distracting other family members from tension-provoking problems. These roles are used as coping mechanisms and by the family system as a set of transactions to maintain homeostasis.

A typology of family coping roles taken on by children raised in alcoholic families also has been suggested by Black (1981), who labeled these as the responsible one, the adjuster, and the placater. Like Wegscheider's family hero, the "responsible one" provides consistency and structure in the home environment, taking over parental roles on a routine basis.

> The responsible child makes life easier for the parents by providing more time for the alcoholic to be preoccupied with drinking, and for the co-alcoholic to be preoccupied with the alcoholic. Whether . . . responsible children are blatantly directed into this role or more subtly fall into it, it is typically a role which brings them comfort. Playing the responsible role provides stability in the life of this oldest, or only, child and in the lives of other family members. These responsible children feel and are very organized. . . . (They) have learned to rely completely on themselves. (pp. 19–20)

The "adjuster" copes with a disorganized family system by detaching, by going along with events as they occur and thinking about them as little as possible. Black's "placater," like Satir's (1967), focuses on the needs of others. In the alcoholic system this process tends to involve an attempt to salve the family's wounds.

> The placater finds the best way to cope, in this inconsistent and tension-filled home, by acting in a way which will lessen his own tension and pain, as well as that of the other family members. This child will spend his early and adolescent years trying to "fix" the sadness, fears, angers and problems of brothers, sisters, and certainly of mom and dad. (Black, 1981, p. 24)

To identify and label a limited number of roles played by children of alcoholics and to assume that these roles differ substantially from those played by children of non-substance-abusing parents may be an oversimplification. But understanding that the alcoholic family is at risk of being dysfunctional and recognizing that children of alcoholics might be required to develop extraordinary mechanisms for coping are important in working with these families.

Black (1986) pointed out that children of alcoholics have to cope with a great deal of stress and at the same time may have fewer physical, social, emotional, and mental resources available to them than do children living in more functional family systems. Their physical resources may be sapped because they are tired as a result of lack of sleep at night, because they have internalized stress, or because they have been abused. (They also may be the victims of fetal alcohol syndrome, which can cause developmental problems in the infants of women who consume large amounts of alcohol during pregnancy.) In some cases, social resources also may be limited; hesitancy to bring other children into the home or to share information about the family may interfere with the formation of intimate relationships. Emotional resources are affected by the pain, fear, and embarrassment that come with unstable living arrangements, financial difficulties, broken promises, accidents, and public intoxication. Even mental resources may be affected by a lack of parental help and by difficulties in maintaining regular school attendance.

Children in this situation are not necessarily poorly adjusted. In many cases they are exceptionally competent. Even children who appear to be coping effectively, however, may share some of the feelings described by Morehouse (1986, pp. 128–129) as characteristic of children of alcoholics.

1. Children feel responsible, directly or indirectly, for their parent's drinking. . . . (They may feel, for instance, that their misbehavior upsets the parent and therefore makes drinking an inevitable response.)
2. Children equate their parent's drinking with not being loved.
3. Children feel angry with the non-alcoholic parent for not making things better and for not providing protection.
4. Children fear that the alcoholic will get hurt, sick, or die as a result of being intoxicated.
5. In situations in which the alcoholic parent is more permissive or affectionate while intoxicated, the adolescent may want the parent to drink but then feels guilty.
6. Children feel confused by the difference between "dry" behavior and "drunk" behavior.
7. Parents' inconsistent behavior makes adolescents reluctant to bring friends home because they never know what to expect.
8. Once children are old enough to realize that alcoholic drinking is frowned upon by others or is "different," they feel shame and embarrassment.

Children who are forced to deal with this kind of pain can benefit from the attention of counselors and other helping adults. They deserve the opportunity to share their previously unexpressed feelings, to hear that they are not to blame for their families' difficulties, to learn less personally taxing mechanisms for coping with distress, and to gain the kind of support that we know is needed by people of all ages.

COUNSELING YOUNG CHILDREN OF ALCOHOLICS

Counseling for children who still live in the alcoholic home environment should concentrate on providing empathy and support and on helping clients to develop coping skills that can serve them effectively both in the current situation and in the future. Ideally, this process should help children deal with their present uncertainties and, concurrently, prevent the development of chronic emotional problems.

One way to look at the appropriate direction for counseling to take is to consider Ackerman's (1983) conceptualization of the family's potential for progressing from a "reactive" to an "active" phase of development.

> The reactive phase is consistently dominated by the behavior of nonalcoholic family members reacting to the alcoholic's behavior. During this time most family members become extremely cautious in their behavior in order to avoid or to further complicate the existing problems of alcoholism. However, by being reactive they are constantly adapting their behavior in order to minimize or survive an unhealthy situation. (p. 11)

Thus, the reactive phase is characterized by attempts of family members to deny the existence of the alcohol problem—even to themselves. Parents try to protect children from the situation by covering up problems and by avoiding discussion of unpleasant realities. The reactive phase is characterized by social disengagement, with the family becoming isolated from others. Emotional disengagement also occurs, with children learning to deny their negative emotions.

The kinds of coping roles described by Wegscheider and by Black may become rigidified. Ackerman's notion, however, is that a family can move from a reactive to an active phase.

> The main difference between the active and reactive phases is the response of the nonalcoholic family member even though the alcoholic is still drinking. Rather than being passive to the effects on themselves from alcoholism, they begin to take an active interest in themselves. . . . In this manner, the family begins to "de-center" itself from alcoholism. . . . They are willing to abandon their anonymity in exchange for help and a viable alternative to how they have been existing. (Ackerman, 1983, p. 28)

The most useful approach to take with children of alcoholics may be to help them move from a reactive to an active state. If children are isolated in their home environments, counseling should help them reach out to others. If children are afraid of their feelings, counseling should help them recognize and express their previously forbidden emotions. If children feel they are alone in their situations, counseling should convince them that others share their problems. Children of alcoholics also need to know that their attempts to meet their own needs are in no way detrimental to other family members. These counseling goals probably can be accomplished most successfully in group, rather than individual, settings.

As Brown and Sunshine (1982) pointed out:

One of the primary tasks in the treatment of the latency-age child from an alcoholic home is to help the child bear the burden of the shameful and frightening family secret by bringing it out in the open. This process is immediately relieving to the child and causes her or him to feel less isolated. For this reason and because children from alcoholic homes often have deficits in the areas of social development and peer interaction, group is the treatment of choice. (p. 70)

Morehouse (1986) stated that a group situation is also most appropriate for treatment of adolescent children of alcoholics, suggesting that participation in a group reduces isolation, presents a chance to learn about new ways of coping, encourages peer support, provides a laboratory for practice in sharing feelings, allows for confrontation when needed, and enhances readiness for participation in Alateen (a self-help group movement for young people in alcoholic homes).

Group counseling for children of alcoholics should follow a structured process that helps group members understand more about substance dependence but that goes beyond the cognitive dimension to deal with affect and with skill acquisition. A good example of a structured approach is provided by Hastings and Typpo (1984) in a children's book designed to be utilized by a counselor with a child or a group of children. Their design includes materials dealing with the kinds of topics that are likely to meet the needs of the target population, including:

1. Drinking and drug problems (a knowledge-building module discussing the effects of alcohol and other drugs).
2. Feelings (exercises designed to elicit awareness of negative and positive emotions and to explore the use of defenses).
3. Families (discussions of family rules, feelings, and relationships).
4. Coping with problems (exercises eliciting fresh ideas about coping methods, along with suggestions for dealing with some of the more prevalent alcohol-related family problems).
5. Changes (material encouraging children to make changes in the areas over which they do have some control, including taking care of themselves and handling their uncomfortable feelings).
6. Choices (decision-making exercises with an emphasis on the nature of choices).

This structured approach, like many others becoming available for use by counselors, is designed to help children develop the kinds of skills and resources they need for coping with family stress. Underlying most of these approaches is an emphasis on bringing hidden family dynamics to the surface—on recognizing and talking about "the elephant in the living room."

COUNSELING ADULT SONS AND DAUGHTERS OF ALCOHOLICS

People who grow up with that elephant in the living room may develop coping mechanisms that serve them poorly in adulthood. Only a minority of children of alcoholics respond by acting out; these individuals tend to receive some kind of attention or help during their adolescence. Most children in these situations respond instead of exerting control, burying feelings, and doing the best they can to adapt and survive.

Until recently these children received little notice. If anything, their behavior has been seen as mature and well adjusted. But they pay a price for this adjustment—one that many clinicians and writers believe leads to a common set of concerns in adulthood. Seixas and Youcha (1985), for instance, ask adult children of alcoholics whether they identify with the following list of feelings and attitudes:

Lack trust?
Feel isolated and lonely?
Deny or suppress deep feelings?
Feel guilty?
Feel unnecessarily embarrassed and ashamed?
Wish for closeness, yet fear it?
Have a low opinion of yourself?
Feel sad?
Need to control yourself?
Need to control others?
Split the world into all good or all bad?
Have an exaggerated sense of responsibility?
Want desperately to please?
Have trouble standing up for your own needs?
Overreact to personal criticism? (pp. 47–48)

Adult sons and daughters of alcoholics certainly are not the only people who exhibit the attitudes and behaviors listed above. These problems are ubiquitous in our society. Many writers point out, however, that a significant number of adults from alcoholic homes (and, of course, from other dysfunctional family situations) are troubled by difficulty in trusting others, relinquishing control, identifying and expressing feelings, or abandoning behavioral rigidity (Ackerman, 1983; Black, 1981; Seixas & Youcha, 1985; Wegscheider, 1981). Clearly, adult children of alcoholics (ACOAs) who have the opportunity to participate in group situations addressing their specific concerns do seem to sense a commonality in their characteristics.

We're often high achievers, even overachievers, but we also have a knack for sabotaging success, and certainly have difficulty enjoying it. We fear losing control to the point where we're often rigid. We may have terrific social skills, but we feel we're different from other people. We can be perfectionistic and are relentlessly unkind to ourselves. Sometimes to take some of the heat off ourselves, we're relentlessly critical of others. We have a pervasive sense of guilt and of sadness. We feel our heart is a stone, but we cry at dog movies. We lie when it would be just as easy to tell the truth, and we're often brutally honest when we shouldn't be. We have a high tolerance for the bizarre. We're extremely loyal even when loyalty is undeserved. We deal in extremes. We have low self-esteem. Some of us also wisecrack a lot. That was my specialty and I learned it at my mother's knee. (Malone, 1987, p. 54)

Coping mechanisms made necessary by a difficult childhood situation may be less appropriate in mature life styles. The counselor attempting to work with adult children of alcoholics should address these issues in a two-stage process. Black (1986) has suggested that clients must be encouraged to face their fears of loss of control and to express their guilt, sadness, and anger, but that this catharsis then must be replaced with an attempt to learn new behavioral skills. If counselors accept this idea, they then can approach these clients as they would any others—completing a careful assessment of each individual's strengths and deficits and developing a plan for behavioral change based on the client's unique needs.

If client's needs are addressed through a group process, emphasis should be placed on the development of skills such as assertion, relaxation, stress management, and interpersonal communication, depending on the areas that group members need to have addressed. Although the group also can serve as a mechanism for providing information about substance abuse and its effects on family dynamics, it probably is less useful to focus on children of alcoholics as an alcoholism risk group than to stress the individual's potential for successful adaptation and self-control. Attempts to eliminate the individual's sense of isolation and guilt may work best in concert with a referral to one of the many self-help groups for adult children of alcoholics now available in a number of locations.

RESOURCES FOR SELF HELP

Thousands of adult sons and daughters of alcoholics are finding in the "ACOA movement" a chance to explore issues that they might have kept hidden for years. Of course, as with any broadly based movement, there are vast oversimplifications. Stark (1987, p. 62), for instance, quoted an alcoholism program director's reaction to the publicity being given to children of alcoholics:

> I think the label is wonderful news. Finally a lot of these people can say, "Ah! That's what's the matter with me."

Human behavior is too complex to allow an individual to attribute all of his or her personal problems to a single causal agent, just as systems are too complex for people to believe that families with alcoholic members are unique in their dysfunctional characteristics. With this caveat in mind, however, specialists in counseling and human development should recognize the benefits that the self-help phenomenon can offer.

As one woman wrote about her feelings on attending her first ACOA workshop:

> ACOAs are people who have spent the bulk of our lives not feeling. Beneath the shock of recognition that these 40 strangers carried my secret, there was also the recognition that if I kept on with this process, the pain would get much worse before it got better. And beneath that, barely breathing, lay a tiny newborn of hope . . . When the workshop leader started asking questions and people started answering them, I never doubted that this direction was

where health lay. I was hearing my experience validated over and over again. (Malone, 1987, p. 54)

This validation of personal experience provides the under-pinning of activities that are becoming available to children of alcoholics for the first time. The resources that people seem to find useful take two general forms: (a) written and audiovisual materials designed to guide personal exploration and (b) organizations encouraging interpersonal networking among affected individuals.

Written and Audiovisual Material

A body of self-help literature has appeared in recent years. A number of books written for the general public describe the experience of growing up with an alcoholic parent. Of particular interest are several publications that take the form of manuals, providing guidelines and exercises designed to take an individual or group through a healing process. Among the manuals available in popular bookstores are:

Black, C. (1985). *Repeat after me*. Denver: M.A.C. Printing and Publications.

This popular work contains a number of sentence completion exercises that help the individual reader to recognize the effects of past losses and to move ahead unencumbered by blame and judgment. The step-by-step process begins with a series of warm-up exercises and goes on to consider feelings, self-esteem, and family issues.

Tessmer, K. (1986). *Breaking silence: A workbook of adult children of alcoholics*. Santa Rosa, CA: ACAT Press.

This book uses CAT family stories, adapted from the author's earlier work for children, to help ACOAs deal with issues such as anger, fear, guilt, grief, sex roles, relationships, and parents. Guidelines for letter writing to parents, as well as a personal "bill of rights," are included.

McConnell, P. (1986). *Adult children of alcoholics: A workbook for healing*. San Francisco: Harper & Row.

McConnell's book is divided into two general sections. The first section, "The Hurt," focuses on recognizing the beliefs, behaviors, and roles governing the individual's life and making the decision to change. Section Two, "The Healing," helps the individual to confront issues of anger and control and to concentrate on healing, forgiveness, and self-empowerment.

Seixas, J. S., & Youcha, G. (1985). *Children of alcoholics: A survivor's manual*. New York: Harper & Row.

The "survivor's manual" begins with a look back to childhood ("Living in Chaos"), goes on to examine "hangovers from childhood," and, like the other manuals, extends its focus to "climbing out of the trap."

Several films—also appropriate for the lay public—focus on issues relating to alcoholic family systems and on the problems faced by children of alcoholics and other substance abusers. Among these films are:

Alcoholism and the Family (FMS Productions, 1777 N. Vine St., Los Angeles, CA 90028)

> This film discusses the impacts of both active alcoholism and sobriety on the family system. (42 minutes)

Alcoholism: A Family Problem (Health Sciences Consortium, 200 Eastowne Dr., Suite 213, Chapel Hill, NC 27514)

> Based on a stage theory of alcoholism, this film shows the effects on the family during each of three stages in problem development. (13 minutes)

All Bottled Up (AIMS Media, 626 Hustin Ave., Glendale, CA 91201)

> This film depicts a child's viewpoint regarding alcoholic parents. (29 minutes)

Children of Alcoholics (Addiction Research Foundation, 33 Russell St., Toronto, Ontario, Canada M5S 2S1)

> This film examines treatment programs for children of alcoholics. (15 minutes)

Children of Denial (A.C.T., P.O. Box 8536, Newport Beach, CA 92660)

> This film focuses on children of alcoholics and the issues they face in childhood, adolescence, and adulthood. (28 minutes)

The Family Trap (Onsite Training and Consulting, Inc., P.O. Box 3790, Minneapolis, MN 55403)

> A general overview of the impact of alcoholism as a "family illness" is followed by the benefits of intervention and counseling. (30 minutes)

She Drinks a Little (Learning Corporation of America, 1350 Avenue of the Americas, New York, NY 10019)

> This is the story of an adolescent girl with an alcoholic mother. (31 minutes)

Soft is the Heart of a Child (Maryland Center for Public Broadcasting, 11767 Bonita Ave., Owings Mills, MD 21117)

> This dramatization shows the effects of alcoholism on children and other family members. (30 minutes)

The Summer We Moved to Elm Street (McGraw-Hill Films, 330 West 42nd St., New York, NY 10036)

> A father's alcoholism and its impact on a 9-year-old girl and her family are dramatized in this touching film. (30 minutes)

Organizations

A number of organizations provide assistance and opportunities for networking to children of alcoholics. Among the organizations that can provide information concerning COA and ACOA issues are:

Al-Anon Family Group Headquarters, Inc.
P.O. Box 182
Madison Square Station
New York, NY 10010 (212/302-7240)

Children of Alcoholics Foundation, Inc.
200 Park Ave.
New York, NY 10166 (212/949-1404)

National Association for Children of Alcoholics
31706 Coast Highway, Suite 201
South Laguna, CA 92677 (714/499-3899)

National Clearinghouse on Alcohol Information
Box 2345
Rockville, MD 20852 (301/468-2600)

National Council on Alcoholism
12 West 21st St.
New York, NY 10010 (212/206-6770)

CONCLUSION

> What is an adult child of an alcoholic (ACOA)? A person who, when she's drowning, sees someone else's life pass before her eyes. That life is the drinking parent's. (Malone, 1987 p. 50)

The effects of being raised in a family with an alcoholic parent often linger, affecting the individual's attitudes and behaviors long after the acute problems appear to have passed. From childhood through adolescence and adulthood, sons and daughters of alcoholics use survival skills that have helped them cope with the stress of an alcoholic family system but they may serve them poorly as long-term styles of living. Specialists in human development can help affected individuals to surmount these difficulties first by recognizing the pain and isolation of children of alcoholics and then by providing the kind of support, assistance, and information that can enhance the individual's attempts to move ahead.

REFERENCES

Ackerman, R. J. (1983). *Children of alcoholics: A guidebook for educators, therapists and parents (2nd ed.)* Holmes Beach, FL: Learning Publications.

Black, C. (1981). *It will never happen to me.* Denver, M.A.C.

Black, C. (1986, March 14). *Children of alcoholics.* Paper presented in Chicago.

Brown, K. A., & Sunshine, J. (1982). Group treatment of children from alcoholic families. *Social Work with Groups, 5*(1), 65–72.

Goldenberg, I., & Goldenberg, H. (1985). *Family therapy: An overview.* Monterey: Brooks/Cole.

Hastings, J. M., & Typpo, M. H. (1984). *An elephant in the living room.* Minneapolis: CompCare Publications.

Kaufman, E. (1985). *Substance abuse and family therapy.* Orlando: Grune & Stratton.

Malone, M. (1987). Dependent on disorder—Children of alcoholics are finding each other and paths to a better life. *Ms., 15*(8), 50–62.

Minuchin, S. (1979). Constructing a therapeutic reality. In E. Kaufman & P. Kaufmann (Eds.), *Family therapy of drug and alcohol abuse* (pp. 5–18). New York: Gardner Press.

Morehouse, E. R. (1986). Counseling adolescent children of alcoholics in groups. In R. J. Ackerman (Ed.), *Growing in the shadow.* Holmes Beach, FL: Learning Publications.

Satir, V. M. (1967). *Conjoint family therapy (2nd ed.).* Palo Alto, CA: Science & Behavior Books.

Seixas, J. S., and Youcha, G. (1985). *Children of alcoholism: A survivor's manual.* New York: Harper & Row.

Stark, E. (1987). Forgotten victims: Children of alcoholics. *Psychology Today, 21*(1), 58–62.

Steinglass, P. (1978). The conceptualization of marriage from a systems theory perspective. In T. J. Paolino & B. S. McCrady (Eds.), *Marriage and marital therapy: Psychoanalytic, behavioral, and systems theory perspectives* (pp. 298–365). New York: Brunner/Mazel.

Steinglass, P. (1979). Family therapy with alcoholics: A review. In E. Kaufman & P. Kaufmann (Eds.), *Family therapy of drug and alcohol abuse* (pp. 147–186). New York: Gardner Press.

Von Bertalanffy, L. (1968). *General systems theory.* New York: George Braziller.

Wegscheider, S. (1981). *Another chance: Hope and health for the alcoholic family.* Palo Alto, CA: Science & Behavior Books.

Judith Lewis is Professor of Alcoholism Sciences, Governors State University.

THREE: SCHOOL INTERVENTIONS

Jon Carlson and Judith Lewis

The junior and senior high schools have a major influence on adolescents. Unfortunately, their impact is not always positive. For most kids, school is a "necessary evil," with one primary benefit: It's a prime place for socializing. No other non-family setting consumes so much of their time, involves so much attention, and demands so much effort. The actual process of formalized classroom activity is often secondary, and how the students feel is determined largely by the teacher's opinion. Parents often suggest that adolescents ignore the teacher's shortcomings and concentrate on the subject matter, but this is hard to accept, as everything in a classroom is filtered through the teacher's personality.

What can be done about teenagers who are turned off to school and learning, who are disinterested, who are not working up to their capabilities? The first step is to uncover the reason. But in most cases there is no simple answer. Sometimes parents themselves are at fault. With the best intentions in the world, parents tell their kids, "You have to learn to do things you don't like to do," and all too often school falls into that category. Parents foster this attitude because they want their teenagers to realize that schoolwork must take precedence over hobbies and pleasurable activities, but it can backfire if the kids attend school with the sacrifice of all pleasure and fun.

Counselors have trouble providing effective services in today's world. The confusion, uncertainty, and alienation that young people experience today mirror problems that past generations have not faced. Increases in adolescent depression and suicide, use of drugs and alcohol, and the growing number of single-parent families present staggering issues for our society at large. In addition, today's counselors are touched by conditions that professionals of the past were not, such as the effects of unemployment, the rising rate of adult alcoholism, and the alarming prevalence of child abuse. These social conditions cannot be laid solely at the feet of counselors, of course. Crime, violence, and the public's disillusionment with the quality of education in general also have contributed to a disaffected view of counseling services in the school.

These conditions require a more active counselor, one who is willing to experiment and realize that traditional roles and strategies do not alleviate these problems. Although counseling techniques for young people have been improving over

187

the years, many strategies that have consistently not worked have not yet been discarded. But discarding ideas and theories that one has learned in training from respected teachers isn't easy.

Roger Aubrey believes that educational reform is occurring, and that counselors can play an important role in creating "educational excellence." Counselors, however, are currently on the periphery of education. His article discusses the need to develop new strategies so that school counselors' needs, and those of their students, will not be ignored in the midst of the changes that are taking place in schools.

In her article, Elsie Moore discusses inequalities in education and how counselors can help minority youngsters achieve. Often, teenagers from minority backgrounds have low performance because of low expectations. Cultural differences are mistakenly evaluated and understood, which impacts learning and achievement. Minority children are often relegated (or reject themselves) to inferior positions. IQ scores, achievement tests, and other culturally loaded forms of assessment label minority students as not being as capable as others. She gives helpful suggestions to counteract these problems.

Jon Carlson, in his article, presents motivational techniques that build students' feelings of confidence and self-worth. Teenagers must believe in their own importance and worthwhileness. As Elsie Moore noted, discouragement is common in minority youth. Yet discouragement is common among all teenagers who are struggling with identity formation. The specific procedures presented can be used by counselors, parents, teachers, and teenagers themselves.

Merle Ohlsen believes that today's adolescents need, more than ever before, the assistance that can be provided in personal growth and counseling groups. Teenagers do not feel as needed as they did several generations ago on the family farm or in the small family business, and they have much more time on their hands. Money and transportation are readily available, and parents are uncertain about the morals they wish to teach and what to do to enforce their expectations. This article is based on the concept that personal growth experiences teach teens the skills and values needed to live in today's world. Specifically, they help them learn to manage developmental passages and crises, complete unfinished business with significant others, and replace self-defeating behaviors with productive ones.

In the final selection, William Erpenbach and Philip Perrone describe how counselors can develop and utilize power and influence to better meet students' needs. These suggestions and strengths allow counselors to aid adolescents in a meaningful and much improved fashion.

11

Excellence, School Reform, and Counselors

Roger F. Aubrey

In April of 1983, the National Commission on Excellence in Education issued a report entitled *A Nation at Risk: The Imperative for Educational Reform* (Gardner, 1983). Since that time dozens of reports and studies calling for basic changes in education have been presented to the American public. Almost all of them are highly critical of current educational practices and call for sweeping changes. Few mention school counselors or programs linked to the concept of guidance.

This article is concerned primarily with the impact of educational reform on counselors who work in schools and the options before them. To address this concern, it will be necessary to give an overview on educational reform before turning to how this will influence counselors in schools. Finally, the range of response open to counselors will be examined and suggestions offered.

CHANGES IN SCHOOLING: THE CYCLE CONTINUES

Periodically the American public is told that our public educational system is inadequate and in need of fixing. Those doing the telling usually are panels sponsored by some branch of federal or state government or groups funded by a national foundation. Occasionally voices arise within the educational community itself. These voices are seldom heard, however, unless they are linked to some compelling social or economic force outside of the educational establishment.

The 20th century has seen many reforms in schooling. In earlier decades one major change was in extending schooling to millions of young people. Prior to 1900 only 1 in 10 students was given an opportunity to attend secondary school (Cremin, 1961, p. 291). As early as 1889 only 6.7% of the high school age group actually attended high school. By 1909 this figure had almost tripled (15.4%), and by 1930, 73.3% of this age group was attending secondary school (Goodlad, 1985, p. 268).

One of the major social forces propelling the extension of secondary education was the Industrial Revolution. The motive for more schooling was threefold. *First,* the extension of schooling kept a large number of people out of the labor market. *Second,* the need for more and more literate and skilled workers required more education than that offered in the typical elementary school. *Third,* John Dewey and his Progressive movement capitalized on a time of rapid change by demonstrating actual changes in education in areas such as pedagogy, curriculum, teacher training, and school organization.

By the time of the Depression years of the 1930s, the elementary school was no longer considered as terminal. Instead, elementary schooling from this point on came to be viewed as preparatory to high school. High schools at this time, however, were subject to increased criticism on the grounds that they did not reach the gifted, failed to prepare young people for citizenship, did not guide or counsel students well, and contained a curriculum that was unrelated to the lives of young people (Cremin, 1961, p. 252).

Following World War II another major shift in education occurred as a result of the war and a rise in the hopes and aspirations of the American public. Education was extended beyond high school because of the G.I. Bill and a time of new prosperity. Again the critical focus was on secondary schools and how well they prepared youth for the demands of college and the work force.

In 1957 Russia launched Sputnik, and panic hit the educational establishment as government officials pointed at public education for failure to keep us abreast with the Russians. The following year the National Defense Education Act was passed in an effort to beef up secondary and college education. A year later James Conant (1959) began a nationwide study of secondary schools culminating in a series of recommendations calling for changes in curriculum, standards, instruction, and organization. One strong recommendation was that of a mandatory requirement for fulltime school counselors in all of the nation's secondary schools.

WHY REFORM IN THE 1980s?

The reforms in education that occurred in the early and mid-1960s were reflections of events and social forces at that time in history. They also reflected the more healthy economy of that time and national priorities. Since that time, however, our economic picture has changed dramatically. In fact, between 1965 and 1980 financial support for education decreased by 20% (Boyer, 1983, p. 296). Furthermore, funding for education between 1980 and 1984 dropped each year (Odden, 1984, p. 311).

Failure to fund schools does not deter critics of education. Today, schools are blamed for many social changes that took place outside their doors in the 1960s and 1970s. Substance abuse, sexual promiscuity, racism, violence, unemployment, and delinquency are just a few of society's problems that the schools are asked to address. Naturally, basic education is expected to occur as in the past, but new social ills are to be added to the already overcrowded agenda of the schools.

Critics of public education also are to be found in colleges and universities, as well as in government, business, and industry. Colleges want secondary schools to adopt curricula that would prepare all (whether they go on to college or not) for a 4-year college career. Our federal government is worried about public schools because "our once unchallenged preeminence in commerce, industry, science, and technological innovation is being overtaken by competitors throughout the world" (Gardner, 1983, p. 3). The government expects schools to educate young people so we can defend ourselves economically, politically, and militarily against any and all. Finally, the business world wants schools to send forth future employees who will not cost them huge sums of money to train and who are lifelong learners with dependable work habits (National Academy of Science, 1984).

School reformers of the 1980s are numerous and demanding. Their desires for change in schooling are far from uniform, and there is consensus only in a felt need for change. As a consequence, counselors should view any proposals for change from two perspectives. *First,* do the proposals properly address and analyze the problems at hand? *Second,* are the recommendations for change sound and realistic?

THE RATIONALE FOR CHANGE

The vast majority of school reform proposals focus on American secondary schools (Adler, 1982; Boyer, 1983; College Board, 1983; Cusick, 1983; Lightfoot, 1983; Powell, Farrar, & Cohen, 1985; Sizer, 1984). A few, such as John Goodlad (1983), analyze the entire school system from kindergarten through high school. Most proposals mention the need for change in teacher training institutions. Most of the proposals are not based on empirical data or longitudinal studies of schools. Instead they rely either on secondary data or the expertise of the blue-ribbon panel making the recommendations. Few panels include teachers, parents, or pupil support personnel.

The rationale behind the push for change in schools varies from proposal to proposal. Some cite lowered SAT and standardized test scores. Others quote college admission officials and their feeling that high schools are turning out inferior students. Still others cite employers and the business community and their disappointment with the education of young people just entering the labor market. The military adds to this audience with its criticism of school training prior to the entrance of young people into the armed forces. Government officials also add their voices in worrying about our ability to compete with foreign markets with poorly educated students. Finally, advocates of high technology are worried about the quality of schooling now and over the next decade lest they end up with an insufficient number of workers.

Counselors and school people must carefully examine not just the suggested changes but also the stated reasons for educational reform. This is so because if the justification for change is in error, so might be the recommendations. As Sarason (1983) noted: "What the critics have been unable to do is to examine the possibility that there may be something radically wrong in their diagnosis and prescriptions . . . that they may be guilty of that of which they accuse school personnel: inability to accept responsibility for failure and avoidance of the question of what is being taken for granted that should not be taken for granted. When an institution appears over time to be resistant to change from within and without, with money and without money . . . does this not suggest that both critics and educators share some blind spots?" (p. 25).

WHAT REFORMERS WISH

Reformers view change in public schooling from a number of vantage points. Their yardstick for excellence all too frequently is a rise in test scores or an increase in the college-bound. All too infrequently do they employ indices such as a decline in the dropout rate, reduction in violence, less racial and sexual discrimination, better education for the handicapped, lowering of school vandalism, greater student involvement in the local community, and character development.

CATEGORIES OF CHANGE ADDRESSED IN REFORM PROPOSALS

As reform proposals look at schools, a number of areas are covered in the proposals: curriculum and subject-matter content, teaching and instruction, school organization, educational standards, teacher training services, class size, community involvement, leadership, length of school day/year, finances, and student/teacher support.

Curriculum and Subject-Matter Content

People proposing changes in schooling are generally well educated. It should come as no surprise, therefore, that most reform proposals wish a secondary school curriculum that closely resembles pre-college preparation. If anything, most proposals call for an increase in pre-college subjects such as science, mathematics, and foreign language. Many proposals also wish a dramatic decrease in electives, and some think vocational education should be eliminated. The general spirit behind the recommendations is best summed up by Adler (1982), who stated, "The best education for the best is the best education for all" (pp. 6–7). Of concern to counselors and pupil support service specialists is that many reform proposals are inflexible and see a single curriculum for all, with no provision for the non-college-bound or those who are unable to meet heightened standards.

Teaching and Instruction

To improve teaching and instruction in schools, several suggestions recently have been forthcoming. These include merit pay, higher standards, performance-based evaluation, career ladders, higher salaries, a longer working year, smaller classes, more teacher aides, use of noncertified teachers, better inservice training, and greater teacher autonomy. In the area of instruction, recommendations range from team-teaching and deliberate mentoring, to use of more primary source materials, to utilizing coaching as a way of teaching. Most of these suggestions involve the expenditure of a great deal of money. Further, most recommendations would expose teachers to a tremendous amount of public exposure and evaluation. Resistance among teachers and teacher associations already has occurred at the national and state levels and can be expected to continue in proportion to the threat experienced.

School Organization

Reform proposals such as *High School* (Boyer, 1983) and *The Paideia Proposal* (Adler, 1982) advocate a single curriculum track for all high school students. As a consequence, their recommendations regarding school organization are concerned largely with flexibility for laboratory courses and a decrease in class size. Other proposals, such as Goodlad's (1983), intentionally seek to reduce not only class size but units within schools as well. Goodlad would reorganize any school larger than 500–600 students into smaller houses—schools within schools. Under this plan, each house would be "characterized by its own curriculum, students, faculty and counselors—each house is organized vertically so that each contains students from all secondary levels" (p. 311). At the elementary level, instead of houses, students in smaller groups (100) would be assigned to teams of approximately four teachers for 3–4 years to accomplish a more personalized environment.

Other suggested organizational changes seem to follow a pattern of granting greater freedom to teachers in school decision making as well as greater freedom to individual schools in determining and carrying out objectives. One obvious problem here is bureaucracy and the stranglehold that central offices and state officials have on individual schools and teachers.

Educational Standards

Is anyone against higher educational standards, mother, and apple pie? Probably not—or at least until the implications of higher standards are considered in terms of school pushouts, dropouts, and failures. In any event, most reformers wish an increase in intellectual rigor, and this translates into an increase in Carnegie units for graduation; more math, science, and foreign language; greater yearly testing of students (and evaluations of teachers); more grade level retentions; and restrictions for participation in school athletics and extracurricular activities. Needless to say, higher standards for all eventually will translate into lower self-esteem for many, and these concerns ultimately will lead students to the school counselor's door.

Teacher Training

Few are pleased with traditional teacher training programs. Critics see the concern as too many courses centering on methods of teaching and too few on content and subject-matter mastery. The critics also are displeased at the caliber of people entering the teaching profession. They would change this condition by active recruitment, higher salaries, smaller classes, and better working conditions. In addition, people with college degrees other than in teaching would in some cases be allowed to teach (especially in science, math, and foreign language).

Finally, a small but growing number of advocates support the total elimination of undergraduate education degrees. Instead, all future teachers would first earn a Bachelor's degree and then enter a 1-year Master's program in education before joining the teaching ranks. As with the problem of standards, immediate implementation of this type of proposal would severely hinder an already growing teacher shortage and possibly not address the real problems in American education.

Smaller Class Size

Class size has long been a bone in the craw of teachers. Many teachers believe that if their classes were significantly reduced, student learning would improve— and possibly it might. Nonetheless, scant research supports this contention, at least until class size is 15 students or smaller. Naturally, smaller class size would allow teachers to assign, grade, and return more written papers and conceivably reduce discipline problems. Therefore, teachers and most reform proposals glibly suggest drastic reductions in class size and teaching loads with no thought whatsoever of financial costs or how money might be raised to support this recommendation.

Unfortunately, in the cold light of day, this may be the most unrealistic of all recommendations. Consider that in a study conducted in the District of Columbia, it was found that reducing all classes in the district by just *one* pupil per class would cost $4 million dollars per year (McKenzie, 1983, p. 392). Imagine a "significant" reduction of 5, 10, or 12 pupils per year!

Greater Community Involvement

Practically all suggestions for school change wish greater cooperation between schools and the outside community. Many are aware that desegregation and busing had led to what sociologist Morris Janowitz (1981) calls the "disarticulation" between schools and parents. Disarticulation implies a split, separation, or lack of communication. Janowitz believes this disarticulation also has occurred between schools and the workplace. To correct this fault, reformers such as Boyer (1983) desire a greater "ownership" of the schools by the community, including business and industry, parents, citizens, local school boards, state agencies and legislatures, and so on. Many suggestions toward this end include a parent-teacher-student advisory council in each school, a network of community coalitions called "citizens for the public schools," meaningful liaisons between schools and business and industry, and placement of all students for one semester of high school in volunteer work in the community or at school as a service requirement.

Leadership

The simplest way to view leadership in schools is to focus on the school principal and how he or she operates. This is the way most reformers see leadership, and practically all wish to give greater power and autonomy to principals. Many also view the principal not just as a manager or the key authority person but one who is the key educator in the school. For example, Adler (1982) stated that, "The principal should be first and foremost what the title implies—the head teacher, or what in private schools is called the headmaster, leader of the other teachers who are also called masters" (p. 63). This naive perspective on the principal's role belies the myriad tasks that principals perform daily. It also fails to note the leadership roles of department heads, assistant principals, central office personnel, and individual teachers and pupil service specialists.

Luckily, some proposals realize the limitations of the principal as sole leader in the school and advocate greater autonomy and decision making by teachers and other school staff in each separate school. These proposals would see head teachers, small groups of master teachers, and department chairs—not the school principal—as the key people in decisions involving teaching and curriculum. How this is to be achieved is rarely spelled out, but it would be a monumental task in many schools controlled by principals and assistant principals.

Lengthening of School Day/Year

The number of days in a school year varies from state to state, with a range of 180 to 200 days in a school year. Proposals for school reform that significantly increase the number of required Carnegie units for high school graduation definitely would demand an increase both in the length of the school day and the number of school days per year. Such is the case in the most widely publicized reform proposal, *A Nation at Risk* (Gardner, 1983). Framers of this proposal already have advocated an increase in time to a 7-hour school day and a 200- to 220-day school year.

This recommendation is in decided contrast to Goodlad (1983) and others who think the problem is not the length of the school day or year but, rather, the quality of what goes on during that time period. Goodlad believes that, if anything, teachers need less class time and more planning time. Like the reduction of class size, few reform proposals address the issue of costs in increasing the school day and year or the problems this would present to school personnel pursuing advanced degrees during the summer and regular year to meet state certification requirements.

Finances

Few educational reform proposals make solid recommendations to support the financial changes they advocate. This is rather astounding when one considers that practically all of the changes suggested have price tags. As an example, *A Nation at Risk* (Gardner, 1983) makes 38 major recommendations for change in schools, but none deal with monies to support these recommendations. Instead, we are told that, "The Federal Government has the primary responsibility to identify the national interest in education. It should also help fund and support efforts to protect and promote that interest" (p. 33). This statement is naive, to say the least, for it fails to recognize that *less than 10%* of public education costs are covered by the federal government. What requires attention is how state and local governments can continue and possibly increase school funding. The report *High School* (Boyer, 1983) similarly ducks the issue of finances, simply stating: "This report on the American high school has focused on education, not money. But the two, of course, are interlocked" (p. 296).

Finally, a few reformers believe their recommendations actually will save money by changing existing conditions. This is voiced by Goodlad (1983) in claiming that his panel's recommendations call "more for rearranging the use of existing funds and time than for adding resources" (p. 319). It seems safe to say that most proposals for educational change ignore the financial costs behind their recommendations. In so doing, however meritorious the recommendation, they make it easy for those wishing adherence to the status quo to defend their position.

Student/Teacher Support Services

Scant attention is paid in any educational reform proposal to school counselors or student/teacher support services. A bright light shines here and there, as in *High School* (Boyer, 1983), which suggests that "no counselor should have a case load of more than one hundred students" (p. 306). This is in decided contrast to many proposals that see lighter teacher loads, fewer teacher's aides, and smaller class size as the key to return of the teacher-counselor. This person would be a throwback to the 1930s and 1940s, when all teachers were assumed to have guidance responsibilities and counseling ability.

Obviously, the conditions today in schools are quite different from the Depression and World War II days, as is the training of counselors and teachers. Guidance and counseling clearly have been ignored in school reform reports because the authors of these reports focus primarily on what they view as the essentials of schooling: teaching, curriculum, and students. This narrow perspective on education is not surprising. What is taught, how it is taught, and to whom it is taught comprise a neat, tight triangle. The concern for school counselors is primarily one of being viewed on the periphery—outside the mainstream of schooling. We will turn to this concern, and how counselors might improve their image, shortly. First, however, let us look briefly at the major weakness within the educational reform proposals.

THE FLY IN THE OINTMENT

As noted earlier, one glaring weakness in most proposals lies in their failure to link reform measures to means of funding these changes. This indeed limits and stretches the credibility of reform proposals when state and local officials consider implementing costly recommendations. I also have noted the limited perspective of most proposals in concentrating solely on the triangle of teaching, curriculum, and students. (What about school structure and organization, student support services, parents and the greater community, a sound philosophy and rationale of education, handicapped and minorities, citizenship and career development, a realistic plan for implementing school reform, and so on?) If changes in education are to occur, these considerations cannot be put on the back burner or denied. Reformers also fail in most instances to recognize the major social, cultural, political, and economic changes affecting students and schools. These, too, must be addressed if constructive changes are to be brought about.

The real fly in the ointment of school reform, however, is a narrow focus by reformers on the bright, gifted, and intellectually talented in the public school population. The focus of practically all reform proposals is on increasing Carnegie units and providing an exclusive pre-college curriculum. This is justified by organizations such as The College Board, with the glib statement that, "Better preparation for the college-bound will spill over and improve the schooling of those who are not college-bound" (Bailey, 1983, p. 25). Other proposals would grant high school diplomas only on the basis of rigorous testing (of a pre-college curriculum) and exhibited mastery. When asked if this will not result in scores of students being pushed out of school, educators such as Sizer (1984) reply, "Yes, we'll lose kids. The ones bucking the system could find it easier to evade learning" (p. 67).

The elitism in most reform proposals is naive and reflects a private or exclusive suburban school bias. As Oakes (1986) has noted, "There is a single standard posed in the reports, and that standard is undeniably white and middle-class" (p. 74). Rarely is any attention paid in these reports to the tremendous variation in students' intellectual ability and the limitations inherent to setting high and unrealistic standards for all. As Hodgkinson (1982) has noted, many reformers "moved up the high jump bar from four to six feet without giving any additional coaching to the youth who were not clearing the bar when it was set at four feet" (pp. 11–12).

In advocating rigorous pre-college curricula devoid of vocational education and meaningful electives, reformers truly think that a single set of high educational experiences can solve the dual challenge of equity and excellence in education. They fail to see the point raised by Oakes (1986):

Equal educational opportunity does not require the same educational experiences for all individuals, but rather an equal opportunity to develop oneself for an appropriate future in the
worklife of the community. This may, and usually does, necessitate quite different educational experiences for individuals of varying abilities and future roles. Equal educational
opportunity, then, requires the provision of different educational experiences and the proper
match of these educations to individual ability and suitability for future work. In that way
all are served equally well. (p. 64)

Oakes's plea for flexibility in educational expectations takes into account the
staggering school dropout rate for Blacks (39%) and Hispanics (45%) (Bayer,
1983, p. 5). The reform proposals do not. Oakes's point underscores educational
problems in all metropolitan areas today. For example, in Boston the dropout rate
is 50%, 20% of the school population is handicapped, 12% is bilingual, 40% is
educationally and economically disadvantaged, and 70% consists of minority students. Does anyone really believe a standardized pre-college curriculum would
work in Boston? Should the majority of school students anywhere have to be subjected to a curriculum and standards developed for the 32.5% fortunate enough to
graduate from high school and go on to college? (Aubrey, 1985, p. 94).

EXCELLENCE, EDUCATION, AND COUNSELORS

In 1984 the school dropout rate in the United States among 17- and 18-year-old
youth increased from 25% to 27% (Williams, 1984, p. 47). This increase marked
the first time in two decades that the school dropout rate showed an increase, and
it coincided with the first of many rigorous educational reforms. Counselors and
other school personnel, then, might consider that the time may come when not 1 in
4 but *1 in 3* young people will drop or be pushed out of school prematurely.

The wave of reform movements in the 1980s is both similar and dissimilar to
previous reform movements. Today's reforms are the same in that they seek excellence for young people through innovation and change. They are dissimilar in that
today's reforms, unlike those of the 1950s and 1960s, are *focusing on a small proportion of all youth and are driven by economic considerations*. In the words of
two educator-economists, the most recent reform proposals reflect "the shift of
commitment away from equity for bilingual, economically disadvantaged, racially
isolated, and handicapped students in favor of a workforce that would be more
highly qualified to meet the needs of U.S. industry. Indeed, the reports make a
point of justifying their recommendations on the basis of the crucial role that the
schools must play in making the workforce internationally competitive in a world
of high technology" (Carnoy & Levin, 1986, p. 43).

Counselors must not be misled by the current ballyhoo over high technology.
It is true that high tech in some areas requires highly skilled workers. It is also true
that some areas of high tech include the fastest growing occupations in America.
But it it just as true that over the next 10–15 years only 7% of all jobs in this country
will have anything to do with high tech. Similarly, although high tech jobs are new
and fast growing, they employ but a scant number of the labor force. Instead the

service sector is where the vast number of jobs are to be found (Aubrey & D'Andrea, 1984). Jobs in the service sector are replacing former work in industry and production and typically require less training. They also pay less, are more boring and routine, and carry fewer benefits. It is here where high school graduates usually will enter the labor force—and these positions certainly *do not require a pre-college curriculum!*

As gatekeepers to work and education beyond high school, counselors have a tremendous burden in attempting to guide young people over the next few decades. Reforms in education will come and go, and each time they emerge, vested interests will attempt to determine priorities. At this juncture in schooling, the concept of excellence appears to be used as the rationale for major changes in school standards and curricula. These changes, as we have noted, are actually aimed at only one segment of the school population—the college-bound—and could have disastrous consequences for the majority of students—the non-college-bound. Counselors, therefore, need to examine what reformers mean by the term *excellence* and how this concept extends to not just the academically gifted but to all students.

EXCELLENCE AS AN EDUCATIONAL STANDARD

Few people would disagree that excellence is a powerful yardstick for determining educational outcomes. They might disagree, however, in defining this term. Prakash and Waks (1985) have examined this concept carefully and have come up with four definitions of education, each with its own standards of excellence. The first concept sees excellence as *proficiency*. This view is highly technical and measures outcomes by quantitative data such as test scores. Teachers in this scheme are information providers, and educational leaders are managers who supervise teachers who provide knowledge and skills. In this view, teachers are not trusted, and they are "managed" by standard lesson plans, texts, student evaluations, frequent testing, and observation. *A Nation at Risk* (Gardner, 1983) is typical of this view of excellence, in which increased mental proficiency is the bottom line for assessing excellence.

A second view of excellence sees *rationality* as the primary goal of education and calls this "disciplinary initiation." In this view, "disciplinary" means mastery of a specific discipline such as the scientific, the moral, the aesthetic, the humanities, and so on. Unlike the technical, the rational encourages imagination and creativity and does not prize rote memory and the mechanical application of exercises and routines. A rational approach rewards problem solving and application of disciplined thinking. Boyer's (1983) *High School* characterizes this approach, and it is quite similar to how colleges view excellence. It is not seen as something best measured by tests but, rather, by the products of students' work (essays, papers, lab experiments, projects) as evaluated by teachers and others who are masters of a particular discipline. Leaders (principals and supervisors) in this scheme are knowledgeable experts themselves who orchestrate conditions so meaningful learning can occur in the interaction between student, teacher, and content.

A third view of excellence is that of *self-actualization* or personal development. This view of excellence rejects education that simply piles layer upon layer of culture on passive students through master teachers. Instead, this perspective "is shaped by a vision of the individual human being in a lifelong quest for freedom from both biological and social conditioning in search of authenticity. Self-actualization is the end of human development, and hence the organizing principle and standard of excellence for this conception" (Prakash & Waks, 1985, p. 85). Counselors are well aware of this philosophy; it can be found in the works of Carl Rogers, Abraham Maslow, A. S. Neill, and Carl Jung.

A final concept of excellence is that of *social responsibility*. This view recognizes self-actualization as a guiding principle but only in the context of the community as a whole. Self-actualization, therefore, is rejected if the good of any member of society is furthered at the cost of others. John Dewey, who long ago voiced this opinion, believed that the common good for all should be the responsibility of all social institutions, especially the schools. Education in this final concept, thus, is empowerment, and the social responsibility of students and school staff would set the standard of educational excellence.

These four notions of excellence are mentioned at this point to illustrate some very different definitions of excellence. This is important because many who are involved in educational reform seem to think they have a franchise on excellence and how it should be attained. Today, the loudest and most popular of reformers are those stressing standardization, mental proficiency, nationwide achievement testing, and so on. For those working in schools, it seems essential to possess what Ernest Hemingway spoke of as a "built-in crap detector"—a means of determining what has worth and what is fool's gold. Let us now turn to what counselors might do to help themselves and their students in this new wave of educational reform.

WHAT COUNSELORS CAN DO

Counselors have been left out of many reform proposals. Some reformers are aware of counselors but believe that if teaching conditions were vastly improved, teachers and school administrators could replace counselors. In other instances, counselors are seen on the periphery of education, dispensing services when needed but not really essential to the majority of educational outcomes. Counselors, therefore, are ignored for they are not part of the "big picture" of education. Finally, a few reports do acknowledge the hard work of counselors and wish to improve their working conditions along with teachers and others.

What can counselors do to improve their image with their many publics? How can counselors assist the many students who may well turn out to be casualties as standards are increased and higher expectations are placed on all? Do counselors have a role in the current push for educational excellence? If so, what is it?

The suggestions that follow are neither definitive nor panaceas for the problems counselors face with excellence and school reform. Rather, they represent some measures counselors can take to ensure that their presence in schools is known and respected. These suggestions are not presented in order of importance. All are important.

Develop a Knowledge Base

Much of the training and education of counselors is process-oriented. Most Master-level programs emphasize specific skills and techniques such as active listening, group dynamics, reflection of feelings, and so on. Because the emphasis in graduate counseling programs is on process, content is frequently ignored. This is unfortunate for counselors entering schools because teachers and others, often view them as non-educators and only service providers. Granted, in high schools counselors are assumed to have information about colleges and course scheduling. This, however, is not the same as someone having a Master's degree (which means mastery of some discipline) in a specific subject or area (e.g., English, math, science).

To be part of educational excellence, counselors must carve out areas that have meaning and credibility to fellow educators, students, parents, administrators, and the greater community. This means a knowledge base they can "own," claim expertise in, and pass along to others. Counselors are building such a base in educational reform and can further that foundation by collecting more knowledge from the references cited in this article.

Another area with which most counselors are already acquainted is career development. If an area stands out as being the one where counselors can carve an immediate niche in schools, it is in career development. This is really where counseling and guidance began in the schools, but it has been sorely neglected recently. To know and "do" career development is no easy task because it requires constant updating on labor trends, employment statistics, job shifts, and so on. Nonetheless, with the rapid transition to a world of high tech, counselors have to translate what this means to students and their families, as well as to fellow educators.

A related area that counselors might consider is human development and individual differences. Some knowledge of this domain, though usually part of graduate education, is not enough for true expertise. Here again, counselors can create an area of expertise that few in the schools possess but desperately need. The thrust of this suggestion is that counselors can expand their service role to that of an educator as well. To do so, counselors need a recognizable sphere of expertise that is prized by the publics they serve and work with. Many such areas are available if counselors wish to become part of the educational process.

Own a Standard of Excellence

Excellence has been discussed throughout this article. It also is discussed daily by school boards, state department of education officials, parents, legislators, the business community, and educational administrators. The hallmark of most discussions is excellence—what it is, why it is desirable, how it can be attained, how much it will cost, and so on. Each individual counselor working in a school should examine this concept and arrive at his or her own defensible definition of excellence. This will prepare the counselor for discussions and actual changes aimed at improving excellence. It also will allow counselors to raise important considerations when innovations may adversely affect the students they work with. Finally, owning one's own definition of excellence can guide significant changes in counseling efforts.

Build Support Bases

Support bases consist of individuals and groups a counselor can call upon for encouragement and help. They may be fellow counselors, teachers, parents, other pupil service workers, outside agencies, students, and so forth. When the chips are down or aid is needed, they are important allies. Some support groups may be formal groups that a counselor assembles (an ongoing parent, teacher, or pupil service worker group); others may be informal groups or individuals that a counselor cultivates for help and assistance (this is obviously a two-way street). Most counselors already have some support bases. I suggest that these resources be expanded so they can be mobilized in times of need.

Do More Group Work

Working with groups of students, teachers, or parents is much more efficient than is a one-to-one approach. In some cases, it is also more effective as members of a group help one another or provide role models beyond the counselor. I hesitate to say "more" because most counselors already have heard this suggestion for years. Nonetheless, few school counselors do any significant amount of group work; it remains barren and unused.

Learn and Use Computer Technology

The advent of computers can be a real boon to school counselors in three ways. First, at the secondary level computers may in time relieve counselors of much quasi-administrative work in scheduling, attendance, and the like. Second, interactive computer systems allow students to access and acquire information that they otherwise would seek in one-to-one interviews. Third, knowledge of computers should greatly increase counselors' knowledge base and information capacity. For these advantages to become reality, counselors first must step forth and desire them. If they do not, others in the schools will gain these ends.

Monitor Student Progress

As educational reforms are initiated at state and local levels, the impacts of these changes seldom are monitored. Granted, standardized tests often are used to indicate that index of education. What is lacking, however, is someone looking at equally valid indices such as the holding power of the school, increase in grade level retentions, academic stress, and so on. Counselors, as a result of their close contact with students, should be able to look at the school climate as proposals are enforced and students are exposed to new demands. As advocates of students, counselors in some situations may be the only persons examining the impact of reform on the mental health of students—but someone must do this.

Affiliate

To deal with major changes in education alone is difficult. In addition to support groups, counselors who are not affiliated with state, regional, and national associations would do well to consider these resources. For example, in January of 1984, the American Association for Counseling and Development (AACD), the American School Counselor Association (ASCA), and other AACD divisions sponsored a 3-day conference on school excellence. Materials from this conference, as well as other printed material, are available from AACD headquarters. Committees from various AACD divisions, as well as state-level groups, also have been at work on educational reform. At some level all counselors working in schools should affiliate with an organization of their choice that will help them face social, political, and economic forces affecting them and their students.

SUMMARY

For the past three to four years critics of education have swamped the American public with proposals calling for change in schooling. Counselors have not been addressed in many of these proposals—but the changes suggested surely will impact on their lives and those of their students. In particular, the emphasis of a number of current proposals on strengthening educational standards could work to the detriment of many deserving youth. Counselors are urged to become knowledgeable of these proposals and how they define excellence and to develop strategies so their own needs and those of their students will not be ignored as change occurs in schools.

REFERENCES

Adler, M. (1982). *The Paideia proposal: An educational manifesto*. New York: Macmillan.
Aubrey, R. (1985). A counseling perspective on the recent educational reform reports. *School Counselor, 33*, 91–99.
Aubrey, R., & D'Andrea, M. (1984). What counselors should know about high technology. *Counseling & Human Development, 17*, 1–12.
Bailey, A. Y. (1983). The educational equality project: Focus on results. *Phi Delta Kappan, 65*, 22–25.

Boyer, E. (1983). *High school: A report on secondary education in America*. New York: Harper & Row.

Carnoy, M., & Levin, H. (1986). Educational reform and class conflict. *Journal of Education, 168*, 35–46.

College Board. (1983). *Academic preparation for college: What students need to know and be able to do*. New York: College Board.

Conant, J. (1959). *The American high school today: A first report to interested citizens*. New York: McGraw-Hill.

Cremin, L. (1961). *The transformation of the school*. New York: Knopf.

Cusick, P. (1983). *The egalitarian ideal and the American high school*. New York: Longman.

Gardner, D. (1983). *A nation at risk: The imperative for educational reform*. Washington, DC: U.S. Dept. of Education.

Goodlad, J. (1983). *A place called school: Prospects for the future*. New York: McGraw-Hill.

Goodlad, J. (1985, December). The great American schooling experiment. *Phi Delta Kappan*, pp. 266–271.

Hodgkinson, H. (1982, December). What's STILL right with education. *Phi Delta Kappan*, pp. 231–235.

Janowitz, M. (1981, Winter). Why don't things work anymore? *University of Chicago Magazine*, pp. 18–23.

Lightfoot, S. L. (1983). *The good high school: Portraits of character and culture*. New York: Basic Books.

McKenzie, F. D. (1983). The yellow brick road of education. *Harvard Educational Review, 53*, 389–392.

National Academy of Sciences, National Academy of Engineering, and Institute of Medicine. (1984). *High schools and the changing workplace* (Report of the Panel on Secondary Education and the Changing Workplace). Washington, DC: National Academy Press.

Oakes, J. (1986). Tracking, inequality and the rhetoric of reform: Why schools don't change. *Journal of Education, 168*, 64–80.

Odden, A. (1984). Financing educational excellence. *Phi Delta Kappan, 65*, 311–318.

Powell, A., Farrar, E., & Cohen, D. (1985). *The shopping mall high school: Winners and losers in the educational marketplace*. Boston: Houghton Mifflin.

Prakash, M. S., & Waks, L. J. (1985). Four conceptions of excellence. *Teachers College Record, 87*, 79–101.

Sarason, S. (1983). *Schooling in America: Scapegoat or salvation*. New York: Free Press.

Sizer, T. (1984). *Horace's compromise: The dilemma of the American high school*. Boston: Houghton Mifflin.

Williams, D. (1984, January 16). A report card for the states. *Time*, p. 47.

Roger Aubrey is Director of the Human Development Counseling Program, Peabody College of Vanderbilt University.

12

Enhancing the Educational Attainment Of Minority Youth

Elsie G. J. Moore

Inequalities exist in the life opportunities of young Americans from various social classes and ethnic groups. This is obviously not a new observation. The issue became the focus of considerable sociopolitical concern in the early 1960s as larger segments of our society were confronted with the reality that some groups were experiencing unmitigated intergenerational poverty and social and cultural isolation at a time when the majority was benefiting from prosperity and opportunities for upward mobility in an expanding economy.

Although the historical social forces of segregation and exclusion on the bases of race and national origin undoubtedly had contributed to the problems, legally banning these practices was clearly not sufficient to solve them. The fact remained that most individuals in the excluded groups were not developing the skills and credentials required by an increasingly technical society. That poor children and those from isolated ethnic groups consistently showed lower levels of educational attainment and scholastic achievement was recognized as a major contributor to socioeconomic disparities.

Also, public education clearly was not entirely succeeding as the great "equalizer" in providing—regardless of family background—the opportunity to learn, develop, and achieve. Black Americans, Hispanics, Puerto Ricans, and other ethnic minority children were not developing literacy and mathematic skills at a level necessary to compete with their more advantaged agemates in the majority culture.

Although general agreement existed that the socioeconomic immobility of these groups was strongly related to their lack of educational achievement, considerable disagreement emerged over what factors were contributing to their school failure and how these factors might be mediated by social class and ethnic group membership. Many experimental intervention programs were developed with the common goal of reducing or eliminating the school achievement deficiencies of minority status children. The focus and content of these programs varied depending upon the theoretical orientation of program developers to the nature and causal sequence of factors in minority children's educational difficulties.

In addition to numerous isolated experimental programs, Project Head Start was implemented at the national level in 1965 with federal funds allocated for the War on Poverty. The purpose of this national program for poor and minority status children ages 3 to 5 years was to ameliorate handicaps that prevent children from benefiting from public education, and thereby to increase their potential for upward social mobility.

After more than two decades of educational innovations, interventions, and research, considerable disparities remain in the scholastic achievement and educational attainment of minority status youth and their majority culture peers. Why this is the case and what can be done to facilitate school success of minority status young people are the issues addressed in this article. Suggestions as to how counselors may play a role in enhancing the educational attainment of minority youths are particularly focused upon in this discussion.

A CLOSER LOOK AT THE PROBLEM

Young people from certain ethnic groups consistently show lower levels of educational attainment (i.e., number of years of schooling completed) than their majority culture peers. Blacks and Hispanics, for example, show significantly lower educational attainment than their Anglo counterparts.

Comparative Studies

Recent estimates indicate that, among American youth between ages 18 and 23 in the summer of 1980, the proportion of Blacks who had not obtained a high school diploma was twice that of the White population (32% vs. 16%) (U.S. Department of Defense, 1982). The proportion of Hispanic youths in this age range who had not completed high school was even higher than that of Blacks—42%. Differences in the proportions of these ethnic groups, ages 18 to 22 years, who had completed at least 1 year of postsecondary education (i.e., some college) were not as great as those seen for high school completion, but they were considerable.

Regardless of ethnicity, individuals with more education obtain higher status jobs and, generally, higher salaries. Therefore, educational variation between groups is an important factor in the persistent inequalities in life opportunities and ultimate occupational and income attainment observed between them (Jencks et al., 1979).

Increasingly, educators and social science researchers are focusing not only upon how much schooling young people from various groups complete but also on the level and types of skills they attain while in the educational system. Technological advances have reduced the demand for unskilled and semiskilled workers while increasing the demand for clerical, technical, and professional workers. What this means is that basic literacy *and* numeracy skills are absolute prerequisites for performance in occupations at even the lowest end of the skilled labor continuum. Individuals with basic science, electronics, and mechanical knowledge, as well as basic academic skills (in reading, writing, and mathematics) can be expected to create a competitive advantage in selection for jobs, higher educational placements, and job-training programs leading to higher status and more lucrative careers in today's labor market.

Studies of academic skill development among American school-age children have consistently shown that, on the average, minority youth are not developing basic academic skills, such as reading, writing, mathematics, and science, at the same rate as their White counterparts. The discrepancy in skill development among minority status youth quite clearly relates to social and educational processes that undermine their opportunities for quality education.

This point was substantiated by Coleman et al. (1966) in reporting the results of their national study of the skill development of American school children at various grade levels. The study demonstrated the unevenness with which public education serves individuals from various life circumstances. It alerted educators, social scientists, and policy makers to the fact that Black and other minority status children were not developing even basic academic skills at the same rate as their White agemates, even when they had the same amount of schooling. Subsequent studies such as the periodic National Assessment of Educational Progress, conducted by the Education Commission of the States, and analyses of results of the yearly administration of the Scholastic Aptitude Test (SAT) (see Jones, 1984, for a review of these studies) generally confirm the persistence of ethnic group differences in specific skill development over time.

Profile of American Youth

In 1980 a unique opportunity to examine the skill level of the contemporary American youth population, to assess their vocational potential (as indexed by aptitude test scores) and to compare the performance of persons of varying ethnic and educational backgrounds, resulted from a study sponsored by the Department of Defense in cooperation with the Department of Labor. This study, called *Profile of American Youth*, involved administration of the current version of the Armed Services Vocational Aptitude Battery (ASVAB) to nearly 12,000 young people ages 15 to 22 at the time of testing. The study sample was developed to yield data that could be projected to represent the entire U.S. population in this age range. Because the young people who were administered the ASVAB were participants in the Department of Labor's large-scale study, National Longitudinal Study (NLS) of Youth Labor Force Behavior, a considerable amount of background data were available for each person tested, including educational information, family background data, ethnicity, and so on.

What makes the results from the *Profile of American Youth* study so unique is that the data come from persons of all segments of our society who were sampled by direct home visits. Consequently, they give a much broader picture of the skill development of American young people than tests administered to school children (e.g., the National Assessment of Educational Progress) or to high school seniors who are college-bound [e.g., Scholastic Aptitude Test (SAT) and American College Testing (ACT) program results reported annually]. In addition, because the ASVAB is a broad-range aptitude test battery that assesses not only school-intensive skills such as reading, word knowledge, general science, and mathematics, but also technical skills such as electronics information, mechanical comprehension, and auto and shop information, the Profile study permits an analysis of vocationally relevant skills that usually are not covered in the routine testing of students.

Results of the Profile study revealed that for all American young people, poor and non-poor, Black, Hispanic, and White, the more schooling they complete, the higher are their skill levels in the school-intensive areas and the technical areas. But Black and Hispanic youth who had completed the same amount of schooling as their White peers, including those who had at least some college, generally scored considerably lower than Whites.

As a matter of fact, a clear pattern of increasing difference in level of skill development with education emerged when the performance of Black and White youths was compared. That is, the smallest difference in their scores was seen among those who had completed 8 or fewer years of education, and the greatest difference was seen among those who had completed at least some college. In the case of the Hispanic young people, the smallest differentiation of their skill level relative to White peers also was seen among those who had completed 8 or fewer years of schooling. Beyond this educational level, a larger, but essentially constant, difference was shown in favor of White youth. (See Bock & Moore, 1986, for a complete analysis and discussion of the Profile study results.)

Other Studies

Although researchers consistently have observed considerable differences in the level of skill development of ethnic minority youth as compared to that of their White peers, positive changes are beginning to appear. For example, Burton and Jones (1982), from their analysis of National Assessment of Educational Progress (NAEP) test results for children ages 9 and 13 years old between 1970 and 1980, reported a significant decline in performance differences between Black and White pupils in writing skills, science, mathematics, social studies, and reading. Similarly, Jones (1984) reported a decline in differences between Black and White students in SAT-Verbal and SAT-Mathematics performance between 1976 and 1983.

Even though considerable differences remain between the average scores of Black and White students, these trends of declining differences are encouraging. Why we now are beginning to see encouraging changes in the relative performance of White youth and their ethnic minority peers is difficult to specify. Most observers, however, conceptualize the declining differences as long awaited returns on societal investments in innovations, interventions, and general efforts to improve the quality of education available to ethnic minority youth.

SOME EARLY FALSE-STARTS

In the 1960s and early 1970s the development of most experimental intervention programs aimed at facilitating school success of minority status children was predicated upon the belief that the children's academic difficulties were a consequence of cognitive deficiencies that characterized them at the onset of formal schooling (see Horowitz & Paden, 1973, for a review of these programs). That is, many psychologists, educators, and other authorities assumed that ethnic minority children did not develop prerequisite intellectual skills during the preschool years to allow them to optimally benefit from school instruction. Although theorists at the time differed in their ideas about why the children were deficient (whether the deficiencies were primarily the result of environmental factors or of biological factors), they did generally agree that children from certain ethnic minority groups were disproportionately deficient in the skills necessary for successful school performance and learning.

This notion of pervasive cognitive deficiency among ethnic minority children—particularly Black children—was attributable primarily to the consistent finding that the children on the average scored significantly lower on standardized intelligence tests than did their White peers. Indeed, ethnic group differences in IQ performance and performance on other standardized measures designed to assess learning potential were the empirical bases for assuming that cognitive deficits were the sources of the children's school achievement difficulties.

The logic of this assumption stems from the belief that IQ tests can inform us of the quality of cognitive functioning that characterizes all children and that differences in functioning indicated by variations in test scores play a significant causal role in differentiated school performance (Eckberg, 1979). Both facets of this assumption can be challenged on the basis of accumulated research findings on factors affecting minority children's IQ test performance (see Moore, 1986a, for a discussion of this issue).

In the belief that ethnic minority children suffered from cognitive deficiencies, most of the early programs were designed to provide experiences and instruction that were thought to promote cognitive competency in general and the development of prerequisite academic skills in particular. As might be expected, the effectiveness of those programs typically was evaluated by noting changes in children's IQ scores at the completion of the intervention.

Most of these early programs were successful in boosting the children's IQ scores, but follow-up data revealed that by the third grade the children's scholastic achievement was not significantly different from that of their ethnic peers who had not experienced special preparation for public school entry. Had the programs failed? The unqualified answer is *no,* they had not failed, but many of the guiding assumptions of the programs on which long-term projections for the children's school success were based were in error.

As our knowledge of human developmental processes evolves, we must adjust our assumptions and hypotheses. These early programs based their projections of future school success for the participating children on the assumption that experiences in early infancy and childhood have a lasting effect on the individual—an impact on development throughout the course of development.

Clarke and Clarke (1976) and Brim and Kagan (1980) have compiled evidence from a number of sources to indicate that the effects of early experience, both positive and negative, are not permanent over the life course. Human development is a dynamic process, and individuals change as a result of continual interaction between their person and their changing environments. From this perspective, Ramey and Haskins (1981) concluded that the failure of ethnic minority children to achieve in the public school system consistent with projections made on the basis of their IQ scores after program interventions was attributable to public school characteristics. That is, public schools do not generally provide continued support for these children's intellectual development at the level provided by high quality preschool programs.

The lesson to be learned from early attempts to enhance minority children's educational attainment is rather obvious. Attempts to boost the children's scholastic achievement and attainment cannot be a one-time effort in the preschool years. Efforts to facilitate their academic growth have to be reflected in all segments of the curriculum, in the process of classroom instruction, and in the planning and program development of administrators, teachers, and counselors.

MAKING THE SCHOOLS WORK FOR MINORITY YOUTHS

Each school year a disproportionate number of ethnic minority children are relegated to inferior positions in the curriculum on the basis of test results such as IQ scores and reading readiness assessments (Scarr, 1981). These early school decisions later translate into lower track positions in high school (if the student does not drop out of school from boredom before that time) and generally lower skill development at the completion of their public school experience. The reason for this is that children who are placed in special education classes other than gifted classes often are stereotyped by the larger social system of the school as being not as capable as others.

Teachers, counselors, and other school personnel often use the lower standardized test performance of these children to set a similarly low ceiling on the type, amount, and level of exposure to curriculum materials and on acceptable levels of mastery. Instruction is limited to the level of the test score, with only modest attempts to provide intellectual growth experiences (Haskins, Walton, & Ramey, 1983). Consequently, the children get farther behind their peers who achieve higher curriculum placements early in the schooling process. The effects of this undereducation are cumulative, resulting in greater disparities in skill development between groups at the higher educational levels than at lower levels.

Many unsophisticated users of test data interpret lower scores on standardized measures of the sort mentioned earlier as indicators of fixed deficits. Thus, they feel justified in setting lower educational standards and expectations for children who are thought to be less capable, especially if "hard" evidence, such as a test score, exists to verify that position. Therefore, test data users in the school setting must be aware of the importance of cultural relativity for determining educational potential. Schools and school personnel all too often have a monocultural view (i.e., that of the White middle-class) of what behaviors, skills, attitudes, and values on the part of a pupil and his or her family are indicative of a "high ability" child. This same view generally is reflected in the standardized test measures used to empirically support placement and classification decisions.

Children from different ethnic groups enter this system with learning experiences, skills, attitudes, and achievement orientations derived from their unique socialization experiences, which are quite often different from those expected or even desired by the school (Gilbert, 1985; Shade, 1982). But this does not mean that they have not developed the prerequisite cognitive skills to be successful learners of skills the schools are charged to provide. Schools must become more attuned to ethnic minority children's needs as learners and avoid relying on test scores to account for their failure to do so.

Certainly the standardized test scores of ethnic minority children can be useful—if used wisely and in conjunction with carefully collected observational data of the child in various contexts, not just the school classroom. These data can be used to identify the child's relative strengths and weaknesses in preparation for curriculum placements appropriate for her or his age. But these data must be used to capitalize on apparent strengths in the instructional process, and to plan and implement appropriate remediation, if necessary, to ensure the child's continual academic growth.

The Cultural Context of Educational Processes

School personnel have to recognize that the school context is not a culturally neutral environment. Gilbert (1985) noted that the culture of the school is one that encourages and expects competitive behavior among pupils, demonstrated competency in standard English in oral exchanges, willingness to follow pre-set rules for involvement in the instructional process (e.g., only one person speaks at a time), and that involvement is limited to cognitive participation, not affective and motorical participation.

Shade (1982) suggested that a particular style of information processing is required by the culture of the school for students to be remarkably successful in the educational process. Characteristics of this accepted style of information processing include the spontaneous tendency to focus on the task itself and to ignore the people in the situation, an attending preference for verbal rather than nonverbal cues, abstraction ability that separates ideas and concepts into parts and reconstitutes them into a unified whole, and an analytic thinking style. According to Shade, the schools expect and require cognitive strategies that are "sequential, analytic, and object-oriented" for school success, which means that children who are, as a result of their particular cultural socialization, "universalistic, intuitive, and . . . person oriented" are likely to experience achievement difficulties (p. 238).

More often than not, ethnic minority children enter the schools demonstrating information processing skills, attitudes, and understandings of involvement in the classroom that conflict with the instructional modes and expectations of the typical classroom teacher. Many believe that this mismatch between the skills and orientations to learning that ethnic minority children bring to the school and what the school system expects and values is a major source of the children's achievement difficulties (see Bock & Moore, 1986, for a review of this literature).

If this is the case, adjusting instructional modes to fit the styles of the children rather than attempting to force the children to be responsive to the preestablished style of the school could function to facilitate minority children's achievement. It also might function to facilitate their remaining in school through high school completion to the extent that the adjustment might encourage children's greater feelings of belonging to the system rather than feelings of "foreign-ness."

High Expectations of Pupils' Achievement

Much literature has accumulated on characteristics of so-called effective schools for poor and ethnic minority children—schools wherein these children show high academic achievement. Characteristics of effective schools generally include a strong leader who is knowledgeable about and involved in the instructional program, programs of instruction in reading and mathematics that are systematically implemented and for which goals of instruction are clearly articulated, and high expectations of children's achievement, particularly in basic verbal and numerical skills, by the teachers and administrative staff (Brookover et al., 1978; Edmonds, 1979).

The latter characteristic has been consistently found to affect the achievement of ethnic minority students. Those who experience school settings wherein high academic standards are set and school personnel, particularly teachers, expect them to be successful in achieving the standards show high achievement. Teachers in these situations tend to provide a considerable amount of encouragement, praise, and support for achievement efforts, and the children respond with continued persistence and efforts toward skill mastery.

Unfortunately, many ethnic minority children find themselves in educational settings wherein academic standards are low, as are expectations of their achievement. Why this is the case is not clear, but in these settings ethnic minority children appear to not only fail to achieve skill development at levels that would allow them to be competitive with peers from the majority culture but also develop lower personal standards of achievement and lower expectations of their own achievement potential.

Early Academic and Vocational Counseling

Ogbu (1978) theorized that the high dropout rate and lower scholastic achievement among Black students, in particular result from their lack of awareness of the relevance of the skills taught in school for future career options. If this is the case, teachers, counselors, and other school officials must make special efforts to continually demonstrate the relationship between the academic skills taught and their application to the larger world of work.

Moore (1986b) verified that Black youth have a significantly lower knowledge of the world of work—what people in various occupations actually do—than their White peers. This is perhaps the result of the rather limited representation of career roles available to ethnic minority young people in their home communities. The literature has consistently shown that Black youth, even those who attend college, show a limited range of vocational interests. They tend to gravitate toward the social sciences, education, and the health fields, while White college students favor biological and physical sciences, at least as freshmen (Astin, 1982).

Underrepresentation of ethnic minorities in scientific and technical careers has been the focus of considerable concern in recent years. This is because lucrative career opportunities in the contemporary economy are expanding in these areas. Ethnic minority youth, however, generally do not express an interest in these careers, nor are they prepared to be competitive for educational placements and job-training programs in these areas. Their lack of preparation is related to their lower average mathematics skills and science knowledge upon completion of their secondary education.

The literature clearly reveals that minority youths do not enroll in academic mathematics and science courses in high school in the same proportions as their White peers (Jones, 1984). Large numbers of ethnic minority students who aspire to careers in engineering or other mathematics-related careers, who are perceived as mathematically capable by their teachers and counselors, do not enroll in advanced level mathematics courses in high school. Obviously, better counseling would facilitate their preparation and achievement of career goals.

WHAT CAN COUNSELORS DO?

Counselors' potential to facilitate the educational attainment of minority youth is enormous. Counselors can provide the leadership to develop systematic, comprehensive career exploration programs in elementary, junior high, and high schools that serve large numbers of ethnic minority students and can ensure that these programs are implemented and appropriately evaluated for effectiveness. Counselors can help classroom teachers develop strategies to demonstrate the relationship between skills taught in the classroom and effective, productive functioning in the larger world.

Further, counselors can monitor the use of standardized test results for purposes of classification and placement of ethnic minority students. They also can take the lead in dispelling the myth that any test score is fixed or is a stable index of what the child can achieve. Educating teachers and principals about the appropriate interpretation of standardized test scores would definitely facilitate the achievement efforts of these children.

Counselors can take the lead in developing opportunities for school personnel to explore their own cultural orientations and to consider how their ethnic minority pupils may differ from them on various dimensions. Along this line, teachers also might consider how cultural differences between them and their pupils may negatively impact the learning and achievement of pupils in their charge. Particular attention could be given to the possible mismatch between pupils' typical styles of perceiving and processing information and the style required to achieve under the teacher's preferred mode of instruction.

Finally, counselors can take the lead in educating school personnel on the importance of their expectations for children's achievement striving and attainment. Certainly, teachers and principals need to clarify their performance expectations for ethnic minority students. If they are low, educators should clarify how the expectations were formed and whether they can be verified in fact.

Obviously ethnic minority students' perception of the availability and openness of counselors to meeting with them and discussing their concerns and problems is important. From her study of successful rural Black adolescents, Courtland (1985) reported that many saw school counselors as important providers of academic and personal-social assistance. This component of what the researcher described as "positive school experiences" of these young people is particularly noteworthy in this context.

REFERENCES

Astin, A. W. (1982). *Minorities in American higher education.* San Francisco: Jossey-Bass.

Bock, R. D., & Moore, E. G. J. (1986). *Advantage and disadvantage: A profile of American youth.* Hillsdale, NJ: Lawrence Erlbaum.

Brim, O. G., & Kagan, J. (1980). *Constancy and change in human development.* Cambridge: Harvard University Press.

Brookover, W. B., Schweitzer, J. H., Schneider, J. M., Beady, C. H., Flood, P. K., & Wisenbaker, J. M. (1978). Elementary school climate and school achievement. *American Educational Research Journal, 15,* 301–318.

Burton, N. W., & Jones, L. V. (1982). Recent trends in achievement levels of Black and White youth. *Educational Researcher, 11*(17), 10–14.

Clarke, A. B., & Clarke, A. D. B. (1976). *Early experience: Myth and evidence.* New York: Free Press.

Coleman, J. S., Campbell, E. Q., Hobson, C. J., McPartland, J., Mood, A. M., Weinfeld, F. D., & York, R. L. (1966). *Equality of educational opportunity.* Washington, DC: U.S. Government Printing Office.

Courtland, C. L. (1985). Successful rural Black adolescents: A psycho-social profile. *Adolescence, 20*(77), 129–142.

Eckberg, D. L. (1979). *Intelligence and race.* New York: Praeger.

Edmonds, R. (1979, March/April). Some schools work and more can. *Social Policy,* pp. 28–32.

Gilbert, S. E. II. (1985, October). Improving the success in school of poor Black children. *Phi Delta Kappan,* pp. 133–137.

Haskins, R., Walden, T., & Ramey, C. T. (1983). Teacher and student behavior in high and low ability groups. *Journal of Educational Psychology, 75,* 799–810.

Horowitz, F. D., & Paden, L. (1973). The effectiveness of environmental intervention programs. In B. Caldwell & H. Ricciuti (Eds.), *Review of Child Development Research* (Vol. 3) (pp. 331–402). Chicago: University of Chicago Press.

Jencks, C., Bartlett, S., Corcoran, M., Crouse, J., Eaglesfield, D., Jackson, G., McClelland, K., Mueser, P., Olneck, M., Schwartz, J., Ward, S., & Williams, J. (1979). *Who gets ahead?* New York: Basic Books.

Jones, L. V. (1984). White-Black achievement differences: The narrowing gap. *American Psychologist, 39*(11), 1207–1213.

Moore, E. G. J. (1986a). Family socialization and the IQ test performance of traditionally and transracially adopted black children. *Developmental Psychology, 22,* 317–326.

Moore, E. G. J. (1986b). *The influence of knowledge of the world of work on ethnic group differences in career aspirations.* Paper presented at the Annual Meeting of the American Educational Research Association, San Francisco, CA.

Ogbu, J. (1978). *Minority education and caste.* New York: Academic Press.

Ramey, C. T., & Haskins, R. (1981). Early education, intellectual development and school performance: A reply to Arthur Jensen and J. McVicker Hunt. *Intelligence, 5,* 41–48.

Scarr, S. (1981). Testing *for* children: Assessment and the many determinations of intellectual competence. *American Psychologist, 36*(10), 1159–1166.

Shade, B. (1982). Afro-American cognitive style: A variable in school success. *Review of Educational Research, 52,* 219–244.

U.S. Department of Defense. (1982). *Profile of American youth.* Washington, DC: Dept. of Defense, Office of Assistant Secretary of Defense, Manpower, Reserve Affairs, & Logistics.

Elsie Moore is Associate Professor, Division of Psychology in Education, College of Education, Arizona State University.

13

Motivation: Building Students' Feelings Of Confidence and Self-Worth

Jon Carlson

Educators are constantly confronted with the challenge of motivation—the extent and degree to which they can stimulate students to learn and thereby make talent potentiality a reality. Although we assume that many children could achieve more than they do, in many instances we equate what a child *is* doing with what he or she can do. Motivation depends on the ability of the teaching adult to perceive the untapped resources of the student and to develop techniques using these resources to the best advantage (Dreikurs, Grunwald, & Pepper, 1971).

Motivating students is the most difficult part of teaching them anything. Most teachers feel that they encounter a motivational problem with at least five or six children in a classroom. Yet, for every five unmotivated children are also

—10 who have some motivation, but not enough to perform at their ability level;
—5 who are motivated to perform for the wrong reasons (parental pressure or teacher recognition, for example);
—5 who are motivated to try something but never get beyond trying; they seldom stick with or finish things;
—5 who are always willing to do things as long as someone else provides constant direction and support.

If you are concerned about those five unmotivated kids, take a closer look at the whole group. Look honestly at how well motivated *all* the students are (Drew, Olds, & Olds, 1974).

217

An individual cannot step forward unless he or she has one foot planted firmly on solid ground. We each must believe in our importance and worthwhileness and in our capacity to cope with that not precisely known to us. The unknown attracts and repels, but attraction and repulsion are perceptual phenomena—they reside primarily within the learner rather than being inherent in the stimuli themselves.

Perhaps the single most important factor in motivating students to learn is *encouragement*. Encouragement is a process whereby students' feelings of confidence and self-worth are enhanced through focusing on their assets and strengths. When we frequently acknowledge students' assets, their self-concepts grow and they begin to believe in themselves and their abilities. According to psychiatrist William Glasser (1976), the root of all mental or emotional problems is a feeling of failure or inadequacy. As an educator changes or increases students' feelings of adequacy, he or she increases their ability to function fully. Through the process of encouragement, and by careful planning and organizing, educators can make school work seem more worthwhile, and thereby help pupils stimulate their own learning process. Children who enjoy doing their school work consistently do a better job than do children who are not satisfied with their work.

To encourage students, most teaching professionals will have to change typical communication and behavior patterns. Rather than focusing on children's liabilities, errors, or mistakes, we should point out what children do that we like and value. Most of us think we know what encouragement is. But we believe we are encouraging students when we actually are discouraging them. For example:

> Nancy sat in her chair gazing around the room while her classmates began to work on the new algebra problems. Upon seeing Nancy's hesitation, the teacher walked over and said, "C'mon Nancy, it's easy, you can do it!" Nancy remained detached and thought, "What if I can't do it or what if I can? So what? It's easy."

Despite our good intentions, such methods often do not produce desired outcomes. Rather than motivating, we frequently inhibit or thwart students. Consider the discrepancies between what we say and actually do, as pointed up in Table 1. Obviously, our stated goals and actual practice are not generally in agreement.

We are products of our culture, which until recently was authoritarian, highly critical, and evaluative. As a result, we have become experts at "flaw finding," and we tend to assess ourselves and others in terms of liabilities rather than strengths—a highly discouraging practice. Tearing others down and exposing their weaknesses does not provide "real" motivation. Instead, it causes people to become less vulnerable and less open in the future. Students will probably change their actions to avoid a repeat of the previous situation, but this will be in the form of learning how to avoid punishment rather than learning the concept we had hoped to transmit. Motivation to avoid hurt, embarrassment, and punishment is a natural human instinct.

In contrast, students *do* need help in discovering their assets and strengths. They also need help in assimilating information so that it has meaning for them.

TABLE 1
Our Actions Speak Louder Than Words!

Teacher says:	Teacher does:
1. My students should be responsible and independent.	1. Forces students to perform; does students' work.
2. My students should be good citizens and be respectful and courteous.	2. Talks down to students; criticizes, distrusts, lectures, and punishes students.
3. My students should be happy.	3. Compliments success but dwells on mistakes; tells students they can do better.
4. My students should have concern for others.	4. Shows lack of concern for students by lecturing, reprimanding, scolding, shaming, using students as servants, talking down, giving in at the expense of teacher's own rights.
5. My students should love me.	5. Demands affection but rejects students when teacher is too busy.
6. My students should feel adequate, be courageous, and feel good about themselves.	6. Does too much for students, implying that they are not capable; criticizes, makes fun of, refuses to allow students to try difficult tasks.

Until learners feel good about themselves and can relate to material in a meaningful way, positive learning does not take place.

Any information will affect human behavior only to the degree to which an individual has discovered its personal meaning for him or her. To illustrate this point: Suppose that at breakfast you read the morning paper's statistics on pulmonic stenosis. Thirty-five cases have been reported in your state during the last year. Will this have any effect on your behavior? Probably not. For most readers, that bit of information represents little more than a foreign language. Because it has minimal personal meaning, it will affect your behavior very little. Later in the day you hear mention of pulmonic stenosis and, because you have nothing better to do and a dictionary is handy, you look it up. You learn that this is a disorder of the heart having to do with a narrowing or closing up of the pulmonary artery. You continue to read and discover that it is an affliction with which some children are born. The information now takes on a little more meaning, and you may feel vaguely uncomfortable.

Because most of the readers are concerned with the helping relationship, let us suppose that you hear about a child in a school across town who is afflicted with this disorder. The matter is closer now to your personal concerns and, consequently, it has more effect on your behavior. Perhaps you pay more attention, listen more intently, and even kick around in your mind the matter of pulmonic stenosis.

Now suppose that we give this topic even more personal meaning. Let us say that you are a school counselor who has just read these words in a letter from the mother of a child with whom you have interacted. The mother writes that her child has this disorder and will need surgery in the near future. She asks that you consider the child's potential emotional problems in this regard. The item in the morning paper now has much more personal bearing and produces a number of effects in your behavior. Perhaps you write a note to the mother. You discuss the matter with the child's teacher and other appropriate personnel. It is no longer mere "information." It is something happening to someone who has meaning to you. And because the information has increased personal meaning, your behavior is more sharply focused and more precisely oriented.

Let us go one step further and assume that you have just been told by your doctor that your son or daughter has this disorder. Now, indeed, your behavior is deeply affected. All kinds of things occur that are directly related to your awareness of pulmonic stenosis.

To conceive of this entire concept visually, Figure 1 depicts a person's field of experience. In the very center of this field are the person's concepts of self, all together called the self-concept. At varying distances from this center are the person's perceptions of the rest of the world. The closer the events are perceived to the self, the greater the effects that such perceptions will have in producing behavior. The farther they are toward the periphery of the perceptual field, the less influence they will exert. Plotting the previous discussion about the concept of pulmonic stenosis, one might illustrate the relationship to self on the line A-E and represent it as shown in Figure 1.

The closer that events are perceived to the self, the more likely they will affect behavior in significant ways. This is a basic principle of learning. The challenge of helping people learn, then, becomes one of moving information into closer and more meaningful relationships to self (Combs, Avila, & Purkey, 1971, pp. 92–94). In motivating students, therefore, one must focus on two essential things: encouragement and meaning.

ENCOURAGEMENT

According to Dinkmeyer and McKay (1976), people who want to learn how to effectively encourage others must first eliminate the following attitudes and behaviors:

FIGURE 1   Diagram for the Nature of Learning

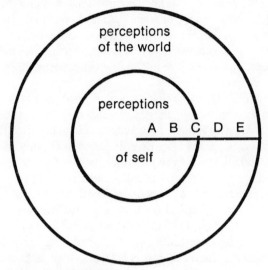

Pulmonic Stenosis

E   Reading the incidence statistics in the newspaper.
D   Looking up the meaning of the term.
C   Hearing that a child across town has the disorder.
B   Finding out that "my" client, Mary Alice, has it.
A   My daughter has it!

   1. *Negative expectations.* Educators' beliefs or expectations of how a student will achieve have an enormous effect upon how the individual actually performs (Rosenthal & Jacobson, 1968). Our expectations are communicated by word and gesture. For example, when we believe that a child cannot do a task, this is communicated some way or another and becomes a sort of self-fulfilling prophecy as the student begins to doubt his or her ability and undertakes the task with less assurance, a lack of confidence—and a greater likelihood or failure.
   2. *Unreasonably high standards.* In an effort to motivate and push students, we frequently establish standards that are virtually impossible for them to meet. Expecting children to do well in *all* areas is a common example. Educators who operate and feel this way are saying in essence that whatever the students do, it is not as good as it should be. Many professionals set standards of performance far beyond the learners' ages and abilities. Students in this type of learning environment learn that "whatever I do, it's not enough, and since I'm not accepted for the way I am (I'm supposed to be something else)—why try at all?"
   3. *Promoting competition among students.* Educators are usually unaware of promoting competition among students and, if aware, perhaps not cognizant of the

results. Most teachers, for example, tend to praise the successful student and ignore or criticize the unsuccessful. Such comparisons, whether deliberate or nondeliberate (such as with a glance or facial gesture) trigger competition. This competition affects not only the learner's strengths but also the weaknesses. As a result, students often choose to concentrate on areas in which they feel they have a better chance to succeed, and to avoid or minimally participate in others in which they are less likely to succeed.

4. *Overambition.* Overambitious teachers want to be the best possible teachers, and to accomplish this, they require that their students demonstrate perfection. This attitude may influence students to not attempt anything unless they are confident of being "perfect" or excelling, and eventually to avoid areas in which failure is a possibility. As a consequence, neither the teacher nor the student develops the courage to take the risk of being imperfect and making mistakes.

5. *Double standards.* Most educators believe that they should have rights and privileges that the students should not have (e.g., teachers who demand that all assignments be turned in on time and then take their time in returning them; administrators who stress punctuality for all students but are themselves tardy; teachers who "mark off" for messy papers but whose own desks and briefcases are in a constant state of disarray).

Students recognize and accept certain privileges of the teaching profession, including responsibility for learning, disciplining unproductive behaviors, and evaluating student performance. But when other questionable rights and privileges are assumed by teachers and denied to students, this communicates to students that they are of lesser value.

6. *Criticism.* Most teaching professionals believe that one way to help students grow is to be critical of their performance and let them know where improvement is needed. We actually dwell on their shortcomings, clearly spelling out that, "You are not OK—I don't accept you as you are, only as you could be." This approach does not help students grow, learn, or improve. It has just the opposite effect. Children become discouraged. Imagine what it would be like if you were constantly reminded of your faults. How would you feel? *People do not feel motivated to change or learn unless they feel good enough about themselves to believe they can improve.*

One must also learn to *separate the deed from the doer.* Children do not always perform as we would like. We must let them know that they are valued as persons no matter how they perform.

> Beth missed five words of 20 on a spelling test. Instead of dwelling on the five errors, the teacher could point out the 15 words that are spelled correctly. Focusing on the positive gives Beth the feeling that she is OK. She is well aware of the five errors; there is no need to point them out. Accepting Beth as she is helps her feel worthwhile as a person and gives her the courage to try (Dinkmeyer & McKay, 1976, pp. 35–36.).

Educators must focus on the positive aspects of students' behavior in order to build the self-concept necessary for motivation. Self-concept is learned behavior.

People are not born hating themselves, and they are not born feeling good about themselves. Everyone's concept of self is learned, and it is learned in part on the basis of feedback from significant others. Some of this feedback is experienced at home, some on the playground, and some at school. It comes from parents, peers, and school personnel. Teachers are an especially significant feedback source, because they provide a steady stream of information that helps form the basis of a young person's developing concept of self.

Studies of teacher-student interaction show that teachers interact with their classroom groups hundreds and hundreds of times each day. Some researchers suggest that these interactions number even into the thousands every day. Regardless of the exact count, teachers' interactions with their students apparently go on at a very rapid pace—so rapid, in fact, that most of these interactions probably cannot be deliberate or even rational.

Teachers are deliberate, rational people before school starts in the mornings. They select their instructional materials, plan learning activities, and anticipate the day's events. But all day long, teacher-student interaction occurs rapidly: "Johnny go to the board." "Everybody take out your books and turn to page 93." "That's not right, Mary; try again." "For goodness sakes, Billy, stop pestering Jenny, or I'll have to keep you after school." And on and on. All day, the teacher "bounces" off the class in a sequence of rapid interactions.

Some teachers have a positive style of bouncing: "Good work." "That's fine, Betty; now explain it to the class so they can all understand." "Attaboy." "You are doing great!" This is positive feedback that tells students they are worthwhile, they do count, they have value, they can make it.

Other teachers, though, have negative bouncing styles. They are critical. They are sarcastic. They humiliate their students and degrade them in minor or important ways. Hundreds of times a day, thousands of times a week, millions and millions of times a year, they provide feedback to their students that implies they are not capable, they are not important, they cannot do it. Such is the stuff out of which negative self-concepts are formed.

If the motivation to learn manifests itself in terms of how young people see themselves, those of us who teach must become instruments of positive feedback (Frymer, 1970).

To feel adequate, students must feel useful and know that their contributions count. School professionals can help students feel useful by identifying their talents and suggesting ways in which they might use these talents to make a contribution to the school or classroom. A list of positive talents and abilities could include:

friendly	aware	popular
highly regarded	anticipating	peaceful
thoughtful	strong	appealing
affectionate	sensitive	determined
well liked	alert	sure
adored	keen	attractive

kind	content	untroubled
"alive"	comfortable	graceful
independent	relaxed	enthusiastic
capable	at ease	eager
happy	wide awake	optimistic
proud	worthy	joyful
gratified	admired	courageous
excited	sympathetic	hopeful
good	concerned	pleased
inspired	appreciated	excited
jolly	secure	interested
warm	glad	turned-on
daring	brave	intelligent

We can help students believe in themselves by our believing in them. We must learn to play down mistakes and to communicate confidence instead. We should be sensitive and alert to point out the positive aspects of their efforts. This involves recognizing improvement as well as final accomplishment.

In getting started in the encouragement process and thereby motivating students, the following points should be kept in mind (Corsini & Painter, 1975):

- *Build on the students' strong points.* Look for good things, including efforts as well as actions.
- *Do not emphasize the students' weak points.* Do not nag, criticize, or spend an undue amount of time talking about what should have been done.
- *Show students what you appreciate.* Some suggested statements could be: "I really enjoy seeing you smile." "I like the neatness of your paper; it's such a pleasure to read." "Thank you for turning in your assignment early; now I have more time to spend on reading it before the avalanche of other papers hits."
- *Be friendly.* A friend takes time to listen and show caring and concern for the students.
- *Show your liking for the students.* A personal comment to a student, a special note, or an arm around the shoulder can convey liking in a meaningful way. Spending time with students during and after class also communicates liking.
- *Suggest small steps in doing a task.* The entire job may seem too much. Give discouraged students a small amount of work to do, and when they finish each of these increments, they will feel encouraged.
- *Use humor.* A wink, a pun, a wiggled nose, or a laugh at oneself can warm relationships. Always laugh *with* students, never at them.
- *Recognize effort.* Recognize attempts at or efforts to do a task even though the job might not be well done. At the initial stages of a new behavior or learning, students particularly need support and encouragement. Once they have developed proficiency in an activity or are beginning to experience success, the secondary reinforcing property of the act itself takes over.

- *Become aware of the interaction between yourself and the students*. Realize that all behavior has a purpose and that many times our responses are counterproductive. For example, students who annoy us to get our attention usually receive lectures on their inappropriate behavior, scolding punishment, or some other form of attention. This attention actually supports the negative behavior rather than eliminates it.
- *Discipline students in silence (actions, not words)*. Angry words are discouraging and seldom true. After taking firm action, resume talking to the student in a friendly manner. Conveying that you still, and always will, respect the student is important. The behavior is what is not acceptable.
- *Do not own the students' problems*. Allow students to solve their own problems; this shows that you have faith in them. Don't be on their backs at all times. Give them flexibility in tending to their own concerns and interests.
- *Do not use rewards and punishments*. These procedures do not encourage students (Bullard, 1970).
- *Accept the students as they are*.
- *Be understanding*. Use empathy and see the world as a student perceives it.

In their classic, *Encouraging Children to Learn,* Don Dinkmeyer and Rudolf Dreikurs (1963) set forth the following nine points to keep in mind when encouraging children:

1. Place value on the child as he or she is.
2. Show faith in the child, enabling him or her to have faith in himself or herself.
3. Sincerely believe in the child's ability and win his or her confidence while building the child's self-respect.
4. Recognize a job well done, and give recognition for effort.
5. Utilize the class group to facilitate and enhance development of the child.
6. Integrate the group so that each child can be sure of his or her place in it.
7. Assist in the development of skills sequentially so as to promote success.
8. Recognize and focus on strengths and assets.
9. Utilize the child's interests to energize constructive activity.

These statements can serve as general guidelines in using the three-step method of encouragement: Identify-Focus-Implement.

Step 1—Identification of Positive Behaviors, Traits, and Efforts

Every activity has something positive about it. If we cannot see it, this is our problem, not the student's. We have been well schooled in discouragement and negative vision. Even when we think we are being helpful and guiding children in positive ways, we are frequently falling into what Corsini and Painter (1975) call the "pitfalls of discouragement." Discouraging statements made prior to behavior include:

Don't get dirty.
Watch yourself.
You aren't old enough
Be careful.
Let me do it for you.
Let me show you how.
I know you can't do it.
If younger children can do it, so can you.
Look at how well your cousin does it.

Discouraging statements made after behavior are, among others:

No, that's not right.
I shouldn't have trusted you.
You could have done better.
I've told you a thousand times . . .
When will you become responsible?
If you'd only listen to me.
If only you weren't so lazy.
You did it again.
Oh, when will you learn?
I'm ashamed of you.
Don't you have any self-respect?
I'll tell your father when he gets home.
You'll be sorry when I'm dead.

The first step in motivating students is to have a clear idea of what you would like to encourage or see changed and what this means in appropriate behavioral terms, including the various movements and efforts that must take place to reach this state. Most people have a difficult time identifying positive behavior. Table 2 offers some samples, along with the associated principle of mental health.

Otto (1973) used the following framework for identifying personality strengths in adults, which is also applicable to children, with modification.

1. *Special aptitudes or resources.* Having hunches or making guesses that usually turn out right; following through on these. Having a "green thumb." Mechanical ability, sales ability, ability in mathematics, skill with hands in constructing or repairing things.

2. *Intellectual strengths.* Applying reasoning ability to problem solving. Intellectual curiosity. Thinking out ideas and expressing them aloud or in writing. Being able to accept new ideas. Original or creative thinking. The ability to learn and enjoy learning.

TABLE 2
Positive Mental Health Principles/Positive Behaviors

Principle	Behaviors
Respects the rights of others	Takes turns Does not monopolize everyone's time Cleans up supplies after an art lesson Does not disturb other students who are working or concentrating on something
Is tolerant of others	Walks slowly so others can keep up Waits quietly while others complete their assignments or tasks Accepts all children and all abilities on the playground Helps students from other cultures with English or comprehending school rules
Is interested in others	Includes/invites others in play Shows concern for absent students Volunteers to help others Talks to and socializes with other students Promotes or suggests social functions
Cooperates with others	Completes assignments on time Works facilitatively in groups Listens to what others say Works with others rather than against them
Encourages others	Notices and acknowledges positive change and good performance in others Focuses on positive aspects of other students Acts optimistic Gives all students a chance when playing games
Is courageous	Takes risks Enjoys novel and different experiences Is calm under pressure of tests Acts enthusiastically toward challenges

(continued)

TABLE 2 (continued)

Has a true sense of self-worth	Likes and validates him/herself Acts in a realistic fashion Understands and accepts his/her assets and liabilities Has the courage to be imperfect
Has a feeling of belonging	Frequently mentions groups to which he/she belongs (e.g., friends, Scouts, sports teams, church clubs) Feels accepted in school and does not need to act out to find his/her place. Makes a positive contribution to a group Exercises a vote/voice in appropriate activities and procedures
Has socially acceptable goals	Works within school rules Is involved in the classroom Cooperates with others and is just and fair Doesn't precipitate fights, and withdraws from physical conflict
Puts forth genuine effort	Tries hard on assignments Does homework Participates in discussions Becomes absorbed and interested in learning
Meets the needs of the situation	Makes good decisions Is able to solve problems Handles spontaneous situations in a responsible manner Does not under- or overreact to assignments
Is willing to share rather than thinking, "How much can I get?"	Readily offers assistance to others Shares lunch, pencils, crayons, etc. More process-oriented than outcome-oriented
Thinks of "we" rather than just "I"	Uses words like "we," "us," and "our" rather than just "I," "me," and "mine" Shows caring and concern for others Frequently offers to share

3. *Education, training and related areas.* All education beyond grade school, including high school, college, advanced study, vocational training, on-the-job training, special courses you have taken, and self-education through study and organized reading. Any high grades. Any scholastic and related honors.

4. *Work, vocation, job or position.* Experience in a particular line of work, as well as having successfully held various positions in various lines. A responsible or supervisory position. Owning or managing your own full-time or part-time enterprise. Job satisfaction, including enjoying your work, good relations with co-workers, feelings of loyalty toward employer or organization, pride in work and duties.

5. *Aesthetic strengths.* Recognizing and enjoying beauty in nature, the arts, or people, and as expressed through the personality of people. Using aesthetic sense to enhance home and physical environment.

6. *Organizational strengths.* Developing and planning sensible short- and long-range goals. Carrying out orders, as well as giving them. Experience in organizing enterprises, projects, club—social, political, or other. Leadership positions in such organizations.

7. *Hobbies and crafts.* All hobbies, crafts, and related interests, including any instruction or training in crafts such as weaving, pottery, and jewelry making. Any other special interests to which you give time.

8. *Expressive arts.* Any type of dancing. Any form of writing (stories, essays, poetry). Sketching, painting, sculpture, modeling with clay. Ability to improvise music or to play a musical instrument. Rhythmic ability.

9. *Health.* Good health represents a strength. Any measures for maintaining or improving your health, including seeking adequate medical treatment at once when needed, yearly medical check-ups, etc.

10. *Sports and outdoor activities.* Active participation in outdoor activities and organized sports, camping, hunting. Regular exercise program.

11. *Imaginative and creative strengths.* Using creativity and imagination for new and different ideas in relation to home, family, job, etc. Developing and extending imaginative and creative abilities.

12. *Relationship strengths.* Ability to meet people easily, make them feel comfortable; ability to talk freely with strangers. Good relations with neighbors. Treating people with consideration, politeness, and respect. Being aware of the needs and feelings of others. Being able to really listen to what others have to say.

Helping others to be aware of their strengths and abilities as well as their shortcomings or problems. Relating to people as individuals, regardless of sex, creed, or race. Giving people the feeling that you understand them.

13. *Emotional strengths*. Ability to give as well as to receive affection or love. Being able to feel a wide range of emotions. Being able to do or express things on the spur of the moment. Ability to "put yourself in other people's shoes," to feel what they feel. Understanding the role of your feelings and emotions in everyday living.

14. *Other strengths*.

- Humor as a source of strength—being able to laugh at yourself and to take kidding at your own expense.
- Liking to adventure or pioneer, to explore new horizons or try new ways.
- Ability to stick your neck out, to risk yourself with people and in situations.
- Perseverance or stick-to-it-iveness; having a strong drive to get things done and doing them.
- Ability to manage finances, evidenced by investments and savings, among other things.
- Knowledge of languages or of different peoples and cultures, through travel, study, or reading.
- Ability to speak in public or to make a public presentation.
- Making the best of your appearance by means of grooming and good choice of clothes.

Step 2—A Focus on the Specific Deed and Not the Doer

Students always deserve our respect as persons even though their behavior frequently is not worthy of respect and support. In motivating students, one must clearly specify what they are *doing* that is positive. Frequently, we make statements like, "You are terrific . . . wonderful . . . super . . . lovable," when students do things we like. The problem with this is that students may assume that the converse is also true—that when they do not please us, they therefore must be terrible, worthless, unlovable. Thus, students are not able to evaluate themselves because they are unclear as to what specific behaviors are appropriate. Clear identification of the positive behaviors is much more encouraging. This concept is illustrated in Table 3.

In addition to specifying the behavior clearly, educators must have a clear idea of the difference between encouraging a student and praising a student. Many teachers believe they are encouraging their students when they are actually praising

TABLE 3
Conparison of Focus on Doer and on Deed

Action	Focus on Doer	Focus on Deed
A student turns in a neat paper	"You're wonderful"	"I really like how clear your paper is. It will be much easier for me to read."
A student volunteers for a difficult assignment	"That's super"	"I like the way you accept challenges."
A student offers to help explain an assignment to another	"You're so considerate"	"I like the way you think of others and offer to help them when you have work of your own."

them. The reason this distinction is so important is that praise can be discouraging. Praise and encouragement are alike in that they focus on positive behaviors, but they are different in their purpose and effect.

Praise is a type of reward given for winning and being best. It is anchored in competition. Praise is an attempt to motivate through external rewards. When praise is used, the praiser is really saying, "If you do something I consider good, I will recognize and value you."

Encouragement, in contrast, is given for effort or for improvement—no matter to what degree. The focus is on assets and strengths as a means for the individual to contribute to the good of all. The helping professional who uses encouragement is not interested in how a student compares with others but rather about the student's accepting himself or herself and developing the courage to face difficult assignments. Because encouragement helps the person feel worthy, it is involved with internal means. Another difference between praise and encouragement is that encouragement can be given at a time when children are not doing well and are facing failure—a time when most people need a pick-me-up.

Praise, like punishment, is a method of social control. Overreliance on praise can produce crippling effects. Children come to believe that their worth depends upon the opinions of others. The conforming child who holds this belief usually succeeds initially in earning praise. But praise may be discouraging to the conforming child. He or she may be willing to cooperate only if praised; if not praised, the child may stop contributing. Also, believing, "I am worthwhile only when I please others" may influence children to make decisions that are detrimental to themselves.

Eventually, discouraged children who hold this belief seldom perform up to adult standards; therefore, they seldom receive praise later on. When they do receive praise on rare occasions, and their reward comes, their behavior may suddenly become worse than it was before, because: (a) they do not believe they are worthy of praise and feel a need to prove how unworthy they are or (b) they fear they can never earn praise again. In effect, they wonder, "What can I do for an encore? I'd better save face by not trying." Thus, praise for the child who is discouraged and desperately needs recognition can have the effect of discouraging the child even more (Dinkmeyer & McKay, 1976, p. 37). Table 4 further clarifies the distinction between praise and encouragement.

Step 3—Implementation Using the Language of Encouragement

To maximize motivation, one must communicate *clearly*. Phrases that minimize our own values and opinions and help students believe in themselves include:

Phrases that demonstrate belief in the student

"I like the way you worked that problem through."
"I like the way you dealt with that."
"I'm pleased that you enjoy reading."
"I'm glad you're satisfied with the project."
"Since you are not satisfied with the project, what do you think you can do so that you will be pleased with it?"
"You look pleased."
"How do you feel about it?"

Phrases that display assurance

"You'll work it out."
"I have confidence in your decision-making skills."
"Wow, that's a tough one, but I'm sure you'll work it out."
"You'll finish it."
"Knowing you, I'm sure you'll do fine."

Phrases that focus on helping and strengths

"Thanks _____ that was a big help."
"It was thoughtful of you to _____ ."
"Thanks, I appreciate _____ , because it makes my job easier."
"I really need your help on _____ ."
"You have skill in _____ . Would you share it with the rest of the group?"

Phrases that recognize effort and progress

"I see you're moving along."
"Wow, look at the progress you've made!" (Be specific and tell how.)

"You're improving at _____ ." (Be specific.)

"You may not feel that you've reached your goal, but look at how far you've come!"

"It looks as though you've really thought this through."

"It looks like you really worked hard on your homework."

To further illustrate the implementation process, Clint Reimer (1967), in his paper, "Some Words of Encouragement," has listed 10 ways of encouraging students.

1. "You do a good job of . . ."
   Children should be encouraged when they do not expect it, when they are not asking for it. It is possible to point out some useful act or contribution in each child. Even a comment about something small and insignificant to us may have great importance to a child.
2. "You have improved in . . ."
   Growth/improvement is something we should expect from all children. They may not be where we would like them to be, but if there is progress, there is less chance for discouragement. Children usually will continue to try if they can see some improvement.
3. "We like (enjoy) you, but we don't like what you do."
   Often, a child feels he or she is not liked after making a mistake or misbehaving. Children should never think they are not liked. It is important to distinguish between the child and the behavior, between the act and the actor.
4. "You can help me (us, the others, etc.) by . . ."
   To feel useful and helpful is important to everyone. Children want to be helpful; we have only to give them the opportunity.
5. "Let's try it together."
   Children who think they must do things perfectly are often afraid to attempt something new for fear of making a mistake or failing.
6. "So you make a mistake; now, what can you learn from your mistake?"
   Nothing can be done about what has happened, but a person can always do something about the future. Mistakes can teach children a great deal, and they will learn if they do not feel embarrassed for having made a mistake.
7. "You would like us to think you can't do it, but we think you can."
   This approach could be used when a child says or conveys the impression that something is too difficult, and he or she hesitates to even try it. If the child tries and fails, he or she has at least had the courage to try. Our expectations, of course, should be consistent with the child's ability and maturity.
8. "Keep trying. Don't give up."
   When a child is trying but not having much success, a comment like that might be helpful.

TABLE 4
Differences Between Praise and Encouragement

PRAISE				ENCOURAGEMENT		
Underlying Characteristics	*Message Sent to Child*	*Possible Results*		*Underlying Characteristics*	*Message Sent to Child*	*Possible Results*
1. Focus is on external control.	"You are worthwhile only when you do what I want." "You cannot and should not be trusted."	Child learns to measure worth by ability to conform; or child rebels (views any form of cooperation as giving in).		1. Focus is on child's ability to manage life constructively.	"I trust you to become responsible and independent."	Child learns courage to be imperfect and willingness to try. Child gains self-confidence and comes to feel responsible for own behavior.
2. Focus is on external evaluation.	"To be worthwhile, you must please me." "Please or perish."	Child learns to measure worth on how well he/she pleases others. Child learns to fear disapproval.		2. Focus is on internal evaluation.	"How you feel about yourself and your own efforts is most important."	Child learns to evaluate own progress and to make own decisions.

3. Rewards come only for well done, completed tasks.	"To be worthwhile, you must meet my standards."	Child develops unrealistic standards and learns to measure worth by how closely he/she reaches perfection. Child learns to dread failure.	3. Recognizes effort and improvement.	"You don't have to be perfect. Effort and improvement are important."	Child learns to value efforts of self and others. Child develops desire to stay with tasks (persistence).
4. Focuses on self-evaluation and personal gain.	"You're the best. You must remain superior to others to be worthwhile."	Child learns to be overcompetitive, to get ahead at the expense of others. Feel worthwhile only when "on top."	4. Focuses on assets, contributions, and appreciation.	"Your contribution counts. We function better with you. We appreciate what you have done."	Child learns to use talents and efforts for good of all, not only for personal gain. Child learns to feel glad for successes of others as well as own successes.

9. "I"m sure you can straighten this out (solve this problem, etc.), but if you need any help, you know where to find me."
   Adults need to express confidence that children are able and will resolve their own conflicts if given a chance.
10. "I can understand how you feel (not sympathy, but empathy), but I'm sure you'll be able to handle it."
    Sympathizing with another person seldom helps him or her, but instead suggests that life has been unfair to that person. Understanding the situation and believing in the child's ability to adjust is of much greater help.

Again, encouragement becomes discouragement if motivated by a desire to establish "good" behavior permanently or by an "I told you so" attitude. For example: "It looks as if you really worked hard on that . . . so why not do it all the time? . . . it's about time . . . see what you can do when you try!" (Dinkmeyer & McKay, 1976, p. 39). But genuine encouragement is to people what water is to plants.

MEANING

Eliminating the described undesirable attitudes and behaviors and providing encouragement are important to the student learning process, but this is not enough to accomplish consistent positive change. We must also work on certain attitudes and methods that will help provide the *meaning* necessary for learning.

1. *Beliefs about the subject.* To know one's subject matter well is not sufficient. Effective teachers strongly believe in the material, its importance, and what they are doing. For effective professional work, knowledge about the subject must be so personally meaningful to the helper as to have the quality of belief.

2. *What are people like?* Effective educators see other people in essentially positive ways. Combs et. al. (1969), in their research, discovered that good teachers saw others as able rather than unable, friendly rather than unfriendly, worthy rather than unworthy, internally- rather that externally-motivated, dependable rather than undependable, helpful rather than hindering.

3. *What am I like?* The helping professions demand the use of self as instrument. Effective operation requires personal interaction. Helpers have the ability to share themselves and, at the same time, must possess the capacity for extraordinary self-discipline. The giving of self called for in the helping professions is probably possible only in the degree to which the helper feels basically fulfilled. The deeply deprived self cannot afford to give itself away. A self must possess a satisfactory degree of adequacy before it can venture commitment and encounter. The task of professional workers is dependent upon entering into some kind of relationship with others. But one cannot have a relationship with a nonentity. Effec-

tive helpers must be *somebodies*. They must possess sufficient personal strength to make sharing possible. They must feel personally adequate in order to work effectively in that role.

The following characteristics have been associated with how effective teachers see themselves identifying with people rather than apart from them; trustworthy rather than untrustworthy; wanted by people rather than unwanted; worthy rather than unworthy.

4. *What are my purposes?* Good teachers have been differentiated from poor ones on the basis of the following purposes: Effective teachers see their task as freeing rather than controlling (i.e., they see the purpose of the helping task as that of assisting, releasing, and facilitating rather than as a matter of manipulating, coercing, blocking, or inhibiting behavior); they are concerned more with larger than smaller issues; they are self-revealing instead of self-concealing; they see themselves as involved with others rather than alienating them; they are process-oriented rather than goal-oriented; they are altruistic, not narcissistic.

5. *Approaches to the task.* Good helpers are more concerned with people matters than with thing matters (their orientation is human rather than oriented toward objects, events, rules, and regulations). They also tend to see their students from an internal rather than an external view; they are more concerned with how things look from the students' point of view than from their own.

Teachers with perceptual organization that encompasses these five areas are highly sensitive to students, purposeful in their work, consistent, self-respectful, and they establish *meaningful* learning through positive regard. The meaning of any event does not reside in the event itself. A common error among teachers is to assume that meaning lies in the subject matter. Meaning is a people problem. It happens in persons. Development of meaning is a creative art occurring as a consequence of people interacting with the world in which they live (Combs, Avila, & Purkey, 1971, p. 84).

Discovering meaning takes time. We need only to recall how long it took us to learn some of the important concepts. One easily forgets this when attempting to help someone else arrive at the same conclusions. When we push the learning process too fast, we may actually destroy the possibilities of the individual discovering meaning at all. Effective teaching requires the quality of *patience*. Motivation is a complex process, not a unique event; its development is dependent on a number of gross and minute events.

REFERENCES

Asselin, C., Nelson, T., & Platt, J. M. (1975). *Teacher study group manual.* Chicago: Alfred Adler Institute.

Bullard, M. (1970). *Human operant behavior and individual psychology in the classroom.* Paper presented at the Ninth Congress of the International Association of Individual Psychology, New York.

Combs, A. W., Avila, D. L., & Purkey, W. W. (1971). *Helping relationships: Basic concepts for the helping professions.* Boston: Allyn & Bacon.

Combs, A. W., et. al. (1969). *Florida studies in the helping professions.* Gainesville, FL: University of Florida Press.

Corsini, R., & Painter, G. (1975). *The practical parent.* New York: Harper & Row.

Dinkmeyer, D., & Dreikurs, R. (1963). *Encouraging children to learn: The encouragement process.* Englewood Cliffs, NJ: Prentice-Hall.

Dinkmeyer, D., & McKay, G. (1976). *Systematic training for effective parenting: Parent's handbook.* Circle Pines, MN: American Guidance Service.

Dreikurs, R., Grunwald, B. B., & Pepper, F. C. (1971). *Maintaining sanity in the classroom.* New York: Harper & Row.

Drew, W. F., Olds, A. R., & Olds, H. F. (1974). *Motivating today's students.* Palo Alto, CA: Learning Handbooks.

Frymer, J. R. (1970). Motivation is what it's all about. *Motivation Quarterly, 1*(1), 1–4.

Glasser, W. (1976). *The positive addiction.* New York: Harper & Row.

Otto, H. A. (1973). *Group methods to actualize human potential: A handbook.* Beverly Hills; Holistic Press.

Reimer, C. (1967). Some words of encouragement. In Vicki Soltz, *Study group leader's manual* (pp. 71–73). Chicago: Alfred Adler Institute.

Rosenthal, R., & Jacobson, L. (1968). *Pygmalion in the classroom.* New York: Holt, Rinehart & Winston.

Jon Carlson is a Psychologist with the Lake Geneva (Wisconsin) Wellness Clinic.

14

Encouraging Personal Growth in School Groups

Merle M. Ohlsen

Frequent family moves, rising divorce rates, weakened extended family influence, changing social norms, and increased use of drugs have heightened children's and youths' need for assistance in their personal development. Elementary school counselors have taken the initiative for programs addressing these concerns by serving as consultants to parents and teachers, as well as by counseling children and parents and by helping teachers introduce personal growth programs in their classrooms (Ohlsen, 1973). Some middle school counselors also have taken the initiative, but most have tended to accept the secondary school counselor's administrative-managerial model (Ohlsen, 1982).

Perhaps today's adolescents need more than ever before the assistance that can be provided in personal growth and counseling groups. They do not feel as needed as they did several generations ago on the family farm or in the small family business, and they have more time on their hands. Many have money and the means of transportation to escape parental supervision. Moreover, parents are not certain about the morals they wish to teach and what to do to enforce their expectations. If both parents work, they also tend to allocate less time to supervision and personal development of their children.

When secondary school counselors participate in curriculum development, seek teachers' and parents' assistance in furthering personal development, learn to function as consultants to teachers and parents, and provide personal growth groups in addition to individual and group counseling, they can help adolescents satisfy their basic needs, which are (Ohlsen, 1977):

1. Search for identity by defining meaningful goals for various facets of life.
2. Increased understanding of their own interests, abilities, and aptitudes.
3. Improving skills for identifying opportunities and for evaluating them in terms of their own interests, abilities, and aptitudes.

4. Increasing interpersonal skills and self-confidence to recognize and solve their problems.
5. Improving interpersonal skills and self-confidence to recognize when decisions are required, how to make them, and how to implement them.
6. Increasing sensitivity to others' needs and improving skills for helping others satisfy their needs.
7. Improving communication skills for conveying real feelings directly to relevant persons, and with consideration for their feelings.
8. Independence to examine what they believe, to make their own decisions, to take reasonable risks, to make their own mistakes, and to learn from their mistakes.
9. Improving interpersonal skills to deal with authority figures in a mature manner—for example, employers, police, and government officials, as well as parents and teachers.
10. Meaningful participation in developing and maintaining limits on their own behavior.
11. Growing knowledge and skills for coping with their physical and emotional changes with maturation.
12. Improving skills for living adult roles. (pp. 177–178)

Affluence and parents' uncertainty about how they should function as parents and what they have a right to expect from their children have contributed to today's youth's special problems in achieving independence. On the one hand, the children want complete independence but, on the other hand, recognize their dependence upon parents to complete their education and establish themselves in their adult roles. They understand the controls that come with financial dependence, but they do not like them. They also recognize that they are not mature enough at times to cope with peer pressure to do something that even *they* do not wish to do, and they elect to act out of deference to parents' expectations rather than to confront the peers who are pressuring them. They desire, and genuinely value, significant older adults' advice, feedback, and support—but they prefer adult-to-adult consultations that allow them to request assistance but with the mutual understanding that they are free to accept or reject the consultant's advice.

Publishers have produced some excellent self-help materials that children and youth can use effectively for personal development (e.g., Cantor & Wilkinson, 1982; Goldstein, Sprafkin, Gershaw, & Klein, 1982). Usually, however, students profit most from these materials when they can share, in a personal growth or counseling group, what they have learned from their reading, decide which ideas they wish to implement, and when they fail in implementing their desired new behaviors, solicit their peers' assistance in learning from their failures. During this process they often discover relevant lifestyle decisions that must be considered, review their priorities, make decisions, pinpoint personal skills they must master in order to implement their decisions, and learn to use role playing to develop these skills before attempting to implement their new behaviors.

INITIATING A PERSONAL GROWTH GROUP

A school counselor must provide, in addition to individual and group counseling, leadership for personal growth groups. To do this, a counselor describes, in classroom presentations (Ohlsen, 1977), the rationale for such group experiences, specifies how these groups function, explains how participants decide what new behaviors they will learn, spells out what they must do to join a group, and non-defensively answers their questions concerning participation. The counselor might also stress that youth have learned to be what they are, and therefore they will be able to learn the new behaviors required for them to function better.

Furthermore, youth tend to more readily accept the problems with which they are concerned when they discover even before they enter the group that *they* will decide whether to join a personal growth group, that *they* will define the new behaviors that *they feel they must learn* to function better, that others whom they admire are struggling with similar problems, and that the problems with which they require assistance can be assigned one of five normal labels. These categories of problems are (Ohlsen, 1983):

1. Recognizing and learning how to cope with developmental tasks.
2. Managing passages.
3. Managing crises.
4. Completing unfinished business with significant others.
5. Learning new behaviors to replace self-defeating ones.

The classroom presentation helps adolescents, in particular, accept themselves as normal human beings who can profit from professional assistance in growing up, increase their hopes for success, and adopt and maintain productive norms within their personal growth groups.

In the classroom presentation, students are offered the opportunity to join a personal growth group. They are not coerced to participate. They are given maximum responsibility for locating the information they require, taught to evaluate and use it in making decisions and in implementing new behaviors, and in deciding what new behaviors they must learn. They also are taught new skills. Role playing is used often to help them better understand themselves and the problem situations with which they require assistance, and to develop the skills they require to implement desired new behaviors (e.g., learning to be more assertive, listen more attentively, convey caring, and manage anger). Although the topics discussed in these groups are often similar to those discussed in counseling groups, the content tends to be less personal and participants tend to be involved for shorter periods of time than in group counseling (five or six weekly sessions, as contrasted with 12–14 in group counseling).

TOPICAL AREAS IN GROWTH GROUPS

Some personal growth groups that are being used effectively in schools specifically address the following areas: intimacy, lifestyle, personal skills, interpersonal skills, affective education, and information giving.

Intimacy

Everyone needs close, intimate relationships with significant others in order to experience love and rich companionship, share dreams, pleasures and successes, and discuss disappointments and failures. Within the very best families a child learns to give and accept love; to listen to feedback, accept it, and use it; to give feedback to others considerately; to be honest, genuine, and considerate; and to be both tender and tough. Older members help the younger ones to recognize the developmental tasks, passages, and crises they must learn to manage, to complete unfinished business with significant others, and to replace the self-defeating behaviors that interfere with satisfaction of intimacy needs.

Intimacy can be learned, but it is more difficult for those who did not learn it gradually as they matured in nurturing families. Even youngsters who question whether the struggle to learn intimacy is worth it usually can be convinced that it is worthwhile when they explore with peers the consequences of not learning the skills required to develop and maintain it. When children and youth seek assistance in developing and maintaining meaningful relationships and discover early in the life of the group that they are accepted for admitting the need for help, for committing themselves to learn new behaviors, and for keeping confidences, they find that they can examine important questions such as:

- What can I expect from an intimate friendship?
- What unfinished business do I have, with whom, that may interfere with developing intimate relationships?
- What must I do to complete this unfinished business?
- What self-defeating behaviors do I have that may interfere with developing intimate relationships?
- What new skills must I develop in order to initiate and maintain intimate relationships?
- Do I have among my acquaintances persons with whom I would like to develop a special relationship? What skills must I develop to initiate and maintain these intimate friendships with each of these persons?
- Do I have among my relatives and former close friends persons with whom I would like to develop closer friendships? What prevents me from developing these relationships (e.g., unfinished business, former failures)?
- If I really wish to develop a special relationship with a new person or persons, do I feel sufficiently secure with someone to discuss the kind of person I am looking for, help me locate such a person, and introduce me to him or her?
- Am I willing to take the risks required to seek out such a person?
- If I were rejected in my initiative, to whom could I turn for feedback that may increase my chances for future successes?
- When I identify these new persons with whom I would like to develop intimate relationships, what must I do differently to function better than I have with

new relationships in the past? What new behaviors and attitudes will enable me to avoid my past mistakes?

- What may I do if, after getting to know these persons better, I decide that I do not want to nurture the relationship? How can I terminate these relationships considerately?

Elementary school children usually obtain help with these problems in classroom discussion groups and group counseling. Secondary school youth sign up for short-term (five or six weekly sessions) personal growth groups offered under titles such as: Developing and Improving Friendships, Getting to Know New People, Improving Your Social Life, Dating, Going Steady, Building Relationships, Learning to Love, Getting Along with Friends, and Getting Along with Parents.

Lifestyle

Lifestyle discussion groups encourage participants to explore a wide range of lifestyle decisions and to decide for themselves what they genuinely prefer rather than to make these decisions by default, as many do. Initial questions include:

- With whom, or at least what type of person, to I prefer to spend most of my time?
- What special interests, hobbies, and activities rate high with me?
- For what reasons do I elect to use or not use drugs, including alcohol?
- What are the unique advantages of highs that I can achieve without drugs?
- For what purposes do I want private time alone?
- How important to me is maintaining a close relationship with my family? . . . my extended family? How can I do this and still achieve independence from them?
- How important is marriage? . . . having children? . . . an active social life? . . . close friends? . . . membership in prestigious groups or organizations? . . . participation in service organizations? . . . political activities?
- Where do religion, worship, and church affiliation fit into my need priorities?
- How ambitious am I? Where does career success fall into my priorities?
- What experiences have given me the most personal satisfactions? . . . greatest self-esteem?

Making it safe for participants to obtain the information they require to understand themselves and the developmental tasks with which they are confronted is not sufficient. The discussion leader also must possess the counseling skills to clarify the choices that do not seem clear to the students, to detect the feelings associated with the choices, to help them discover and discuss these feelings, to consider their ambitions, interests, and values, and to examine the possible rewards and natural consequences of each choice. Rogers (1979) has strongly endorsed this person-centered approach, which enables participants to experience a sense of community, permits diversity, provides a sense of freedom, and allows participants to experience the pain and anxiety associated with genuine responsibility. Participants are encouraged to become increasingly aware of their own abilities, aptitudes, strengths, dreams, interests, and values, and make their own decisions.

As the potency of the personal growth group increases and it becomes more and more like a good counseling group, participants develop greater respect for the individual and his or her right to make lifestyle decisions that they cannot accept for themselves. These experiences enhance participants' acceptance of responsibility for their own personal development, for increased self-esteem, and for tolerance of others' values.

Increasingly, teachers of career guidance courses and leaders of career discussion and counseling groups are encouraging students to consider, early in the life of their group, lifestyle decisions and their implications for career planning. This helps youth recognize that, although career choice is important, it is just one of many lifestyle decisions they must make. It helps them realize how all these choices can either enhance or interfere with career development and, likewise, how career choice can contribute to or interfere with fulfilling other lifestyle decisions. These discussions also encourage participants to develop priorities—to decide for themselves what they are willing to sacrifice to achieve what, and to learn to be sufficiently assertive to cope with significant others who may want to make these crucial decisions for them.

Discussion leaders often find that special additional sessions are required to give participants specific training in determining what information they require, locating it, evaluating it, and deciding how they can use it to make essential decisions. Some discussion leaders add sessions in which they use human potential lab techniques to help participants recognize, accept, and develop their potential. These sessions also help participants learn to detect others' unique potential and encourage them to accept and use it. Further, value clarification techniques can be used in both lifestyle and career discussion groups. Use of human potential labs and value clarification techniques focuses attention on the humanistic approach to career counseling recommended by Bloland and Walker (1981).

Personal Skills

Personal growth groups designed for personal skill development have been used to help individuals cope with a wide range of problems such as: (a) extinguishing phobias, stage fright, and test anxiety, (b) learning to manage stress, weight problems, serious illness, terminal illness in the family, grieving, and pain, (c) developing the self-discipline (and maturity required) to manage time and to develop good study habits, and (d) stopping drinking, smoking, and use of drugs.

Extinguishing Specific Fears

Counselors who are prepared in behavioral counseling techniques have used desensitization to extinguish phobias, stage fright, and test anxiety. Briefly, desensitization involves six steps:

1. Describing the process and its potential benefits to prospective participants and helping each decide whether to join a group.
2. Helping each participant describe the threatening event/situation(s).
3. Arranging the feared events/situations in a hierarchy from least feared to most feared (e.g., hearing the teacher announce a future examination as least feared and every level of fear up to actually having the teacher hand the student the exam and announce time limits).
4. Teaching participants how to relax when confronted with their stresses.
5. Teaching each participant while in a relaxed state to visualize himself or herself in a threatening situation and alternating that with visualizing himself or herself in a nonthreatening situation, gradually increasing the number of seconds spent visualizing self in a threatened state to a point of desensitization at that step in the hierarchy, then following the same procedure of desensitization for each subsequent step in the hierarchy (and when the participant gets tense, dropping back to the previous step, where he or she was relaxed, and repeating the process).
6. Encouraging group members to discuss what they learned about managing their feelings and exploring how they can generalize these learnings to similar new situations.

Perhaps the most research has been published on use of this technique to desensitize youth to *test anxiety* (e.g., Horne & Matson, 1977).

Many otherwise "normal" persons who suffer from debilitating fears could profit from this type of assistance—the student who has mastered the essential material covered in a test but gets sick, performs poorly, or skips the exam; the student who has mastered the material and organized it to give an excellent speech but either presents ideas poorly or doesn't show up to give the speech; the businessman who is required to travel a lot but, because of a deathly fear of flying, either wastes hours in ground travel or flies and suffers needlessly. Obviously, desensitization cannot be substituted for a student's mastery of essential knowledge and skills, but it can be used in personal growth groups to help participants learn to manage their fears.

Managing Stress

Another similar problem is managing stress. Failing to manage stress not only makes one miserable, but it also can result in serious health problems such as ulcers, high blood pressure, heart trouble, and cancer. Most persons who have stress problems are what is known as Type A people: ambitious, hurried, aggressive, impatient. They appraise their worth in terms of the number of their accomplishments. Though most Type A persons probably would not want to become less ambitious and more relaxed Type B persons, many are willing to examine their lifestyles and priorities, to meditate and relax, to master the interpersonal skills necessary to be more assertive and to develop more intimate, satisfying relationships with significant others.

In personal growth and counseling groups, participants are learning to recognize and manage stress procedures (Glasser, 1976; Lazarus, 1977; Madders, 1979; Selye, 1974; Truch, 1980). They are learning to recognize early signs of conflict and a power struggle and to deal with the relevant persons while the stress is still more manageable. They are discovering their self-defeating behaviors and learning the new behaviors they must master to replace old, ineffective ones such as letting others use and abuse them. Examples would be learning to be sufficiently assertive to cope with harassment by rebellious teenagers or sexual harassment by one's employer. With encouragement, feedback, and skill development, people under stress discover that they do not have to allow even those whom they love very much to hurt them, that they can learn some specific things that will enable them to cope better with significant others.

At the close of a presentation to a sixth-grade class, a boy made a comment to me that illustrates how unfinished business contributes to stress: "I think I know what you mean by unfinished business hurting us. I floated into kindergarten, eager and excited to learn. I could hardly wait to learn to read. People have let all the air out of my balloon and loaded it with rocks—unfinished business." Discussion groups can help children like this identify their unfinished business and develop the interpersonal skills needed to complete it and reduce the related stress.

Discussion groups also can help participants reduce stress by helping them define more realistic goals, by teaching them relaxation techniques, and by helping them examine their priorities. Everyone must learn to live with some stress. In fact, healthy people learn to *use* it. But individuals must learn to recognize when they need help in managing stress—when they are confronted with a number of stressful events at one time or within a relatively brief time, or when they are weak during recovery from illness, for example. Fortunately, a variety of stress tests have been developed to help laypersons recognize stress early (Vickery, 1980, 1981). These tests were developed to help individuals assess whether they are experiencing hurtful levels of stress and to encourage them to identify and implement essential changes in their lives.

Assertiveness Training

Assertiveness training is designed to help participants stand up for their own rights, cope with others who use and abuse them (and create unnecessary stress in their lives), and still be warm, loving, considerate human beings (Cotler & Guerra,

1978; Kahn, 1979; Lange & Jakubowski, 1978). It also can increase their self-esteem and help them develop the courage and self-confidence to master the interpersonal skills required to develop intimate relationships. Some for whom this training is essential worry that they will replace their unassertive, self-defeating behavior with agressiveness. Therefore, the trainer must differentiate clearly at the outset between aggressive and assertive behavior, help participants identify specific persons in specific situations that require assistance, help them decide precisely what they must learn to do differently to be assertive, practice the desired new behaviors in their group with use of role playing and with others between sessions, and solicit feedback from other members (Ohlsen, 1977, chapter 7).

Leaders are encouraged to make a recording (preferably video) of these role-played interactions. After the group has processed a role-played scene from spontaneous recall, participants usually profit from the recording. Frequently, the group learns most with which to assist the help seeker by first using and processing a role reversal, then having the help seeker play his or her own role.

Coping with Illness, Dying, and Grief

Terminal illness, and even serious illness, is difficult for the patient and members of the family to manage. It is something teachers and counselors should be alert to and help students cope with. Increasingly, hospitals are employing counselors to help these patients and the members of their families. In hospitals the first groups of this nature were designed for cancer patients and their families. When the patient and family can be helped by one or two sessions, this is usually done without assigning them to a group. But commonly the counselor has one or two sessions for the terminally ill and then adds the patient to a functioning group of terminally ill patients. Later the patient is counseled with his or her family. At first the counselor tries to help the patient discuss his or her anger and disappointments, to complete important unfinished business with significant others, and after exploring whether the patient believes that he or she has done everything possible to get well, to accept death. Kubler-Ross (1969) found that most terminally ill patients with whom she had worked knew they were terminally ill even before they were told, tended to pass through five stages in learning to accept death, and appreciated her help in learning to face death and to complete important unfinished business with others.

Lest readers conclude that coping with terminal illness and grieving is not a problem among their students, they are urged to check this out. The grief process is not limited to death and dying. Adults often fail to notice how deeply a child grieves over the loss of a pet or the loss of a friend who moves away. They also worry about what may happen to a loved one. Beginning elementary school counselors are often surprised at the number of children who seek assistance with these problems when given an "opening." Counselors also tend to be pleasantly surprised by the sensitivity children can learn to express in helping each other cope with these problems.

Developing Self-Discipline

Personal discipline is required to develop good work habits. Students who have poor study skills require systematic instruction in developing good study skills and time management. Even more difficult is to motivate them. Frequently these students have given up on school success or question whether they could succeed even if they tried much harder. Usually these issues must be dealt with before study skills can be improved. These students can be influenced by peers who believe in them and insist that they accept responsibility for improving their own choices. The group can provide a vehicle for this peer impact.

Eliminating Addictive Habits

Mental health centers have developed some excellent programs for drug abuse and for helping people to quit smoking. Counselors can adapt these programs for use in schools (Aubrey, 1971; Webb, Egger, & Reynolds, 1978; Zoller & Weiss, 1981). Although Synanon methods (Higgins, 1972; Martin, 1972; Sugarman, 1973) have been used primarily in residential settings, the methods can be adapted to school use. Similar discussion-type groups have been used to help smokers, workaholics, and compulsive eaters.

Most drug addicts, and even many heavy users of marijuana whose primary friends are drug-dependent, require intensive treatment over a considerable time in a sheltered environment from which they can be released for short periods as they gradually learn to accept responsibility for managing their own lives. Even young drug users are difficult to help, but some can be reached in discussion groups—especially when the groups include strong peer models who have made the decision to not use drugs and have developed the personal skills required to develop and maintain satisfying personal relationships.

The non-drug-using participants must be briefed about how drug users got to be what they are. Usually they have been either pampered or neglected, often reared by adults who did not care enough or were not strong enough to discipline them. When they got into trouble, they may have been rescued by significant others (and thus unknowingly reinforced for their drug use). They tend to be weak, immature, and irresponsible. They doubt that they can break their habit, and they are not motivated to do so. Drug users will not likely be sufficiently motivated to change until they realize precisely how they are destroying themselves and the persons whom they claim to love, that they are teaching their significant others to hate them, and that peers whom they admire believe they can be helped, encourage them to change, and make a commitment to help them change (Horne & Ohlsen, 1982, chapter 15).

Consequently, peer helpers must be selected with great care, helped to define specific new behaviors that they are committed to learn, taught to reinforce only the drug users' new behaviors, and allow the drug users to suffer the natural consequences of their failures. These helpers must learn to be a wholesome support group rather than to function as a "rescue service." They must accept heavy responsibilities and not be destroyed by the drug user's failures. When they learn to do these things, they can experience increased self-esteem and maturity. The rewards are great.

In addition to initiating good programs for students, counselors should help students and parents appraise smoking, weight control, and drug clinics. Many of these are staffed by uncertified or unlicensed persons who make dramatic claims, advertise cleverly, and use colorful techniques such as hypnosis. Usually the leaders of these clinics fail to deal with the problems underlying or associated with excessive eating, smoking, or drug use and make no provision for follow-up. Smokers must learn what they can do instead of lighting up when they feel awkward or uncomfortable. Obsessive eaters must learn what they can do instead of eating when they feel anxious, lonely, or depressed. Drug users must develop new friendships with non-drug users and learn to achieve highs without drugs instead of using drugs as a crutch. Each must examine the lifestyle issues involved, consciously decide what new lifestyle changes are necessary to make, and identify persons to reinforce the desired new behaviors in order to extinguish the undesirable habit.

Promoting Decision Making

A final example of a personal management skill that school counselors can teach students in personal growth groups is decision making. Some specific applications are:

- Think about a specific instance in which you were confronted with a situation that required you to make and implement a decision. With what would you have liked help? From whom did you solicit help? Did you make and implement the decision? If not, why not? With what unfinished business are you left . . . with whom?
- Think about two other instances: one in which you are pleased with your performance, and another in which you feel you performed badly. How did these two situations differ? What persons were involved in each? What new skills and attitudes must you develop to correct the deficiencies in the latter?
- What decisions should you make right now? What information do you require to make these decisions? How can you use this information in the decision-making process? What are your alternatives? What is involved in choosing an alternative and implementing it? What new skills must you master to implement it?

Behavioral counseling techniques, especially social modeling, have been used effectively to supplement discussion groups. These treatments also motivate participants to seek needed information, make decisions, and learn to take the risks required to implement decisions.

The "Fiddler Game" also can be used for these purposes. Perhaps readers will remember Tevye in *Fiddler on the Roof* examining the pros and cons of an issue. When this idea is used to teach decision making, the leader first teaches the client to state and clarify the choice to be made. Assume that Bob is faced with a choice between accepting an apprenticeship offer or admission to a preferred college. The group helps him explore whether he is leaning toward the apprenticeship or college admission. If he says that he is leaning toward accepting the apprenticeship, he is asked to tell the others *why* in a most convincing way. When Bob seems to have run out of material, he is asked to state as convincingly as possible his arguments for turning down the apprenticeship and accepting the college admission. Then he is asked to make his choice on the basis of what he knows. Finally, the other members give him feedback and help him explore whether he needs any more information and, if so, where he can get it. They also agree on a time when he will report his decision and tell what he has done to implement it.

Persons who are dependent, or at least do not know how to make and implement decisions, are usually resented by their significant others. Ironically, when these dependent persons begin to learn to make decisions and behave more independently, their significant others often get upset, and perhaps even unknowingly reinforce dependent behavior. Though these significant others may complain bitterly about the person's indecisiveness and dependency, they have learned to live with it. The group leader should alert help seekers to this problem and encourage them to explore with fellow group members how they can share their goals with significant others and enlist their reinforcement of specific desired new behaviors.

Interpersonal Skills

Implementation of *personal* skills often depends upon development of *interpersonal* skills—or at least the practice of desired new behaviors in one's personal growth or counseling group. Fortunately, most of the techniques mentioned in the previous section on personal skills can be used here, too.

Whereas personal skill sessions are designed primarily to help individuals develop the skills and self-confidence to manage problems they face in daily living, interpersonal skill sessions are designed to help individuals cope with specific relationship problems with specific significant others. Frequently, both types of skills are required in dealing with some persons. An example is the 12th grade girl who believed her chemistry teacher had graded her unfairly. In group sessions she first described the development of her relationship with this teacher, then examined her feelings concerning what happened, and finally decided what she must do to resolve the problem. By the time she had resolved the problem, she had completed several special group sessions allocated to assertiveness training, decided when she would talk to the teacher, role-played several scenes in which she practiced talking to him, and shared with the group her successes in resolving the problem.

Other examples of groups designed to help students develop interpersonal skills are discussed under the headings of completing unfinished business, negotiating differences, managing conflict, and developing leadership. Usually, separate groups are organized for each. When a counselor introduces the idea of such groups, the first volunteers tend to participate in more than one of the separate groups.

Completing Unfinished Business

Completing unfinished business with significant others usually begins with helping participants discover with *whom* they have *what* unfinished business and the negative consequences of evading completion. Next they are helped to clarify precisely how they neglected or hurt whom or were hurt or neglected by whom; to decide precisely what positive feelings they need to express to whom; to identify the persons with whom they have to resolve the pain associated with hurt, neglect, or disappointment; to develop the interpersonal skills required to discuss the problems with the relevant persons and complete the unfinished business; and to generalize their learnings to other situations. Many find that writing a letter to the target person(s) is helpful. The letter is to include the answers to these three questions:

- How do I feel toward you? (The group aids the fellow help seeker in identifying the positive feelings and stating them convincingly, and then identifying the negative feelings and communicating them considerately.)
- How have you hurt me?
- What do I need from you now?

The letter writers are encouraged to schedule a specific time to discuss their letter with the target person when they deliver it and to invite the target person to write a similar letter before discussing the initial letter. Even when the target person refuses to read the letter or talk about it, the senders usually experience considerable relief because they tried to complete the unfinished business.

Though most people tend to believe at first that their unfinished business involves primarily negative feelings, they are usually pleased to discover that perhaps even more unfinished business involves missed opportunities resulting from a failure to express positive feelings. For example, Keith met a girl with whom he had a pleasant date, but he failed to tell her that he genuinely enjoyed the date, that he liked her, and that he would like another date. Had he not discussed this unfinished business in his personal growth group, he probably would have allowed his shyness and fear of failure to be self-defeating. With the assistance of fellow group members, he clarified how he really felt toward the girl, decided what he wanted to say to her, and practiced it in several role-played scenes. This prepared him to complete his unfinished business and to begin the process of building a good relationship with the girl.

In helping individuals complete their unfinished business, counselors must be sensitive to the participants' feelings about unfinished business. Perhaps they did not try to convey their real feelings for fear that the target person would laugh at them or reject their positive feelings. Participants also may doubt whether they possess the communication skills to convey their feelings well. On the other hand, when they harbor negative feelings, they may not know how to schedule a time and place to talk, present their feelings effectively, and confront the target person. They may question whether the target person cares enough to complete the unfinished business or whether anything can be done to salvage the relationship. They may even want some more revenge before trying to complete the business. In any case, helping group members to discover and examine these underlying feelings usually helps prepare them to complete their unfinished business. The use of client-centered, behavioral techniques facilitates the process (Ohlsen, 1983).

Negotiating Differences

Persons who genuinely care about each other and are committed to developing lasting relationships must periodically review what they can expect from each other and learn to negotiate their differences. Many serious conflicts result when one or the other assumes that he or she knows what he or she can expect from the other and never checks it out or recognizes differences and treats them as deficiencies. Usually groups with this focus are organized for couples, but they may be organized for other dyads such as parent-child and supervisor-employee. Even dyads who get along well are usually surprised when they write down independently what each has a right to expect from the other and then compare their lists. Though they often need to be taught how to negotiate their differences and how to use the feedback that observers in the group can provide, they are pleased to discover that it is something they can learn to do.

Managing Conflict

Similarly, everyone must learn to manage conflict. Members of a personal growth group are most effective when they are able to help individuals in the group to:

1. Describe specific situations in which they need help in coping with conflict with specific persons.
2. Identify the earliest possible clues that suggested a developing conflict.
3. Help the individual select and prepare group members to role-play the scene in which the conflict occurred (Ohlsen, 1977, chapter 7).
4. Role-play the scene with another playing the student's own role (role reversal) while the student plays the role of the chief adversary (role reversal), and process it.

5. Replay the scene with the student playing his or her own role while the student who played the role initially plays the adversary role, and process it.
6. Explore additional alternative ways of coping with the adversary.
7. Explore ways in which the conflict could have been handled better if it had been dealt with when the first clues of a developing conflict were noted.

Developing Leadership

Finally, school counselors are encouraged to assist with leadership development. Again, several approaches may be used, but some of the best work in this area has been done by National Training Laboratory (e.g., Bradford, Gibb, & Benne, 1964; Cartwright & Zanders, 1968; Golembiewski, 1972). Perhaps Grater's (1959) model is one of the easiest for school counselors to use.

Basically, students are organized into personal growth groups that are managed much like a counseling group except that the discussion content is limited to the problems students meet as student leaders. Counselors usually accept a few more students in each group (11 or 12 instead of 8), encourage participants to read more printed materials, invite participants to observe each other while conducting meetings, and ask them to return to the group to provide feedback. During group sessions, students are encouraged to discuss the problems they meet as leaders, define specific new leadership behaviors they must learn, discuss the problems they meet in implementing new behaviors, and generalize their new learnings into other leadership roles.

Affective Education

Classroom discussion have helped elementary school children obtain the information they desire, cope with developmental tasks, accept, manage, and enjoy their emotions, and improve the learning climate in their classrooms. Both DUSO (Dinkmeyer, 1972) and Magic Circle (Ball, 1972) have been used to assist children with the last two. By selecting all the members for a counseling group from a single classroom, I (Ohlsen, 1977) have been able to involve the clients in classroom discussions that teach classmates to manage the developmental tasks with which the clients have learned to cope.

In introducing classroom discussions, the counselor must be certain that the teacher and students understand precisely how a classroom discussion differs from a regular class discussion. First, it is a special 20–30 minute period set aside, usually once a week, to discuss special topics not normally discussed in their other classes. Students select the topic for the day. This is their special opportunity to obtain answers to questions and explore ways of handling common problems. Even when the discussion leader is their regular teacher, the teacher is more student-centered than when conducting another class. The teacher-leader is more sensitive to their feelings, exhibits more caring, and tries harder to discover relevance in every student's contributions. The teacher also tries extra hard to help the student(s) who requested the topic to locate the needed information and use it to implement desired new behaviors.

Guidance courses and units have been taught for many years at the secondary level. Years ago, Shimberg and Katz (1962) concluded that these courses could not be substituted for individual counseling but that they could be used to increase students' understanding of themselves and the factors they must consider in educational and career planning. Career units and courses, and special units designed for exploration of lifestyle decisions, continue to be used to stimulate career development and appraisal of abilities, aptitudes, and interests.

A few secondary schools have encouraged students enrolled in cooperative education programs to participate in weekly work experience seminars. Here, students are encouraged to share their success at work, examine what they are learning on the job, look at their own work attitudes and employers' expectations, evaluate their failures, and learn to profit from the feedback they receive from fellow enrollees, their teachers, and their employers. Role playing often is used to help them convey what happened on the job and to obtain feedback for coping with these problems. The seminar discussions often motivate them to reevaluate their career plans, consider new careers, and explore new educational opportunities.

Where guidance oriented classes have been most successful, teachers of these courses have understood and accepted the objectives of the program, were provided adequate teaching materials, believed that they were competent to do the work, and were backed up by a good counseling program. Most youth, and even adults in mid-life career change, require more than the answers to their questions concerning careers and their abilities, aptitudes, and interests. They also require assistance in accepting what they learn about themselves and their preferred careers, developing the courage to implement their decisions, reevaluating their plans, and coping with significant others who want to make decisions for them.

Many elementary school teachers have had some preparation in conducting the type of classroom discussions recommended by Sonstegard and Dreikurs (1973). They are more apt to initiate programs when their schools employ competent counselors or school psychologists who can demonstrate effective classroom discussions, observe them when they first start the program, and offer helpful, considerate feedback.

Information Giving

Even when information is provided in accepting personal growth groups, it may not be accepted because the information does not fit into the information seeker's perception of his or her situation. Consequently, the counselor must be sensitive to detect when participants are tempted to ignore the information they requested because it is threatening or upsetting. Therefore, merely answering participants' questions with the best available facts is not sufficient, and neither is teaching them where to locate the resources for finding their own answers. Participants also must be helped to recognize and manage the feelings that prevent them from evaluating, accepting, and using the information required to make their decisions. Even an information-giving group requires better counseling competencies of the discussion leader than most professionals have realized (Ohlsen, 1983, chapter 5).

Children's significant adults often have difficulty answering their questions. When parents, pastors, teachers, and counselors develop the competencies to answer children's questions, they usually can cope with adolescents' and adults' queries: Why did Mommy go away? Why does my stomach hurt so much? Am I going to die from this hurt? What will the doctor do to me? Why do you lock your bedroom door? How can I tell if God hears my prayers?

Fortunate are the children who discover early in life that every question that genuinely concerns them deserves the best answer they and the adults in their life can find. Not only must adults recognize when they lack the facts to answer a child's question but, perhaps even more important, adults also must be able to teach children to locate their own answers, help them translate the facts into language they understand, and reinforce their curiosity and motivation to seek their own answers.

Before counselors can do any of these, they must listen to the child carefully to detect precisely what the child wants to know, clarify the questions asked, and detect and manage any discomfort or embarrassment the counselor experiences in answering the child's questions. When a child asks difficult or embarrassing questions, counselors must admit their discomfort, but also convey the commitment to help the child find the information requested. The counselor also must answer children's questions, try to empathize with them, capture their perspective, and not talk down to them. Every adult also must learn to cope with children asking difficult questions at inopportune times, such as when busily doing something that requires concentration and not distraction. Difficult as it may be, the adult must stop and give the child undivided attention, or if that is not possible, tell the child when he or she will help find the answer to the questions. Answers often involve morals, values, and prejudices along with the information. Whether information seekers are adults or children, they must be encouraged to discuss their reactions to what they learn and to request assistance in digesting it, evaluating it, and incorporating it into their perceptions of self and their situations.

Children who have grown up in a nurturing home have learned to ask their questions and participate in finding their answers. They have been encouraged to become increasingly better acquainted with their interests, abilities, aptitudes, morals, and values. They have been guided in discovering where they can succeed, what requires extra effort to master, and what may require remedial instruction to achieve desired success. They have been encouraged to recognize deficiencies and decide which they will learn to live with and which they are willing to make the effort required to correct. Those who have not learned these skills in nurturing homes as children can learn them as adolescents and even as adults.

SUMMARY

This article presents a rationale for school counselors to participate in curriculum development, to serve as consultants to teachers and parents, and to offer students personal growth experiences in discussion groups. These groups can help children and youth learn to manage developmental tasks, passages, and crises, complete unfinished business with significant others, and replace self-defeating behaviors with productive ones. The topics discussed in these groups cover a wide range, such as career planning, developing new friendships, earning recognition in the classroom, learning to get along with teachers, and coming to recognize and consciously make lifestyle decisions.

The best results tend to be achieved in these groups when the counselor clearly describes the groups to prospective participants, answers their questions, and encourages them to prepare for group participation. Even when the personal growth group is primarily an information-giving one, counselors must be sufficiently competent to detect when a participant is tempted to reject the information requested because it is threatening. With the proper background and skills, counselors should see obvious benefits in the use of personal growth groups in schools.

REFERENCES

Aubrey, R. F. (1971). School-community drug prevention programs. *Personnel & Guidance Journal, 50*, 17–24.

Ball, G. (1972). *Magic Circle at school.* La Mesa, CA: Human Development Training Institute.

Bloland, P. A., & Walker, B.A. (1981). A humanistic existential perspective on career counseling. *Vocational Guidance Quarterly, 29*, 197–204.

Bradford, L. P., Gibb, J. R., & Benne, K. D. (1964). *T-group theory and laboratory method.* New York: Wiley.

Cantor, S., & Wilkinson, J. (1982). *Social skills manual.* Somerset, NJ: John Wiley & Sons.

Cartwright, D., & Zanders, A. (1968). *Group dynamics: Research and theory.* New York: Harper & Row.

Cotler, S. B., & Guerra, J. J. (1975). *Assertiveness training: A humanistic behavioral guide to self-dignity.* Champaign, IL: Research Press.

Dinkmeyer, D. (1972). *DUSO D–1C and D–2C Kits.* Circle Pines, MN: American Guidance Service.

Glasser, W. (1976). *Positive addiction.* New York: Harper & Row.

Goldstein, A. P., Sprafkin, R. P., Gershaw, N. J., & Klein, P. (1982). *Skillstreaming the adolescent.* Champaign, IL: Research Press.

Golembiewski, R. T. (1972). *Renewing organizations: The laboratory approach to planned change.* Itasca, IL: F. E. Peacock Publishers.

Grater, H. A. (1959). Changes in self and other attitudes in leadership training groups. *Personnel & Guidance Journal, 37*, 493–496.

Higgins, A. (1972, August). Synanon is for people who never learned to live. *Dodge News Magazine*, pp. 21–23.

Horne, A. M., & Matson, J. L. (1977). A comparison of modeling, desensitization, flooding, study skills, and control groups for reducing test anxiety. *Behavior Therapy, 8*, 1–8.

Horne, A. M., & Ohlsen, M. M. (Eds.). (1982). *Family counseling and therapy.* Itasca, IL: F. E. Peacock Publishers.

Kahn, S. E. (1979). Adding effect to assertion training. *Personnel & Guidance Journal, 57*, 424–426.

Kubler-Ross, E. (1969). *On death and dying.* New York: Macmillan.

Lange, A. J., & Jakubowski, P. (1978). *Responsible assertive behavior: Cognitive-behavioral procedures for trainees.* Champaign, IL: Research Press.

Lazarus, R. S. (1977). *Stress and coping*. New York: Columbia University Press.

Madders, J. (1979). *Stress and relaxation*. New York: Arco.

Martin, P. M. (1972, September 20). Is God at halfway house? *Christian Century*, pp. 733–736.

*Ohlsen, M. M. (Ed.). (1973). *Counseling children in groups: A forum*. New York: Holt, Rinehart & Winston.

Ohlsen, M. M. (1977). *Group counseling*. New York: Holt, Rinehart & Winston, 1977.

Ohlsen, M. M. (1982). Theories of school counseling. *Contemporary Education, 53*, 186–189.

Ohlsen, M. M. (1983). *Introduction to counseling*.Itasca, IL: F. E. Peacock Publishers.

Rogers, C. R. (1979). Groups in two cultures. *Personnel & Guidance Journal, 58*, 11–15.

Selye, H. *Stress without distress*. (1974). New York: Signet Books.

Shimberg, B., & Katz, N. R. (1962). Evaluation of a guidance text. *Personnel & Guidance Journal, 41*, 131–132.

Sonstegard, M. A., & Dreikurs, R. (1973). The Adlerian approach to group counseling of children. In M. M. Ohlsen (Ed.), *Counseling children in groups: A forum*. New York: Holt, Rinehart & Winston.

Sugarman, B. (1973). *Daytop Village: A therapeutic community*. New York: Holt, Rinehart & Winston, 1973.

Truch, S. (1980). *Teacher burn out and what to do about it*. Novato, CA: Academic Therapy Publications.

Vickery, D. M. (1980). *Life plan for your health*.Reading, MA: Addison-Wesley.

Vickery, D. M. (1981). What's your life score? *Reader's Digest, 118*, 128–130.

Webb, R. A. J., Egger, G. J., & Reynolds, I. (1978). Prediction and prevention of drug abuse. *Journal of Drug Education, 8*, 221–230.

Zoller, U., & Weiss, S. (1981). Hashish and marijuana: An innovative, interdisciplinary drug education curriculum program for high schools. *Journal of Drug Education, 11*, 37–46.

See especially chapter 3, by Sonstegard and Dreikurs; chapter 9, by Hawes; and Appendix A, by Ohlsen.

Merle Ohlsen is Professor Emeritus of Educational Psychology, University of Illinois; Holmstedt Distinguished Professor Emeritus, Indiana State University; and counselor in private practice, Champaign, IL.

15

School Counselors— Using Power and Influence to Better Meet Student Needs

William J. Erpenbach and Philip A. Perrone

School counselors have *power,* and counselors can exercise this power and their personal influence to help schools better meet *all* the developmental needs of pupils. In our view, power is employed in schools to determine curricula (what is to be taught and when), to establish instructional parameters or guidelines regarding the nature of pupil-teacher interactions, to allocate human and fiscal resources, and to make a myriad of other decisions such as who does what, when.

Power is assigned to or assumed by administrators, teachers, and occupants of other roles such as counselor, psychologist, and social worker. Power is reflected in terms of "role" responsibilities and the consequences when these responsibilities are unmet or the role occupant is interfered with in the pursuit of legitimate goals. Holders of power can be influenced through interpersonal dynamics that may be employed in forthright as well as Machiavellian ways.

We join a host of others in calling upon school counselors to recognize and accept the legitimate power inherent in their role and to apply this power in ways that support efforts to better meet students' learning needs and educational goals. Pietrofesa and Vriend (1971, p. 39) have voiced a similar advocacy—albeit phrased differently:

> Counselors can no longer afford to be subservient in the educational enterprise. They cannot allow themselves to be tossed hither and yon based on the whims of administrators and teachers. Cooperatively much can be done for the proper definition of counselor role. But

counselors must be willing to stand up and be counted. Counselors, because they are "facilitators" and are warm human beings, are too often conflict-avoidant in their behavior. Confrontation, at times, may be what is most needed.

Commenting on the recent recognition by counseling professionals of the need to participate in political action (the application of power being inherent in the practice of politics in education), Aubrey and Lewis (1983, p. 13) helped to place the need for political action in a professional perspective by noting: "One factor that is too rarely recognized . . . is the importance of using such action not just to protect funding and services but also to impact on the general social and economic environments that affect client populations." Participation in political action involves the development and application of a power base.

Over a decade ago, Erpenbach (1976) underscored how important it is for counselors to become political:

> Unfortunately, all too often school counselors have not demanded an adequate (if any) role in making decisions regarding the programs and policies to be set forth in legislation and guidelines determined by the legislative and executive branches of the state and federal governments. It ought to be clear by now that these processes affect the quality, quantity, and mode of services that may or may not be delivered to young people through school guidance programs. Too many counselors have been more than willing to let these decisions be made by others. Further, too many counselors seem unwilling or unable to communicate to policy makers from the local to the federal level what contributions they are making in the schools. Counselors must be interested in and knowledgeable about who gets what, where, when, and how. That's what politics is all about.

This and other calls for political action by counselors remain unheeded.

One could ask: Why counselors? Why should school counselors be expected to understand the application of power and influence in schools? What does the use of power and influence have to do with the goals of education and the role of counselor? Tied closely to the answers to these questions are changing public expectations for the role and function of school counselors. One of the principal expectations for guidance and counseling that emerged during the 1970s was that *school counselors would directly help students achieve desired goals by effecting changes in the school system* (Hollis, 1978). Some persons (Podemski & Childers, 1980) have described this as the *change agent* role. Wrenn (1983, p. 324) believes that counselors must be more willing to take risks. Calling for counselors to be realists, he stated: "This means accepting the changes and uncertainties of the contemporary society and taking action appropriate to such changes." In calling for counselors to be more risk-taking in view of major social changes, he aptly described a far too common perception of counselors:

> Counselors are also thought to be rather passive, accepting individuals who often work in situations where the rules and working conditions are determined by others. These working expectations often reduce the counselor's effectiveness with the clients to whom he or she is dedicated, and yet the counselor often accepts them with only mild mutterings of discontent. There is seldom an aggressive and persistent attempt to change the attitudes of the critics or to improve the environments that influence counseling effectiveness. (p. 323)

Silverman (1975, p. 1) observed that "counselors are located in positions within their school settings which will allow them to be catalysts for change." In an article titled, "The Counselor as Catalyst for Renewal," he argued for counselors to be "problem recognizers and problem solvers" as agents for *institutional growth*. The term *ombudsman* has also been used to characterize a more contemporary role for school counselors.

USING POWER TO WHAT ENDS?

Whether we use the term *change agent* or *ombudsman,* there is an expectation of action and the association of power with these terms. According to Podemski and Childers (1980, p. 169), change agents are "individuals who strive to change the status quo when they feel that it is hurting the individuals whom they are trying to help." They further observed that, "In the change agent role, the counselor is concerned with organizational development as well as the shaping and reformation of the school's curriculum, program, and the organization itself to meet more effectively the needs of students, parents and the community" (p. 173).

In light of the challenges facing public schools today, Porter (1982) envisions a threefold role for the school counselor:

1. The counselor has the responsibility for the student's personal and social understanding and skills.
2. The counselor should be the major resource for career and educational information.
3. The counselor should assume the responsibility for linking educational and employability-occupational forms of preparation. (p. 588)

Aubrey (1970) has observed that the counselor's flexible schedule in the school makes him or her the logical intervener on behalf of students when considering all the societal forces confronting students' lives. He stated:

> The counselor has more freedom of movement during the school day than teachers, and therefore accessibility to a greater variety of individuals and resultant feedback concerning the institution. Coupled with this advantage is the training and experience of the counselor, which should enable him [or her] to obtain more "inside" information from students than the typical teacher. This does not mean the counselor divulges all of this information. However, a first-rate counselor should have a wealth of information concerning the pulse-rate of the school and its total impact on the school population.

> A final answer to "why the counselor?" comes from the requirements of the role itself. Unlike teachers, counselors are charged with following the continuity of youngsters beyond a semester or school year. Counselors in many instances are assigned to a group of students for a period of from three to six years. Over this period of time, only the counselor has the responsibility for following the academic and emotional development of the student. It therefore behooves counselors to carefully scrutinize the curricular and social experiences prescribed by the school for this entire period of time. If these seem detrimental to the development of students, the counselor must intervene before harm is done.

We believe school counselors who work to solidify their efforts and expand or refine their guidance programs can do so more effectively by understanding and channeling those forces and resources that underlie policy development and program implementation in their schools. It is one thing to realize that schools typically spend more on maintaining their ground, more on their band and music programs, and more on student athletics than they do on guidance and counseling K-12—especially grades 7-12. It also should be disconcerting to realize that schools similarly spend more on treatment than on prevention activities. Counselor-to-pupil ratios of 1:500 result in *less than 10 hours* of individual attention and counseling available for each student from *grade 7 through graduation* (less than 30 minutes annually).

On the other hand, to marshal the necessary resources and develop the action plans to achieve a higher priority for guidance in the schools is an entirely different thing. Wrenn (1983, p. 323) has offered this sage advice: "It is the counselors themselves who must fight for the service to others which they believe to be so essential to our society, or see the services sadly eroded or wiped out." He continued in this vein to describe a dramatic example of the power that has become inherent in the school counselor's role and, thus, in the school guidance program:

> Counselors are expected to show some concern for the dropouts and the discontented. The average daily attendance figure determines the budget of the school and must be protected if the school is to survive. Counselors are compassionate and concerned with the unhappy student for that student's own sake, but the concern has now a pragmatic twist: dropouts, for any reason, threaten the school's continued existence. School . . . counseling is more than love. (pp. 324–325)

Porter (1982) argued exceptionally well for school counselors to take a system-wide view of changing expectations and roles and, in turn, to examine their impact on *individuals* within the system—teachers, other counselors, administrators, and students. For counselors to fulfill their responsibilities, they will have to assume both change agent/leadership and managerial roles. Porter also reminded school counselors: "If we're going to be key players, we must understand the rules and know the strategy of the game. We are part of a system that must respond to consumer needs" (p. 589). What many school counselors fail to realize is that leading educators and administrators believe school counselors could assume far more significant roles as leaders in educational reform and are prepared to support counselors in such an endeavor—an endeavor that involves *creation of a power base and the judicious use of that power.*

POWER SOURCES FROM WITHOUT

An understanding and appreciation of their very potent power base, combined with administrator support and their flexible schedules, gives school counselors considerable latitude in determining when and how to intervene on behalf of students who appear to be on a collision course with school policy and procedures.

Aubrey (1970) formulated guidelines for school counselors to follow in identifying "key intervention points for large segments of school populations," suggesting seven such intervention points.

1. When the school is unresponsive to student needs.
2. When the school is miseducative or abusive to students.
3. When the school fails to respond to pressing or changing social conditions.
4. When the school fails to incorporate new techniques, practices, and methods that might benefit its members.
5. When the means for maintaining and supporting the institution become ends in themselves and work to the detriment of students.
6. When the institution fails to provide for difficult transition periods in the lives of young people.
7. When the development of an individual indicates excessive difficulty in dealing with the tasks of a specific stage leading to maturation. (pp. 7–9)

Aubrey also commented on the counselor's behavior dilemma in light of conflicting expectations of counselor roles and responsibilities that often arise should he or she wish to engage in change agentry on behalf of counselees: ". . . the question for counselors often comes down to a simple choice between meeting the needs of counselees or adhering to the demands of the institution. This is obviously not an easy choice in such matters as confidentiality, injustice to students, inappropriate curricula, incompetent teachers, and unresponsive administrators" (p. 6).

The potential for conflict and confusion extends to the use of power among counselors themselves. To many, counseling and the use of power may seem antithetical. Counseling is commonly perceived as a soothing or smoothing process, and counselors (regardless of work setting) see themselves and are seen as warm, caring persons who help people (clients) feel better. For years, school counselors have been challenged by a variety of publics to be more risk taking, to become change agents. Unfortunately, many school counselors have avoided or rejected this challenge seemingly because change agentry suggests the use of power, and power implies confrontation. We strongly encourage counselors to accept the challenge of becoming change agents and in so doing recognize and *accept the power inherent in the role of counselor*. Counselors will require and likely need to find ways of gaining administrative support in order to assume the personal responsibility required to enact the change agentry role, as this involves considerable risk-taking.

Over a decade ago, Cook (1973) took the position that counselors have no legitimate power base accruing from an authority role (line-staff organizational plan). Our position is different, but we do see the value in counselors exercising the concept of "synergic power" as introduced by Cook. Quoting the earlier work of Craig (1972), Cook pointed out that synergic power is derived "not from manipulating rewards or punishments" (p.7) but, as described by Craig:

. . . from guiding and helping other persons in doing four things . . . First, helping people clarify their discontents and, perhaps, identify the source of their discontents. Second, helping people visualize paths to those goals. And fourth, helping each person discover specifically what he [or she] can and must do to attain, or at least to approach, his [or her] shared and unique goals. (p. 7)

We take the position that *the person of the school counselor provides the energy or sustaining force needed to exercise the power inherent in the counselor role*. Rather than listing separately several personality attributes that, combined, would represent the basis for being assertive within the role of counselor (assertiveness being associated with exercising influence and power), we have chosen to merge school counselor and personality within the context of the situations wherein power brokering occurs—specifically, resolving conflicts and problem solving in behalf of students. It goes beyond the scope of this article to elaborate upon the variables that would modify school counselors' approaches to power brokering, but we have tried to identify the major variables that will influence how counselors function in power brokering situations by raising a series of questions:

- Is the conflict between individuals or between an individual and an institution?
- Is one or the other, or neither, willing to compromise?
- Does one or the other, or neither, have the resources or information needed to compromise?
- Does the conflict resolution have an effect on other individuals or institutions that will resist change?

The answers to these questions have crucial implications for how school counselors would proceed in conflict resolution or problem-solving situations, given their role and commitment to helping students meet needs and achieve personal goals in light of institutional goals and constraints.

Developing and Experiencing Power

We have identified five attributes, which, when fused into a comprehensive program, create a legitimate power base for school counselors:

1. A global perspective relative to a targeted individual or a group of individuals with an understanding of the targets' many environments.
2. A role definition and set of functions that are flexible, allowing counselors to readily adapt as circumstances require.
3. The opportunity to readily interact with targeted individuals and members of all significant referent groups.
4. Access to confidential information regarding targeted populations.
5. A role of gatekeeper as evidenced in information dispensation, placement, and referral functions.

Counselors can follow four steps to fully utilize their power on behalf of students:

1. Become aware of the power base and accept the responsibilities that go with exercising power.
2. Understand on a personal level how to activate one's power base.
3. Communicate to others the essence of counselor power and gain administrative support.
4. Implement one's power on behalf of targeted individuals and groups with administrative support.

One example of power brokering at the system-wide level has been discussed by Atkinson, Skipworth, and Stevens (1983). In an article entitled, "Inundating the School Board with Support for Counselors: An Eleventh Hour Strategy for Saving An Endangered Species," they described how counselors in the Santa Barbara, California, High School District met a threat to abolish all counselor positions there and the strategies employed to successfully defeat the proposed school staff realignment plan. Several months later (October, 1983), in the "Feedback" column of a subsequent issue of the journal, John Rothney commented:

> The administration plan was defeated, but was the procedure sufficient to justify its use in defending the place of counselors in schools? Do we have to inundate school boards with emotional and vocal appeals instead of providing evidence that counselors can make so many contributions that they are indispensable? Do we have to resort to the use of high pressure techniques that are more suitable for the market place than for the professional scene?

Rothney argued that current and longitudinal data are the most effective way to support the need for school counselors.

Our position is that both strong political action and data that demonstrate the worth of the guidance program seem to be needed. On occasion, counselors have to get other people's attention—especially decision-makers'—and counselors may be more successful in this through the application of political power than solely by providing evaluative data. The effective application of power can be more relevant than the use of data or statistics for certain situations, whereas data may be more relevant in others. Sustaining any gain, however, would seemingly be dependent on appropriately employing both power and data.

Furthermore, counselors must differentiate between a power *base* and a power *source*. This places the exercise of power back on the individual. In the case of school counselors, their power base is embedded in the guidance program. The guidance program provides both form and direction—an identity—for school guidance.

Aubrey (1970) has pointed out that the counselor's flexible schedule makes him or her the logical intervener on behalf of students in schools. Podemski and Childers (1980, pp. 171–172) aptly described a distinct organizational dimension of schools that supports the counselor's position as change agent and the concept of power inherent in the counselor's role—*staff authority combined with a flexible schedule*. Podemski and Childers defined staff authority as "advisory and supportive in nature . . . grounded in the special knowledge and skills of the occupant of the staff position." In contrast to line authority, which permits one to direct the work of subordinates, Podemski and Childers argued forcefully that staff authority is more advantageous to the counselor.

Staff authority has two special advantages for school counselors. The first is that recommendations, based on specialized knowledge and skills, can be viewed as learned opinions as opposed to personal preferences or experiences. Such recommendations are more likely to be accepted by fellow staff members. The second special advantage concerns freedom from line responsibility. Experience and research support the notion that counselors' recommendations stemming from staff authority are more likely to be viewed as being for the organizational good in contrast to possibly being self-fulfilling. Again, experience and research seem to support the conclusion that in the schools there is a tendency for persons with line authority to offer recommendations more beneficial to solely their areas of responsibility. From a staff authority base of reference, the counselor is less likely to exercise bias in formulating recommendations.

The mix of staff authority and flexible schedules can lead to conflicts between teachers and school counselors, as well as between district administrators, principals, and counselors. The potential for this conflict can be heightened when the counselor assumes the role of change agent. As Aubrey (1970, p. 6) has pointed out, the acid test usually arises when the counselor works with an individual "with a legitimate grievance in direct conflict with established school norms." The perceptive, sensitive counselor who has mainstreamed herself or himself into the school, who regularly communicates with teachers and others, who doesn't operate in a vacuum, will be better able to fathom the trials and travails of such acid tests.

We have pointed out that access to confidential information and the role of gatekeeper and dispenser of information also serve to form a legitimate power base for counselors. Podemski and Childers (1980, p. 172) believe that, "The confidential status of the counselor is unquestioned and is perhaps the most singular advantage of the counselor." They described two ways in which access to data enhances the counselor's position/power in the school's organizational structure:

> First, counselors have access to many forms of school-based data, such as attendance figures and trends, drop-out rates, course selection figures, opinions of graduates, figures related to types and frequency of discipline, failure rates, standardized test scores, and information on building use. Counselors' recommendations are data-based, and thus can carry additional weight over more subjective recommendations. The second data-related advantage is the counselor's prerogative to collect new data in areas the counselor may identify as important. Through data collection and analysis, the counselor can assess organizational needs, sense problems, and facilitate change. (pp. 172–173)

Federal laws such as the Family Educational Rights and Privacy Act (Public Law 93–380), court decisions, and state laws—when they exist—in areas such as pupil records and privileged communications/confidentiality add significantly to the counselor's legitimate power base to function in the school.

Access to data and confidentiality of information also expose counselors to a myriad of potential conflicts between themselves and their various publics. Yet, this access and information are crucial to their daily functioning. Talbutt and Hummel (1982) offered the following cautions for school counselors:

1. Court rulings and the professional literature have indicated that unless a particular profession is granted privileged communication by statute, none exists.
2. Public school counselors and other professionals face potential civil litigation in a number of areas. The courts have suggested that counselors will be judged according to standards common to their profession. Should professional conduct fall below that standard, they could be judged negligent. Also, counselors have a duty to take action when the client or others are in danger.
3. Many state laws require that educators, including counselors, social workers, and others, report child abuse. Some laws grant immunity from litigation to those reporting child abuse unless the action resulted from malice.
4. The courts, as well as the professional literature, have advised professionals against counseling and treating students in areas that go beyond their skill and training.
5. Professionals, including school counselors, should be aware and keep abreast of current legal and ethical issues in their field. This is an evolving area of continuous changes.
6. In conflict situations in which counselors find their loyalties divided and have doubts about the proper professional and legal behavior, they should elicit advice from other professionals and legal advice from attorneys working for local school boards who have access to the office of the Attorney General.
7. Educators should be familiar with and follow all pertinent materials published by the State Board of Education.
8. Counselors should be familiar with the standards of conduct appropriate for their profession. Failing to behave according to acceptable professional conduct or going beyond one's legitimate function can result in litigation. (pp. 10–11)

Recent technological developments also hold significant implications for school counselors regarding data collection, storage, maintenance, and access. The virtual explosion of technology regarding the use of computers in the schools has made itself felt dramatically in the counselor's office. As Wilson and Rotter (1982) have commented:

> There is no doubt that technology will play an important part in our lives in Third Wave society. From microprocessors to microcomputers, technology will be available to students throughout the school. From entering notes from counseling sessions to testing to research to programming, counselors will increasingly make use of technology to maximize efficiency and proficiency. (p. 356)

Using Power in Work Settings

If counselors are to be proactive and effectively exercise power, counselor role and function must be utilized within the context of a comprehensive guidance program. Because the relationship of the guidance program to the school's goals and objectives is the foundation from which counselor power is derived, counselors must understand the institution and clearly identify primary purposes of the organization that employs them.

Though it is assumed that counselors would be more effective power brokers if they would maintain a neutral position when individuals and institutions are in conflict, neutrality is hardly a tenable position for counselors. First, the counselor is employed by an "institution" (i.e., school), which hardly places the counselor in a neutral position as perceived by either the employer or non-employer. Second, in nearly all conflict situations—which is where the counselor would need to utilize power—the institution invariably is more "powerful" than the individual. In practice, counselors likely need to side with the individual in conflict situations involving institutions to help achieve a balance in resolving conflicts. A question that readily comes to mind is whether employing institutions would willingly hire counselors with the understanding that, in situations when the institution could or should bend, counselors would be advocates of individuals "against" the institution.

Counselors usually must minimize conflict and keep the use of power to a minimum if individual-institutional interchanges stand a chance of being resolved in favor of the individual. Skill in reframing, restructuring, and redefining are the essence of counselor effectiveness in situations involving power, and the five attributes that serve as the counselor's power base and the counselor's personal characteristics are fundamental to successfully exercising power to resolve conflicts.

Porter (1982), a former state superintendent of public education, offered some interesting insights in this area. He believes that many other educators see counselors as either too passive or too reactive. Porter sees counselors as needing to develop greater political savvy if they are to become a more crucial element in the schooling process. To Porter, "Political savvy means much more than lobbying. It requires taking an active leadership role in the community and school, insisting that quality as well as equality characterize the educational experience" (p. 590).

POWER AS A CONFLICT RESOLUTION TOOL

As previously mentioned, counselor power can be used to resolve conflicts or resolve problems that inevitably arise when individual needs and institutional parameters play off one another. In effect, the counselor's role and function in these situations is similar to that of any professional engaged in planning and design activities. The work of Nadler, Perrone, Seabold, and Yussen (1984) details the elements involved in planning and design activities ranging in scope from individual career planning to the more complex planning done in business and industry and by governments. The importance of sustained use of counselor power becomes evident when considering the complex nature of conflict resolution and problem solving that are specific forms of planning and design. In their work, the above authors also identified the personal attributes of those who engage successfully in planning and design activities. We believe these personal attributes reflect the energy, commitment, and creativity that individuals must exercise as counselors.

Planning and design as a strategy in conflict resolution involves a host of variables. Three sets of variables come into play during the course of problem solving and conflict resolution. First are *structural* variables, which range along continua from:

—well-defined purpose(s) to ill-defined purpose(s).
—identifiable problem elements to unknown problem elements.
—few problem elements to several.
—many available problem resolving resources to few.
—most obstacles to problem solving identified to few identified obstacles.
—one to several persons involved in seeking a solution.

In addition to structural variables, *process* variables include:

—clarifying both individual and institutional purpose(s).
—identifying the structural variables listed above.
—restructuring, reframing, and creating alternative solutions.
—identifying and utilizing resources.
—mapping a plan of attack.
—carrying out the plan (or assisting in carrying out the plan).
—conducting ongoing evaluation and redirection.

The third set of variables that enter into problem solving are *contextual,* which are essentially attudinal and value-laden. Contextual variables range from:

—placing considerable importance to little importance regarding problem resolution.
—perceiving low to high levels of personal efficacy (power).
—being willing to take low- to high-level risks.
—maintaining low to high levels of interpersonal communication (trust).

SOURCES OF POWER FROM WITHIN

Having described the complex nature of problem solving and conflict resolution from a planning and design framework, we return to the personal attributes that provide the sustaining energy of counselor power. Two sets of personal attributes characterize an effective counselor. The first set underscores the importance of *creative* thought and behavior:

—an expansion orientation, which is necessary in order to consider the structural, process, and contextual variables and integrate them into hypotheses.

—open-mindedness, which is required to consider the relative and tangential nature of problems and solutions.

—innovation, which is essential in reframing and redefining.

—risk taking, which suggests a secure person who is willing to take calculated chances and challenge both sides in a conflict situation.

—imagination, which is required to see beyond the present while completely engaged in the present.

The second set of personal variables, which speaks to counselor *efficiency,* includes:

—the ability to discriminate and differentiate among purposes, activities, processes, and outcomes.

—the ability to generalize and recognize patterns.

—the ability to anticipate and consider means-ends relationships.

—being responsible and attributing to oneself and others the capability of achieving stated goals.

—being able to compromise and help others compromise without compromising the counselor's values.

POWER, POLITICS, PROGRAMS, AND THE PROFESSION

The effective use of counselor power requires that more emphasis be placed on developing personal commitment and social-political understanding in the pre-service and in-service training of counselors. During 1983-84, the Association for Counselor Education and Supervision/American School Counselor Association Joint Committee on School Counseling (Thomas & Myrick, 1984) conducted a series of workshops and hearings to gather information considered helpful in identifying future directions of school counseling. Recommendations resulting from this study that hold substantial implications for the work of counselor educators and counselor supervisors are paraphrased as follows:

—More renewal and retraining programs should be developed and offered to counselors in relation to a K-12 developmental guidance program.

—Counselors should be given more assistance in measuring outcomes of their work.

—Counselors need to learn how politics affects their work and must be provided leadership in order to increase political activity.

—Counselors need training in the use of computers and other high technology.

—Counselors need to receive more training in crisis intervention, conflict resolution, and developing outreach programs.

—Counselor educators and school counselors need dialogue and cooperative planning to assure that training programs are responsive to the needs of school counselors.

Strengths of the school counseling profession, as identified by the Joint Committee, that can serve as a foundation for building strong developmental guidance programs include the following:

1. Counselors who were knowledgeable about interpersonal relationships, human development, school law and procedures, and community resources were particularly valued.
2. Counselors are generally seen as having a positive attitude, which in turn affects the school climate. Flexibility [both in personality and role—we would add] seemed to be one of their most praiseworthy characteristics.
3. Also seen as a special strength was the professional perspective that comes with being a counselor. That is, counselors emphasize developmental and preventive approaches to education and they are primarily child- or student-centered.
4. The different roles and functions of a counselor, especially considering their uniqueness to a school, were seen as strengths: consultants to teachers and parents on law (e.g., PL 94–142) and school procedures, school adjustment; educational and occupational placement of students; coordination of services; and the encouragement of teaming and use of special services. But, above all, the major role seen as a strength was that of being a student advocate and an ombudsman.

Among the various professional and personal needs and concerns, counselors expressed the following:

1. Counselors are in a very stressful work situation and they often feel powerless in making decisions about their roles and functions.
2. Generally, counselors are perceived as politically naive and there is a need for more proactive efforts by counselors regarding their professional role and image.
3. [In terms of professional development, counselors need] more professional leadership; more research and accountability; more school counselor positions; better funding; more public awareness; more involvement and support from administrators; and more relevant counselor education.

Our position is that counselors will not successfully address these shortcomings without becoming more assertive and without exercising more of the power that they do indeed control.

Among the recommendations offered in the report of this committee were the following:

It is recommended that counselors be given more assistance in measuring the outcomes of their work, establishing credibility through accountability studies, and telling others of their effectiveness. Public awareness is essential to helping counselors obtain more administrative and public support. [Recommendation #2]

It is recommended that the counselors become more professionally involved and take a more active role in legislative efforts. Increased awareness of how politics affect the work of counselors is the first step, and then the next step is increased political activity. [Recommendation #3]

Counselors can learn to use and access the five elements that constitute *the power base of the counseling profession*. Assuming that the person occupying the counselor role is the power source places considerable responsibility on the individual to make things happen and, in turn, underscores the importance of selecting and retaining individuals in the field who not only can master the elements of counselor power, but also can personally exercise the power that is available. It seems unlikely that counselor preparation programs place sufficient emphasis on developing personal and professional power. Emphasizing the importance of personal and professional power also underscores the importance of counselor's avoiding burn-out and seeking professional assistance when burn-out does occur.

PUTTING IT ALL TOGETHER

For years, counselors have been challenged to become effective change agents—which we interpret to mean that counselors have been urged to marshal and use their power when needed. Counselors have seldom exercised their power, however, so no guidelines exist on how to guard against the abuse of counselor power. We believe a few cautions are in order.

The five characteristics of the profession that have been cited as the counselor's power base also should serve to define the limits or parameters within which counselors are free to exercise their power. Although counselors have a *global perspective* of the school, counselors should define the parameters of their global perspective. Defining limits or setting parameters helps ensure that counselors will be held accountable and hold themselves accountable for people and situations within their prescribed domain. If counselors go beyond these parameters for any reason, they risk abusing as well as diffusing their power base.

To define counselor role and function in *flexible* terms has proven difficult, if not impossible. Defining and communicating role and function further serve to set parameters within which counselors exercise their power. If parameters on philosophy (overall perspective), role, and function are established, *targeted people, information, and gatekeeper* parameters are effectively established. Staying within these parameters ensures that counselors will not abuse their power base.

We have tried to make the case that the person occupying the role of counselor is the power source. Professional ethics that outline the parameters of counselor behavior in general terms serve to guard against the abuse of power by the counselor person. An articulated philosophy, role, and function statement and communication of professional ethics serve to further define and limit the possible abuse of counselor power. Van Hoose (1980, p. 3) noted that, "Even if it were desirable to do so, counselors probably could not actually rule ethics out of their work. . . . The world in which we live requires daily confrontation with ethical issues." He suggested that counselors can analyze their approach to ethical decision making by considering the following sequence of questions:

1. What is the problem or dilemma? . . .
2. Do any rules or guiding principles exist to help resolve the dilemma? . . .
3. What are the possible and probable courses of action? . . .
4. What are the potential consequences for each course of action? . . .
5. What is the best course of action? (pp.10–11)

In the final analysis, counselor behavior and both the awareness of this behavior and the expectations of parents, students, teachers, administrators, and others regarding counselor role and function will be the ultimate determiners of the degree and the form of legitimate power that will accrue to school counselors. Counselors' delivery on these expectations will best solidify the counselors' place and functioning the school.

The next several years strike us particularly pivotal to the future of school counseling. Opportunities for growth and improvement will be abundant. One example is the current national movement in school improvement. School counselors—by training, through daily experiences with students, teachers, and parents, and as a result of their location in the line and staff continuum—can make significant contributions to improving our nation's schools.

Another similar opportunity rests with the need to improve school climate in order to enhance students' learning. In the 1984-85 Annual Edition of the National Education Association's journal, *Today's Education* (Fischer, 1984), eight elementary, middle, and high schools across the nation are featured as "a panorama of excellence" in America's schools. These schools were selected because of various factors that combine to make them uniquely effective. Yet all share certain commonalities: close teacher-parent-student relationships; positive school climate; high school spirit; and pride in accomplishments. School counselors can make major contributions in these areas, which are fundamental in the creation of a healthy school environment (school climate).

A final example we believe provides ample evidence of the legitimate power that accrues to school counselors—and, thus, enhances their effectiveness—can be seen in the counselor role and function expectations reflected in the article, "16th Annual Gallup Poll of the Public's Attitudes Toward the Public Schools" (Gallup, 1984). When questioned about the importance of 25 possible goals of education (18 of the 25 goals reflect student outcomes that should be directly addressed in any comprehensive school guidance program), nine of the top 10 rated goals of education—those ranked as important by 50% or more of the national totals—pertain to desired outcomes of a school guidance program. The most telling examples are:

1. To develop an understanding about different kinds of jobs and careers, including their requirements and rewards. [third highest ranked goal]
2. To help students make realistic plans for what they will do after high school graduation. [sixth highest ranked goal]
3. To develop the ability to live in a complex and changing world. [seventh highest ranked goal] (p. 38)

The opportunities and challenges are there. Counselors can acquire and effectively use their power in elementary and secondary schools to better enable students to meet their unique needs and to achieve personally meaningful and socially relevant goals.

REFERENCES

Atkinson, D. R., Skipworth, D., & Stevens, F. (1983). Inundating the school board with support for counselors: An eleventh hour strategy for saving an endangered species. *Personnel & Guidance Journal, 61*(7), 387–389.

Aubrey, R. F. (1970). Some strategies for guidance intervention. *Focus on Guidance, 3* (2), 1–12.

Aubrey, R. F., & Lewis, J. (1983). Social issues and the counseling profession in the 1980s and 1990s. *Counseling & Human Development, 15* (10), 1–15.

Cook, D. R. (1973). The counselor and the power structure. *Focus on Guidance, 5* (5), 1–10.

Craig, J. H. (1972). *The psychology of power and the power of psychologists.* Berkeley, CA: Center for the Study of Power.

Erpenbach, W. J. (1976). School counseling—survival and expansion through politics. *School Counselor, 24* (1), 2–3.

Fischer, B. (1984). America's schools: A panorama of excellence. *Today's Education* (1984–85 Annual Edition).

Gallup, G. H. (1984). The 16th annual Gallup poll of the public's attitudes toward the public schools. *Phi Delta Kappan, 66* (1), 23–38.

Hollis, J. W. (1978). Guidance and counseling in schools: An historical approach. In *The status of guidance and counseling in the nation's schools.* Washington, DC: American Personnel & Guidance Association.

Nadler, G., Perrone, P. A., Seabold, D., & Yussen, S. (1984). *Teaching planning and design skills* (mimeo). Madison, WI: Guidance Institute for Talented Students, University of Wisconsin.

Pietrofesa, J. J., & Vriend, J. (1971). *The school counselor as a professional.* Itasca, IL: F. E. Peacock Publishers.

Podemski, R. S., & Childers, J. H., Jr. (1980). The counselor as change agent: An organizational analysis. *School Counselor, 27,* 169–174.

Porter, J. W. (1982). The counselor as educationalist. *Personnel & Guidance Journal, 60* (10), 588–590.

Rothney, J. W. M. (1983). Defending the place of school counselors (Feedback). *Personnel & Guidance Journal, 62* (2), 119.

Silverman, R. J. (1975). The counselor as catalyst for renewal. *Focus on Guidance, 7* (8), 1–10.

Talbutt, L. C., & Hummel, D. L. (1982). Legal and ethical issues impacting on counselors. *Counseling & Human Development, 14*(6), 1–12.

Thomas, D., & Myrick, B. (1984). *ACES/ASCA committee on school counseling preliminary report.* Unpublished paper.

Van Hoose, W. H. (1980). Ethics and counseling. *Counseling & Human Development, 13*(1), 1–12.

Wilson, N. H., & Rotter, J. C. (1982). School counseling: A look into the future. *Personnel & Guidance Journal, 60* (6), 353–357.

Wrenn, C. G. (1983). The fighting, risk-taking counselor. *Personnel & Guidance Journal, 61* (6), 323–326.

William Erpenbach is Director of the Bureau for Pupil Services, Department of Public Instruction, State of Wisconsin. Philip Perrone is Professor of Counseling and Guidance, University of Wisconsin, Madison.

Index of Contributors